THE CITY BUILDERS

Andrea Kap '95

Studies in Urban and Social Change

Published by Blackwell in association with the *International Journal of Urban and Regional Research*. Series editors: Chris Pickvance, Ivan Szelenyi, and John Walton

Published

Divided Cities
Susan S. Fainstein, Ian Gordon, and Michael Harloe (eds)

Fragmented Societies
Enzo Mingione

The City Builders
Susan S. Fainstein

Forthcoming

Post-Fordism
Ash Amin (ed.)

The Resources of Poverty
Mercedes Gonzalez de la Rocha

Social Rented Housing in Europe and America
Michael Harloe

Cities after Socialism
Michael Harloe, Ivan Szelenyi, and Gregory Andrusz

Urban Social Movements and the State
Margit Mayer

Free Markets and Food Riots
John Walton and David Seddon

THE CITY BUILDERS

PROPERTY, POLITICS, AND PLANNING IN LONDON AND NEW YORK

Susan S. Fainstein

BLACKWELL
Oxford UK & Cambridge USA

First published 1994

Blackwell Publishers
238 Main Street
Cambridge, Massachusetts 02142
USA

108 Cowley Road
Oxford OX4 1JF
UK

Library of Congress Cataloguing-in-Publication Data

Fainstein, Susan S.
  The city builders: property, politics, and planning in London and
New York / Susan S. Fainstein.
    p. cm. – (Studies in urban and social change)
  Includes bibliographical references and index.
    ISBN 0-631-18243-8 (acid-free paper). – ISBN 0-631-18244-6 (pbk.
  : acid free paper)
    1. Urban renewal–England–London. 2. Urban renewal–New York
(N.Y.) 3. Real Estate development–England–London. 4. Real estate
development–New York (N.Y.) 5. Urban policy–England–London.
6. Urban policy–New York (N.Y.) I. Title. II. Series.
HT178.G72L56365 1994   93-17858
307.76'09421–dc20   CIP

British Library Cataloguing in Publication Data
A CIP catalogue record for this book is available from
the British Library.

Typeset in 10.5pt on 12pt Baskerville
by TecSet Ltd, Wallington, Surrey

Printed in Great Britain by Biddles Ltd, Guildford

This book is printed on acid-free paper

Contents

Figures

The author would like to thank the following organizations for supplying illustrations and allowing them to be reproduced: Stanhope Properties (2.2), City of Westminster Council (2.3), 42nd Street Redevelopment Corporation (6.1), Forest City Ratner Companies (7.4), the Battery Park City Authority (8.1 to 8.3), and the London Docklands Development Corporation (9.1 to 9.4).

Tables

Preface

I conceived this book at a time when the property industry was rapidly transforming the character of metropolitan areas in the United States and the United Kingdom. Not only were annual construction rates at their highest points since the boom years of the early 1970s, but new development was creating a strikingly different urban form from that of the preceding area. No longer were we seeing a thinning of the core and a simple decentralization of urban functions to suburbia. Rather new construction was producing reconcentration in urban centers and intensifying development within clusters on the periphery. Although planners had long urged denser development, the scattered islands of intense use (surrounded by ever-increasing sprawl in the US case), did not result from planners' conceptions of desirable spatial patterns. Even when the restructured metropolis incorporated planning priniciples in isolated developments, its overall fragmentation contravened them. Instead it represented the confluence of an explosion of speculative building for profit and a surging demand for space within a context of local incentives to growth and national policy antagonistic to regulation.

Nowhere within the western world had development proceeded at so strong a pace and produced such a visible effect on the environment as in the London and New York metropolitan areas in the 1980s. In these two cities not only was a proliferation of new large office buildings replacing smaller structures within the old cores, but enormous, highly visible mixed-use projects were springing up on vacant or derelict land. Two of these – the Docklands in London and Battery Park City in New York – came to symbolize the economic and social transformation of the eighties. Built for finance and advanced service firms, their opulence asserted the dominance that those two industries and their employees had assumed over the metropolitan economy.

My purpose was to investigate the economic, political, technological, and cultural factors that caused developers to make the decisions that were shaping the physical form of these two cities. It was my belief that the contemporary urban built environment did not represent an uncomplicated response to demand but rather that developers both molded demand and responded to public-sector initiatives and regulations. While the locational choices of firms that ultimately occupied new structures had been much studied, the strategies of speculative developers were less well understood. Given the long lead time and resource mobilization involved in major construction efforts, developers could not respond immediately to an existing market. Instead they based their calculations on the availability of financing, governmental incentives, community acquiescence, and anticipated demand. I was interested in discovering the criteria underlying their predictions.

During the course of my research, however, the developmental juggernaut that had begun rolling during the early 1980s on both sides of the Atlantic abruptly halted. While my interest in the forces guiding development decisions continued, I became concerned also with the causes of the extremely cyclical behavior of the property development industry and with its impact on urban economic stability. By 1987 it had become apparent that both London and New York would have surpluses of commercial and luxury residential space in the 1990s. Yet developers were continuing to propose and gain financing for projects seemingly doomed to stand empty upon completion, making inevitable the sharp downturn that did indeed mark the early nineties. *Why?* This situation caused me to question further the underlying logic of property development and to inquire into its similarities to, and differences from, other forms of commodity production.

Ultimately the purpose of my inquiry, applicable in times of both expansion and contraction within property markets, became an understanding of the factors influencing the dynamic of real-estate development and, in turn, the influence of that dynamic on the prosperity and attractiveness of urban areas. I sought to explore this dynamic by investigating the reasoning and strategies adopted by key actors in property development, the struggles that occurred among them, the extent to which various participants got their way, and the impact that development had on urban life. In focusing on London and New

York, I both examined property development in the places where the stakes were biggest and addressed subsidiary questions concerning the effect of world city status on urban form and locational patterns.

The stimulus to this book came from numerous sources. Like most scholars my selection of topics derives from personal predilections. I have always preferred the excitement of living in a city to pastoral meditation, and my lifelong commitment to studying central cities reflects this bias, as did my choice, seven years ago, to abandon suburban residence for a loft in the heart of Manhattan. Since my first trip to London thirty years ago, I have appreciated the civilized values and greater provision for working-class people incorporated in that metropolis. My desire to see those virtues adopted in American cities had led me many years earlier to embark on comparative research. But whereas I had once thought that New York was becoming more like London, recently I had been struck by the movement of London toward the New York model. My unhappiness at this outcome – even as many others seemed to be celebrating it – led me to try to understand its causes.

I am grateful to Michael Edwards, Patsy Healey, Thomas Hoover, Ann Markusen, Peter Marcuse, Michael Pryke, and George Sternlieb for reading and commenting on all or portions of the manuscript. I wish also to thank a number of people who have helped me by clarifying some of the issues raised here or giving me access to material; these include Nisar Ahmed, Bob Colenutt, Matthew Drennan, Chris Hamnett, Joan Reutershan, Hank Savitch, Neil Smith, Ken Young, Therese Byrne of Salomon Brothers, Albert Golding of Tower Hamlets, Marie Hill of the Real Estate Board of New York, Amer Hirmis of the London Planning Advisory Committee, Jon McMillan of the Battery Park City Authority, and Tony Mannerino of the New York City Economic Development Corporation. Many people cheerfully submitted to interviews, even when they suspected that my conclusions were likely to be critical of their point of view. I was extremely impressed by the graciousness, articulateness, and cogent analyses of many of the individuals within the real-estate industry and the public sector to whom I talked. I feel rather embarrassed at finding fault with them and hope they find it in their hearts to forgive me.

I have had the extraordinary benefit over the years of extended conversations with a circle of urbanists, whose ideas and idealism have affected me significantly and are woven into the arguments of this book. As well as some of the people already mentioned, these include: Janet Abu-Lughod, Manuel Castells, Lily Hoffman, Michael Harloe, Dennis Judd, John Logan, Enzo Mingione, John Mollenkopf, David Perry, Edmond Preteceille, Saskia Sassen, Richard Sennett, and Michael Peter Smith. Finally, I wish to express special appreciation to three people.

Sydney Sporle so greatly facilitated my research in London that I cannot imagine how I would have proceeded without his intellectual and logistical help. My editor at Blackwell, Simon Prosser, worked diligently on the manuscript in the tradition of editors of old, when book publishers were concerned with the content as well as the marketability of books. He was constantly interested in and sustaining of my endeavor. Norman Fainstein read and commented on each chapter in each of its iterations. Although, unlike much of my previous work, this book was not written in official collaboration with him, his intellectual influence and moral support underpin the entire effort.

Support for the research was provided by the Rutgers University Research Council; the Rutgers University President's Council on International Programs; the Rutgers University Center for the Critical Analysis of Contemporary Culture; and the Social Science Research Council. My graduate research assistants at Rutgers ably performed a number of boring but important chores, and I wish to thank Susana Fried, Grant Saff, Lissa LaManna, and Denise Nickel for their contributions. Anna Crean receives my appreciation for her secretarial assistance. Michael Siegel prepared the maps and Clifford Hirst the index.

Most of this book consists of newly published material. Parts of it, however, contain revised versions of work that I have published elsewhere. Articles and book chapters on which I have drawn are listed below, and I am grateful to the publishers for permission to use them: "The Second New York Fiscal Crisis," *International Journal of Urban and Regional Research*, 16 (March 1992), 129–37; "Promoting Economic Development: Urban Planning in the United States and the United Kingdom." *Journal of the American Planning Association*, 57 (Winter 1991), 22–33; "Rejoinder to: Questions of Abstraction in Studies in the New Urban Politics," *Journal of Urban Affairs*, 13 (1991), 281–7; "Politics and State Policy in Economic Restructuring," in Susan S. Fainstein, Ian Gordon, and Michael Harloe, eds, *Divided Cities: London and New York in the Contemporary World*. Oxford, UK, and Cambridge, Mass.: Blackwell, 1992, 203–35 (Ken Young, co-author); "Economics, Politics, and Development Policy: The Convergence of New York and London," *International Journal of Urban and Regional Research*, 14 (December 1990), 553–75; "The Politics of Land Use Planning in New York City," *Journal of the American Planning Association*, 53 (Spring 1987), 237–48 (Norman I. Fainstein, co-author); "The Politics of Criteria: Planning for the Redevelopment of Times Square," in Frank Fischer and John Forester, eds, *Confronting Values in Policy Analysis*, Sage Publications, 1987, 232–47; "The Redevelopment of Forty-Second Street," *City Almanac*, 18 (Fall 1985), 2–12; "Government Programs for Commercial Redevelopment In Poor Neighborhoods: The

Cases of Spitalfields in East London and Downtown Brooklyn, New York," *Environment and Planning A,* 26 (1994), 3–22.

Susan S. Fainstein
New York City

1

Economic Restructuring and Redevelopment

Our image of a city consists not only of people but also of buildings – the homes, offices, and factories in which residents and workers live and produce. This built environment forms contours which structure social relations, causing commonalities of gender, sexual orientation, race, ethnicity, and class to assume spatial identities. Social groups, in turn, imprint themselves physically on the urban structure through the formation of communities, competition for territory, and segregation – in other words, through clustering, the erection of boundaries, and establishing distance.[1] Urban physical form also constrains and stimulates economic activity. The built environment etches the division in time and distance between home and work and generates the milieu in which productive enterprises relate to each other. As a source of wealth through the real-estate industry, a cost of doing business, and an asset and expense for households, physical structures are a critical element in the urban economy.

The distinction between the use of real estate for human activity and its market role is often summarized as the difference between use and exchange values (Logan and Molotch, 1987). Frequent tension between the two functions has provoked the community resistance to redevelopment and highway programs and the endemic antagonism between neighborhood groups and development agencies which have marked urban politics in the United States and the United Kingdom in recent years. The immense stakes involved have meant that decisions of real-estate developers and the outcomes of struggles over the uses of urban land have become crucial elements in forming the future character of the urban economy.

For policy-makers, encouragement of real estate development seems to offer a way of dealing with otherwise intractable economic and social problems. Governments have promoted physical change with the expectations that better-looking cities are also better cities, that excluding poor people from central locations will eliminate the causes of "blight" rather than moving it elsewhere, and that property development equals economic development. The quandary for local political officials is that they must depend on the private sector to finance most economic expansion, and they have only very limited tools for attracting expansion to their jurisdictions. Their heavy reliance on the property sector partly results from their greater ability to influence it than other industries. How much government programs for urban redevelopment actually do stimulate business is, however, an open issue (Turok, 1992).

This inquiry is intended both to respond to theoretical questions concerning the building of cities and also to address important policy issues for community groups and local governments. Within the academic literature, the economic and political forces that shape real-estate development and its social consequences are the subject of considerable debate. Does real estate development simply respond to speculative gambles by individuals out to make fast profits or is it an answer to genuine social needs? Does the type of development that characterized the 1980s in New York and London inevitably generate "two cities" – one for the rich and one for the poor? Do the subsidies that governments direct toward the property sector represent a sellout by politicians and planners to capitalists or a method by which the public can, with a small investment, gain employment and public amenities as externalities of development schemes? Progrowth coalitions, consisting of business groups and public officials, have expressed confidence in the efficacy of public-private partnerships as engines of economic expansion. Neighborhood groups have frequently, although not always, opposed large-scale redevelopment because they have feared its environmental effects and its tendency to displace low-income residents and small businesses. Other critics, tracing back to the economist, Henry George, have asserted that the profits from development are created by the whole community and are illegitimately appropriated by property owners. Generally leftist scholars have supported the pessimistic view on the causes and results of development, while conservatives have celebrated its entrepreneurial base and transforming consequences.

A major aim of this study is to discover the conditions under which the speculative property-development sector invests in a place and the role of the public sector in providing those conditions. Evaluation of the impacts of publicly supported physical development is more difficult, since there are many confounding variables, but it is a further goal.

PHYSICAL DEVELOPMENT AND THE CONTEST OVER URBAN SPACE

Since the mid-1970s American and British local governments in their policies toward property development have aimed more at stimulating economically productive activities than at enhancing the quality of life for residents. To achieve their objectives they have promoted the construction of commercial space over housing and public facilities. Even though many of the new skyscrapers, festive malls, and downtown atriums produced by commercial developers have arguably created more attractive cities, the provision of amenities has been only a secondary purpose of redevelopment efforts.

Economic development strategies have typically involved subsidies and regulatory relief to development firms, as well as to businesses that could be expected to engage in long-term productive activity.[2] Indeed, in both London and New York, stimulation of commercial property development was the most important growth strategy used by government in the 1980s. Yet only for a short time in the middle of the decade did business expansion appear hampered by a shortage of office space. Public incentives for construction were not a response to a bottleneck that was stifling investment. Instead, the authorities in London and New York hoped that, by loosening regulations and offering subsidies, they would cause developers to offer higher quality, cheaper space. They intended that the lowered costs would draw leading businesses to these dense central areas. Evidently policy-makers believed that an increase in the supply of competitively priced, first-class space would create its own demand.

Two recent reports, *London: World City* and *New York Ascendant*, written at the behest of governments in London and New York, embody the strategic considerations that guided policy-makers.[3] The documents are typical of a number of such efforts in Britain and the United States, which attempted to chart a course that would capitalize on service-sector advantages in the face of a continuing decline of manufacturing. Like most of these plans they were intended as guides to action and were not officially adopted as legally binding policies. Nevertheless, they represent a reasonable summary of the attitudes of public officials and private-sector leaders toward the likely prospects for economic growth.

The writers of the reports perceive the principal advantages of London and New York to be their world city status. They defend the governmental policies of the eighties and justify what they regard as the only practical course for attaining economic prosperity within their high-cost environments. In explaining their emphasis on a few industries, they point out that, despite out-migration of manufacturing and wholesaling enterprises, these two financial capitals have increased their prominence as centers for investment markets, banking, and business services. In their discussion of growth strategies, they call for heightened targeting of these core service businesses by lowering their operating costs. The London report stresses reducing business costs through improving telecommunications and transport and expanding the central business district. As well as identifying these ways in which government can assist the private sector, the report of the New York Commission endorses offering loans and tax subsidies to attract business to less expensive locations within the city.

Analyses of the development industry

Although government agencies play an important role in affecting the physical environment, the main progenitor of changes in physical form within London and New York is the private real estate development industry.[4] Examination of real-estate investment decisions reveals the ways in which urban redevelopment is channelled at the same time by broad political and economic imperatives and by the industry's own specific *modus operandi*. An analysis of its operations shows how economic and social forces create its opportunities and hazards and, in turn, how its strategies etch themselves into the set of possibilities that exist for economic and social interaction.

To a greater extent than I initially anticipated when starting this research, I found that not just economic and political pressures but personality and gender factors affect the development industry. Development continues to be a highly entrepreneurial industry, and particular enterprises strongly reflect the aspirations of the men who run them. Although women now constitute a significant proportion of real-estate brokers, men continue almost totally to dominate the major development firms. As I have studied the large projects that have changed the faces of London and New York, I have been struck by the extent to which they have been driven by individual male egos that find self-expression in building tall buildings and imprinting their personae on the landscape.

Despite its key economic role and political influence, the development industry has only recently become the focus of serious political-economic analysis. For almost a decade David Harvey was virtually alone in examining real estate development from a broad theoretical perspective.[5]

More recently, especially in the United Kingdom, social scientists have begun to subject the property industry to extensive empirical and theoretical investigation.[6] American interest in this subject has also picked up, and several works examining the history, dynamics, and impacts of real-estate investment have recently appeared.[7] The bulk of scholarship, however, remains within the domain of academic programs that train real-estate practitioners. As would be expected in such a context, the emphasis is on how to do it rather than why it is done and what is its social impact. Within the United States a considerable popular literature on real-estate development tends toward hagiography of developer-heroes rather than critical analysis. In a typical example, Douglas Frantz (1991, p. 3) extols "the men who shaped and built Rincon Center [a project in San Francisco], the dreamers who seek riches and immortality by launching great buildings onto today's urban landscapes."[8]

Urban redevelopment has received far more scholarly attention than the real-estate sector alone (see appendix A for an analysis of different theoretical approaches). Studies of redevelopment, however, have largely focused on governmental rather than private decision-making. Although they have investigated the influence of private developers on public policy, they have taken the motives and responses of property investors as givens rather than inquiring into their sources. This book attempts to address that omission, while taking as its starting point the scenario which the redevelopment literature has fairly consistently chronicled and which is recounted below. For in most American and (for the last fifteen years) most British cities, there is a typical story of urban redevelopment.[9] The research reported in this book is directed at filling in the gaps in this story, not at contradicting it

THE TYPICAL REDEVELOPMENT SCENARIO

The story goes as follows: In the past twenty years almost all the major metropolitan areas of the advanced capitalist world have been affected by changes in the national and international economic system such that they have either attracted a surge of capital and well-to-do people or suffered from disinvestment and population withdrawal.[10] In both advancing and declining cities, growth has been a contested issue, and groups have mobilized to affect population and capital flows, either to limit or attract development. Within the United States business groups, usually in concert with political leaders, have promoted growth and tried to impose their objectives within the context of elite coalitions, of which Pittsburgh's Allegheny Conference is the prototype (Molotch, 1980; Mollenkopf, 1978).[11] Urban movements, driven by equity, preservationist, and environmental concerns, have opposed subsidized downtown redevelopment and unregulated profit-driven expansion. They have also, although less frequently, promoted alternative plans for neighborhood redevelopment. The outcomes of these contests have varied. Regardless, however, of whether the result has been growth or decline, greater or less equity, deal making on a project-by-project basis rather than comprehensive planning has been the main vehicle for determining the uses of space.

Overall, business interests have dominated the negotiations among government, community, and the private sector on the content of redevelopment. They have been supported by elite and middle-class consumers seeking downtown "improvements" and attractive, centrally located housing. Neighborhood and lower-income groups have received some gains in some places from redevelopment. Generally, however, the urban poor, ethnic communities, and small businesses have suffered increased economic and locational marginalization as a consequence. Central business district (CBD) expansion has increased property values in areas of low-income occupancy, forcing out residents, raising their living expenses, and breaking up communities. The emphasis on office-based employment within most large redevelopment schemes has reinforced the decline of manufacturing jobs and contributed to the employment difficulties of unskilled workers. While businesses have received direct subsidies, taxpayers at large have borne the costs and received benefits only as they have trickled down.

US/UK redevelopment experiences

British and American experiences differed before the 1980s. Redevelopment in Britain conformed less closely to the logic of private capital than in the US (N. Fainstein and S. Fainstein, 1978). The intimate relationship between local elected officials and real estate interests that is a hallmark of US local government, wherein developers are the largest contributors to municipal political campaigns, did not (and still does not) exist in Britain. British local authorities restricted private development and built millions of units of council (i.e. public) housing, whereas "slum clearance" was a major component of the American urban renewal program, resulting in the demolition but not the replacement of tens of thousands of units of poor people's housing. In addition, land taking for highway building produced an even greater loss of units.

In Britain social housing (i.e. publicly owned or subsidized housing at below-market rents) was placed throughout metropolitan areas, minimizing gross ethnic and income segregation. American public housing, while much more limited in scope, was available only to the poorest residents and was usually located in low-income areas (Harloe et al., 1992). Urban renewal efforts, often derisively labelled "Negro removal" programs by their opponents, targeted ghetto areas that were near to business centers or to more affluent residential districts. Their intent was either to extend the more prosperous area or to cordon it off from the threat of lower-class invasion. Their effect was to displace nonwhite residents into more isolated, homogeneously minority territories.

As in the United States, British local authorities raised revenues through taxation on business and residential property ("rates"). Unlike their American equivalents, however, British local governments that could not meet the service demands on them through internal sources received a compensating central government grant. They therefore did not need to attract business and high-income residents to maintain themselves, and could afford to be more attuned to the negative environmental and social impacts of growth.

During the periods when the Labour Party controlled the British central government, it enacted measures to limit the gain that private developers could achieve through enhanced property values resulting from attaining planning permission on a piece of land. Under the Community Land Act of 1975, adopted during the third postwar Labour government, local authorities were granted the power to acquire land needed for development at a price below market value.[12] Developers would then lease the land from the local authority at market rents. The difference in value would constitute a development tax on landowners of about 70 percent. The purpose was to ensure that the community as a whole would recoup most of the development value of land. Local authorities largely failed to implement the scheme, and the Conservatives dismantled it; nevertheless, while in existence it acted as a deterrent to speculative increases in land prices (see Balchin et al., 1988, chapter 9).

Despite these differences, the British and American cases during the twenty years preceding the 1979 ascendance of Conservative government in the UK did not wholly diverge. Under the American urban renewal program, public authorities had tried to attract developers by putting roads, sewers, and amenities into land that municipalities had acquired for redevelopment. Similar efforts began early in London's outer boroughs. Thus, for example, in Croydon, where 6.5 million square feet of office space was constructed in the 1960s, the council made a major effort to reduce the costs of development through providing basic infrastructure (see Saunders, 1979).

As in the US, a major surge of speculative commercial construction occurred in the UK in the early 1970s. The British expansion began when the Conservative central government increased credit as a means to stimulate the economy. While its action was not specifically directed at the property sector, it set off an intense building boom (Ambrose, 1986, pp. 98–103). Despite the government's commitment to decentralizing population and economic activity out of London, much of the new construction arose in the core, and the Cities of London and Westminster, which made up the commercial center of the metropolis, increasingly took on the look of Manhattan (Pickvance, 1981). Parallel to the experience in a number of US cities, office growth in the center of London led to gentrification of adjacent areas, while government subsidies to owner occupancy hastened the transformation of private rental into owner-occupied units (Hamnett and Randolph, 1988; Badcock, 1984, pp. 162–8). Despite many greater controls on development in Britain, its 1970s boom ended like its American counterpart in a wave of defaults and bankruptcies.

In the latter part of the 1970s, as had been the case in the US for a much longer time, commercial redevelopment became a specific tool of British urban policy. Thus the Labour government, in its growing economic desperation, encouraged commercial expansion into low-income areas next to the City of London (i.e. the financial district) well before the Thatcher regime took office and contrary to its avowed commitment to preserving working-class jobs and expanding the supply of affordable housing (Forman, 1989).

During the 1980s development policies in the UK and US converged.[13] The British Urban Development Corporations (UDCs), modelled after similar American ventures, insulated development projects from public input. Governed by independent boards and reporting only to the central government, they acted as the planning authorities for redevelopment areas. The consequence was the removal of decision-making powers from the local councils. The UDCs were oriented toward stimulating the private market rather than comprehensive planning. In another case of transatlantic cross-fertilization, the majority of American states, although not the federal government, adopted the British innovation of the enterprise zone. Put in place early in the Thatcher regime, enterprise zones are designated geographic areas where firms are rewarded for investments with a variety of tax incentives, regulatory relief, and access to financing (Green, 1991).

In general, the dominant objective in both countries was to use public powers to assist the private sector with a minimum of regulatory intervention. Earlier emphases in redevelopment programs on the provision of housing, public amenities, and targeted benefits to low-income people were downplayed, as aggregate economic growth – measured by the amount of private investment "leveraged" – became the criterion of program success.

The sponsors of the regeneration programs of the eighties claimed that they had achieved a remarkable reversal in the trajectory of inner-city decline. Numerous studies, however, have characterized this growth as extremely uneven in its impacts, primarily benefiting highly skilled professionals and managers and offering very little for workers displaced from manufacturing industries except low-paid service-sector jobs. Moreover, as economic restructuring and contraction of social benefits produced a broadening income gap, growing social inequality expressed itself spatially in the increasing residential segregation of rich and poor, black and white. Rapid development also produced undesirable environmental effects. While the gleaming new projects upgraded the seedy appearance of many old core areas and brought middle-class consumers back to previously abandoned centers, their bulk and density often overwhelmed their surroundings, stifled diversity, and, in the crowded centers of London and New York, overloaded transportation and pedestrian facilities.[14]

The downturn of the nineties has reduced the pressure on inner-city land and thus is stemming the negative environmental impacts of the extravagant ventures of the previous years. It has also caused at least a temporary halt to gentrification. The end of growth, however, is not likely to produce a turnaround in either the widening gap between rich and poor or the governmental pursuit of private investment through subsidies to real estate developers. As firms cut back employment and the property slump continues, city governments are likely to become ever more frantic in their efforts to bring in capital. Thus, the dependence on developers for projects that offer hope of revival will continue and with it the set of programs that offers them inducements to develop.

THEORETICAL CONTROVERSIES

In the study of urban redevelopment the recognition that localities are embedded within a global economic system whose overall contours do not respond to local initiatives has caused a debate over the efficacy of local action. Urban redevelopment efforts have taken place within the larger framework of the hypermobility of capital and intensified national and international economic competition. These factors have seemingly inexorably caused the decline of manufacturing and the flight of employment from older cities. Within this context social scientists have questioned whether, regardless of who controls the local regime, local actors can affect their economies and carry out redistributional policies.[15]

Can local officials produce growth with equity?

The feverish attempts by governments around the world to attract business challenge the view of economic determinists that market forces will by themselves allocate economic functions to their optimum locations. Interestingly, this belief in the power of the market is held not just by conservative economists but also by progressive critics of government subsidies to business (see Swanstrom, 1988). Both argue that businesses do not choose a location because governmental incentives are available but rather because of factors like the price of labor or the presence of clients, which immediately affect production costs or marketing effectiveness. Accordingly, businesses do not choose a location because of governmentally proffered concessions but simply take advantage of them to enhance their profits at the expense of taxpayers.[16]

Paul Peterson, in his influential book, *City Limits* (1981), considers that local governments can affect the economic situation of their jurisdictions even though they cannot directly improve the welfare of their poorer citizens. He explicitly repudiates the possibility of redistributive actions by local governments, contending that they must pursue growth and cannot enact redistributional policies without sacrificing their competitive positions. For Peterson, if municipal officials attempt to assist poor people, thereby scaring away businesses through increasing their tax burden, they will have nothing to redistribute.

In response, Sanders and Stone (1987) maintain that political conflict determines who wins and who loses from the redevelopment process; while they do not explicitly stipulate an alternative path to redevelopment, they imply that it can be achieved through community-based rather than downtown expansion. In other words, local politics matters in determining both the geographic targets of redevelopment programs and who benefits from them. According to this school of thought, urban policy-makers do not have to submit to the logic of capitalism; if they do so, it is because of political pressure rather than economic necessity (Logan and Swanstrom, 1990a).

Is the issue resolvable?

There are several ways to address the issue of local autonomy. Differences between American and European cities and variation among cities that had similar economic bases thirty years ago imply that cultural and political factors influence the capability of cities to fit into new economic niches (see M.P. Smith, 1988, chapter 1). Within the United States, where local governments have a much greater say over levels of welfare spending than in the United Kingdom, economically comparable cities spend different amounts of money on poor people, indicating that the extent to which cities engage in redistribution is not simply determined by competition among localities. At the same time, the downward pressure on social welfare expenses that has characterized all the advanced capitalist countries since the mid-1970s points to serious restrictions on local deviationism (Gourevitch, 1986).

Definitive conclusions based on observation are, however, impossible: for every example of local activity resulting in regeneration or redistribution, there is a counter-example of seemingly insurmountable external forces. My own position is that incentives to investors do make a difference, and that growth can be combined with greater equity than has typically been the outcome of redevelopment programs. But perhaps the farthest one can go in addressing the issue is to identify areas of indeterminacy that potentially can be seized locally within the overall capitalist economic structure – that is, to identify courses of action that can produce lesser or greater growth, more or less progressive social policies, without expecting either an inevitable economic trajectory resulting from market position or socialism in one city deriving from effective political action. The research and policy problem then becomes to recognize those decisional points, rather than to inquire whether localities matter in general. The subject of investigation therefore switches to the strategies followed by local actors, the factors influencing their choices, and how and under what circumstances these strategies affect what happens. My intention is to raise these issues within London and New York in relation to the striking transformations that have occurred in their built environments in the last fifteen years.[17]

Space

A number of urban geographers have been assertive in contending that space matters.[18] For them spatial relations are part of society's underlying structure. Regardless of whether economy or politics has primacy in affecting the location of social groups and economic enterprises, the configuring of space that contributes to and ensues from locational decisions remains crucial in affecting human relations.

Within this intellectual framework, explanations for the marked acceleration of real-estate development in global cities during the 1980s hinge on the spatial causes and effects of the heightened role of financial capital and business services within the world economic system. As production sites and financial markets have become increasingly dispersed throughout the world, financial firms and investment advisers respond to the need for global coordination and trading.[19] In turn, core areas become crucial for the deal-making in which the expanding financial industry engages (Sassen, 1991; Amin and Thrift, 1992). By offering a venue for face-to-face encounters among the numerous parties to high-level negotiations, central areas that had lost their former value as manufacturing, rail, or port facilities find a renewed role. Space at different scales thus enters into the process at two points: the compact area of the urban core allows the structuring of deals; and the distant spaces of the world economy require integration through financial coordination so that raw materials, labor, and capital in various locations can be brought together in a production function.

It is actually difficult to find anyone who explicitly denies that spatial relationships are important and thus the "debate" over space is rather one-sided. Rather, geographers accuse others of ignoring them,[20] resulting in what Edward Soja terms a "hidden history of spatialization" (1989, p. 47). Fundamental to the argument of Soja and other geographers is the contention that uneven spatial development is basic to the dynamics of capitalist investment (see N. Smith, 1984). As this thesis applies narrowly to urban redevelopment, it explains why redevelopment of core areas can be extremely profitable. The underlying reasoning is that central city land occupied by low-income residents, marginal businesses, or derelict facilities sells for a value much lower than its potential price. If, however, the land is transformed through demolition or rehabilitation of existing structures and conversion of ownership and occupancy, it becomes suitable for highly remunerative development.[21] For gentrification of residential areas, buildings that were broken up into small flats are reconfigured into larger units and their initial occupants displaced; for commercial construction, small holdings are usually consolidated into large tracts allowing unified ownership and management. The huge gains available to investors derive from the previously undervalued nature of the property – without uneven development such speculative advantages could not be achieved.

What matters when?

In the controversies over what matters, there are two opposing tendencies: one is to overly polarize the issue so that only structure or only agency, only economics or only politics, only space or only history becomes the determinant of outcomes; the other is to say that everything matters. The intellectual framework that is used in this book privileges the economic and spatial structures in the sense that they, more than other structures, restrict choice in regard to strategies intended to further economic well-being. Everything may matter, but not equally. Nevertheless, uncertainty over the strategies adopted by other actors, the contradictions between individual and social rationality, the power of ideology in shaping human constructions of rational behavior, and the force of non-economic motivation – all these factors make the consequences of particular actions indeterminate. And, of course, the aggregate of individual actions constantly both reproduces and transforms the economic and spatial structure. The investigator's task becomes to figure out not what matters in general, but what matters when, for what result.

According to this approach, developers, politicians, and local activists are important within a restricted range of variation, and the character of the urban regime is a key element in determining the differences in redevelopment efforts among cities (see appendix A). Even if the *primum mobile* of service-led growth is the world economy, the unfolding of the process involves initiatives and responses within particular places (Massey, 1984). The strategies and actions that produce urban redevelopment within the spaces of London and New York comprise my subject matter.

LONDON AND NEW YORK

Why study London and New York? In the first place, London and New York – with Tokyo – are the preeminent global cities, performing a vital function of command and control within the contemporary world system.[22] The contributions of property developers to the situations of global cities have so far been little explored, apart from investigations of the financial industry.[23] Development firms, however, differ from purely financial institutions in their physicality and greater volatility. Their connection to globalization and overall economic stability, as well as their symbiotic relationship to the financial institutions that dominate the economies of global cities, require further inquiry.

Second, London and New York are ideal sites for the exploration of property-led redevelopment because the impact of the real-estate industry within them during the 1980s was so uniquely large. Both cities were the locations of several mammoth projects as well as a range of lesser enterprises. Moreover, real-estate activity in the two cities generated some of the greatest fortunes made during that period of rampant money-making and became symbolic of the spirit of the era.

The reversal of economic decline in London and New York in the 1980s was based in considerable part on a property boom (see appendix B for employment data on the two cities). The erection of such flashy projects as Trump Tower in Manhattan and Broadgate in London symbolized the creation of new wealth and seemingly testified to growing general prosperity. And indeed the flurry of new construction coincided with a major expansion in employment, income, and tax revenues. On both sides of the Atlantic, policies promoting physical redevelopment through public-private partnerships were heralded as the key to economic success.

The real-estate crash of the nineties, accompanied by sharp economic contraction, has, however, called this model into question. Not only have empty office buildings and apartment houses acted as a direct drag on economic activity, but the heavy commitment made by major financial institutions to the real estate industry has threatened the soundness of major banks. The real-estate slump has affected cities throughout the United States and the United Kingdom. It has, however, been particularly significant in London and New York, where the world's major developers are located, and where financial institutions both finance and consume large amounts of space.

LOCAL CONDITIONS AND NATIONAL CONTEXTS

London and New York also make a particularly useful comparison because their striking similarities simplify efforts at understanding the influence of national differences. The economic histories of the two metropolises have proceeded so synchronously as to highlight the roots of social and policy dissimilarities in politics and culture. Both cities developed as great ports; both act as centers of international trade – and the requirements for financing that trade caused them both to become the locations of the world's most important financial markets. Each has been the financial capital of the dominant global economic power, and each faces increased competition from other world centers. While the United Kingdom's international economic position has declined, London continues to hold its place as a financial capital. In both cities manufacturing employment diminished by half between the middle sixties and the end of the eighties, while office employment increased (although far more dramatically in New York). Changes in employment were signified spatially in an expansion of office space, including major government-sponsored development schemes, and pressure on conveniently located housing (S. Fainstein, 1990b). The two cities each have inner-city concentrations of poverty and are surrounded by affluent suburban rings. In both, manufacturing jobs have moved out of easy access for the inner-city poor.

New York and London, however, have strikingly different political institutions. New York is governed by a mayor and council; governmental departments report to the mayor's office. London is divided into 33 localities, each headed by a council larger than the one that governs all

New York. The borough councils are organized in a fashion similar to Parliament, with the leader of the majority party acting as the head of an executive committee, each of whose members has responsibility for a particular governmental function. New York's government has considerable autonomy from higher levels of government, although its charter and its revenue-raising measures must be approved by the government of the state of New York. London's local authorities are strictly subordinate to the central government, which can overrule any local action; they have no intermediate authorities to which they are responsible, and at this time no overall coordinating body exists for the metropolis.

The systems of local government in the UK and the US have become less alike in the recent past. The elimination in 1986 of the metropolitan layer of government in Britain's largest conurbations has partly recapitulated the American situation in which regions consist of numerous, uncoordinated municipalities. Nowhere in the United States, however, do agglomerations exist on the scale of London's core area without an overarching general-purpose government. In addition, the move by the central government to exert ever greater fiscal and policy control over local government restricts home rule to an extent unimaginable in the United States. Just a short while ago Labour control of the Greater London Council (GLC) allowed it to pursue a course strikingly at variance with national policy – for example, by sharply reducing public transit fares and by engaging in economic planning. Once the Thatcher government eliminated the GLC and other metropolitan authorities, however, the possibility of significant deviation became totally blocked.

Other institutional differences abound. The mayor of New York determines the city's political direction; no similar figure exists in London. On the other hand, the London borough councils are much more powerful than New York's community boards, providing an important mechanism for the expression of community-based interests. London is organized by competing political parties with articulated programs. New York is virtually a one-party city, but the governing Democratic Party has no machinery for enforcing a program and, in reality, has no program to impose; essentially, public officials act independently of party control.

Nationally, there are quite dissimilar policy frameworks, although these differences have lessened considerably in the last fifteen years as Conservative governments in the United Kingdom have seriously reduced the state's role in planning and social welfare (S. Fainstein and Young, 1992). Throughout most of the twentieth century the British state took a much stronger role than the US government in promoting and regulating development. It constructed new towns, built council housing, and prohibited private investment in improvements on land unless they received specific planning permission. In the US the government engaged in very little direct construction activity, preferring to offer incentives to the private sector; although it did build public housing, the total amount produced was minuscule compared to what was achieved in the UK (Buck and N. Fainstein, 1992). The US government also did much less than the British to provide public social-service and recreational facilities.

The British party system also continues to diverge from the American one. It remains far more programmatic and has become even more centralized. It has become a three-party system; and at the city level there is not the single-party dominance that characterizes most big American municipalities and has shaped New York politics during the postwar years. The elimination of the metropolitan level of government has meant no one party has control throughout London; rather, party control varies among the 33 borough councils. In 1991 Conservatives and Labour each held a majority in sixteen, with one council controlled by the Liberal Democrats.

Despite these important differences, London and New York increasingly share some political and social characteristics. Government agencies in each city have actively pursued private investment and have met strong opposition from neighborhood and preservationist forces. Borough councils in London and community boards in New York are comparable forums in which planning issues are first debated. In both cities ethnic divisions exacerbate conflict over turf. While systems of local finance differ, they are becoming more similar in requiring increased dependence on locally raised revenue. Both cities have a majority of renter households and systems of rent regulation, although they have had increasing levels of owner occupancy. During the 1980s each operated in a national context of conservative, market-oriented ideological ascendancy but had strong internal political forces demanding continued state intervention within a significant tradition of state-sponsored social-service and housing provision. Indeed New York has been the most "European" of American cities in the historic activism of its government.

The two cities have also both experienced important changes in the relations between men and women, which have expressed themselves in economic transformation, new family structures, and changed consciousness. These in turn have both affected and been affected by the uses of space, as women have sought access to work, better housing, and assistance in their parenting roles. The increased participation of women in the labor force and the strains they have felt as a consequence of the "double burden" of home and work have expanded their need for convenient job locations, better transportation systems, and day care. Their heightened political activism has intensified the community rebellion against systems of housing, land use, and transportation that do not take their needs into account.

The governing regimes of the two cities have followed very similar redevelopment strategies with very similar results. During the 1980s restructuring of the urban environment took place under comparable economic pressures and in the name of similar conservative ideologies. Economic factors did not determine these ideologies; the power of ideological formulations, however, reinforced the restructuring process within the economic and spatial systems of London and New York. The increasing integration of the world economy heightened the importance of these two global cities, as the worldwide investment opportunities of their dominant financial industries increased. At the same time globalization threatened their status through the challenge of increased competition from other aspirants for their economic niche.

METHODOLOGY

I carried out the research on which this book is based sporadically over seven years, although mainly between 1989 and 1992. Data is drawn from interviews; statistical material published by governmental, academic, and business sources; property company reports; publications of community groups; and academic studies. I conducted about 100 in-depth interviews with developers, officers of financial institutions, public and private-sector planners, chartered surveyors, politicians, community leaders, and knowledgeable observers in the two cities.[24] Respondents were selected by a reputational method, in which I relied on informants to supply me with the names of others who could be helpful to my endeavor. I chose respondents either because they were prominent actors in the redevelopment arena or because they were particularly well informed. Generalizations were made when the comments of several independent informants were in agreement. In many respects my technique more closely resembled investigative journalism than standard social science. I have repeated the views of informants because they seemed to me insightful rather than because they represented a statistical average. Because I guaranteed anonymity to the people I interviewed, I do not usually quote them by name.

All comparative research runs into difficulties in the matching up of comparable units and data. Methods for record-keeping and calculation are never uniform from country to country. The problem is exacerbated when the unit of analysis is a city, where jurisdictional lines do not coincide with physical or economic borders.[25] Descriptive statistics for cities often derive from estimates using very small samples. Sometimes statistics do not exist at all for the comparable area, and it is necessary to construct them from data on other territorial units. London and New York present especially perplexing situations, because London no longer has an official boundary while New York City only forms the core of an area that sprawls over three states. For reasons of practicality the analysis in this book will largely be restricted to London within the green belt (the territory of the terminated Greater London Council) and New York City. For both places the labor market area extends much farther than the political jurisdiction; the cores under discussion here, however, comprise most of the spaces that have been subject to redevelopment, which is the focus of my study.

KEY ISSUES

The main objects of my inquiry are the local economic, political, social, and environmental contributions to and consequences of property-led redevelopment.[26] I ask the question: *What is the logic of urban redevelopment and its consequences?* The assumption, however, is that this logic is not abstract but constructed, containing inductive as well as deductive elements.

I focus on the aims and effects of redevelopment policy and on the real-estate industry as an economic sector. Policy-makers and scholars seem to believe property development is a simple response to economic opportunity, that there is an obvious determining capitalist logic to which it conforms. According to this reasoning, if there is a demand for office or residential space, then developers will come along and fill it, and if governmental programs let developers build more and larger projects, then they will make more money. My premise instead is that the development industry constructs and perceives opportunity through the beliefs and actions of its leaders operating under conditions of uncertainty. Real-estate developers participate in a dynamic process in which they sell themselves to governments, financial institutions, and renters, combat their opponents, and estimate their competitors' intentions. They do not merely react to an objective situation, but operate within a subjective environment partly of their own creation. Often they build projects with little chance of success and press for governmental policies that may not be in the best long-term interests of their industry. Because personal rewards are not wholly tied to the ultimate profitability of projects, individuals within both government and the industry often succumb to wishful thinking in pushing for ever more, ever larger development.

One of my main purposes is to outline the broad characteristics of the real estate industry and of real-estate markets within London and New York. I examine the relationships between politicians, community groups, and developers; I investigate as well interactions among advisers, financiers, and developers within the property industries of London and New York. Several key questions structure my inquiry:

1 What is the relationship between economic restructuring and the conditions of real-estate development? In what ways is redevelopment both a functional response to and a causal agent of restructuring?

2 What contradictions are incorporated in urban redevelopment policy? On what basis do real-estate developers select their projects? What are the causes and consequences of property cycles in capitalist development? How does redevelopment policy combine with capitalist logic to produce an oversupply of space?

3 How is the real-estate industry affected by government programs? How does it influence political regimes? What explains the redevelopment policy of the local public sector? What are the roles of planners and the functions of urban planning?

4 What are the similarities and differences in redevelopment activities in London and New York, two cities with similar economic bases but quite different institutional traditions?

5 What are the special characteristics of real estate as an economic sector? Does it contribute to real urban economic growth or only to growth in fictitious capital, where fictitious capital refers to increases in the paper value of assets because of anticipated future gains? (Is fictitious capital a useful concept?)[27]

6 By what criteria should we evaluate the redevelopment process? Who wins and who loses in it, under what conditions?

7 How can redevelopment be incorporated into a realistic, progressive policy for economic growth?

The inquiry conforms to a "realist" methodology in which the point is not to delineate a general process that occurs at all times in all places. Rather the objective is to understand the mix of general and specific factors that create the London and New York of this moment in time, with the expectation that other cities displaying similar characteristics will share similar outcomes but also that other cities will be different precisely because of the existence of London and New York. To put this another way, we have to understand the processes creating London and New York in order to find out why other cities take on other functions. There is no single model of the late twentieth century metropolis, but rather there is a hierarchy of places with some monopolizing particular, specialized niches. Because the financial capitals of the United Kingdom and the United States are in London and New York, other cities differ from them even though they are affected by them. New York and London are special cases, but their atypicality makes them worth studying, not because they present a model of all other cities but because they exemplify a certain, and especially influential, class of city.

NOTES

1   Neil Smith (1992, p. 74) comments on the two meanings of the concept of scale: "It is not only material scale worked and reworked as landscape [i.e., physical proximity and distance], but it is also the scale of resolution or abstraction which we employ for understanding social relationships, whatever their geographical imprinting." By the latter he means, for example, how we choose a definition of closeness or remoteness that allows us to identify a community or an outgroup, a neighbor or an outsider.

2   While other industries have received subsidies through loans, grants, tax relief, and job training, the sums involved overall have been considerably less than those directed at real-estate development.

3   London Planning Advisory Committee (1991); Commission on the Year 2000 (1987). The London Planning Advisory Committee (LPAC) is composed of members of the 33 borough councils and gives advice to the London Office of the UK Department of the Environment. The Commission on the Year 2000 was a specially appointed group of notables brought together by Mayor Edward I. Koch.

4   I shall use the terms real estate and property development interchangeably, although the former term is exclusively an American usage.

5   See Harvey (1973); see also Lamarche (1976); Massey and Catalano (1978). An important contribution to the discussion in the early 1980s was contained in a number of the pieces in Dear and Scott (1981), especially those by Shoukry Roweis and Allen Scott, Chris Pickvance, and Martin Boddy.

6   See especially Balchin et al. (1988); (1990); Healey et al. (1992); Healey and Nabarro (1990); Healey and Barrett (1990); Ball et al. (1985); Hamnett and Randolph (1988); and the series of working papers on the property industry published by the University of Bristol jointly with the Service Industries Research Centre (SIRC), Portsmouth Polytechnic.

Much of the reason for greater activity in Britain than in the United States is the existence of chartered surveying as an academic and professional field in the UK and its absence in the US. Training of chartered surveyors involves study of all aspects of the property industry, including public policy, and in its inclusiveness and more academic orientation differs substantially from the training of real-estate professionals in the United States.

Serious work on property development is also underway in Australia. Berry and Huxley (1992) and Low and Moser (1990) contain portions of longer works in progress. In Finland Anne Haila (*inter alia* 1988, 1991) has also written extensively on the subject.

7   See Downs (1985); Feagin and Parker (1990); Frieden and Sagalyn (1990); Weiss (1989); Logan (1992).

8   Other examples are Shachtman (1991) and Sobel (1989). Shachtman (1991, p. 7) comments that "these men and their peers [New York City's developers] . . . shared a love of soaring buildings that was more than an appreciation of their worth as pieces of property." In his subtitle, "Master Builder," Sobel (1990)

sets the tone for his discussion of Trammell Crow, one of the largest US developers.

9 Exceptions are the "progressive" cities, where political leadership elected by leftist or anti-developer constituencies has sought to channel development away from typical trickle-down programs oriented toward central business districts into neighborhood endeavors and to extract large public benefits from for-profit developers. See Clavel (1986) for a study of five such progressive cities; Krumholz and Forester (1990) for an examination of the Cleveland experience; Squires et al. (1987) on Chicago under Mayor Harold Washington; Lawless (1990) on the changing tactics of Labour authorities in Sheffield; Goss (1988), who chronicles the experience of the London Labour borough of Southwark; and Brindley et al. (1989), who examine "popular planning" within a London borough and "public-investment planning" in Glasgow. Of the various progressive cities described in the literature, only a minority have managed to maintain a consistent posture over the course of several elected administrations.

10 References to the literature from which this story derives are contained in appendix A.

11 Organized in 1943 under the leadership of Richard King Mellon, head of Pittsburgh's leading bank, the Allegheny Conference drew up the plans for the transformation of Pittsburgh from a manufacturing to a service city. The public sector's role was primarily the reactive one of implementing the Allegheny Conference's strategies. The partnership between private and public sectors was institutionalized within the city's Urban Redevelopment Authority. (See Sbragia, 1990.)

12 The first two postwar Labour governments sought to nationalize all undeveloped land.

13 A number of studies are explicitly comparative and reach something of a consensus concerning the similarities in the impact of global economic restructuring on UK and US cities and on the direction of urban policy in the two countries. See Parkinson et al. (1988); Barnekov, Boyle, and Rich (1989); Savitch (1988); A. King (1990); Sassen (1991); S. Fainstein et al. (1992); Zukin (1992).

14 Among the many studies that reach the conclusions summarized in this paragraph see Parkinson and Judd (1988), Squires (1989), and Logan and Swanstrom (1990) on growth strategies and their economic and social impacts; see Ambrose (1986), Sennett (1990), and Sorkin (1992) on impacts on diversity and the environment.

15 See Cooke, 1989; Harloe et al., 1990; N. Smith, 1987; M.P. Smith, 1988; S. Fainstein, 1990a.

16 Nestor Rodriguez and Joe Feagin (1986), whose thesis is also rooted in a left critique of governmental action, come to a contrary conclusion regarding the efficacy of local action. They investigated the factors historically causing cities to occupy specialized positions in the world economic system. They deny that the capture of a niche results from the logic of the invisible hand – that is, it is not simply a product of automatic response to market forces. They argue

instead that the existence of specialized economic centers is rooted in the political actions of business leaders, who force their ambitions on local government, which acts as an agent of their interests both in directly providing them with assistance and in lobbying higher levels of government. Thus, which one of a limited group of competitors for a particular spot – e.g. financial center, oil service industry capital – prevails depends on the activities of local business and governmental elites.

17   This book focuses on activities within the two cities. In her study of New York, London, and Tokyo, Saskia Sassen (1991) is more ambitious and subjects the patterns of international investment and population movements underlying the global city phenomenon to intensive analysis.

18   Not surprisingly political scientists affirm the salience of politics, while geographers insist on the importance of space.

19   Castells (1989) also strongly emphasizes the coordinating function of financial capital in overcoming the friction of distance in his discussion of New York City.

20   The ambiguity of the antecedent to "them" here is deliberate. One suspects that the concern is not just over omissions in regard to spatial determinants but also to the isolation of the discipline from other social sciences.

21   N. Smith (1979) invented the term "rent gap" to describe this potential as it applies to the gentrification of housing.

22   See Friedmann and Wolff (1982) and Friedmann (1986) for presentation of the "global city hypothesis." For recent research on global cities see Savitch (1988); A. King (1990); Sassen (1991); Fujita (1991); Mollenkopf and Castells (1991); S. Fainstein et al. (1992); Sudjic (1992).

23   Saskia Sassen (1991) is the most searching in her inquiry into the root causes of global city status, but she fails to differentiate the behavior of the real-estate industry from that of financial and business services. She does, however, include Tokyo in her investigation. Its absence from my study results from personal constraints rather than any intellectually justifiable cause.

24   I carried out almost all of the interviews personally, but a small number of the New York ones were conducted by a research assistant.

25   N. Smith (1987) comments that "the very constitution of the urban and regional scales is being utterly transformed by the restructuring process" (p. 64). His remark emanates from a critique of the British Changing Urban and Regional Systems (CURS) study for its scale criteria in demarcating localities. Any choice of an empirical object, however, runs into a boundary problem by necessarily biasing the investigation toward the dominant processes within the chosen area.

26   Patsy Healey and Susan Barrett (1990, p. 90) support a similar approach:

> The critical task for the analyst seeking to understand the processes of production of the built environment is an examination of how such *external pressures are reflected in and affected by the way individual agents determine their strategies and conduct their relationships as they deal with specific projects and issues, and as they consider their future stream of activities.* (Italics in original)

28 Harvey (1982) provides an extensive discussion of "fictitious capital." While real property is a significant component of fictitious capital, the term includes all values based on anticipated revenues and thus is not specifically spatial. Its management requires evaluation of investment opportunities, structuring of deals, and allocation of capital

2

The Development Industry and Urban Redevelopment

The development industry is in some ways the basic industry of New York City.

Linda Davidoff [1]

Some day a sociologist in the business faculty of one of the great universities will take it into his [sic] head to study the development of the commercial property business in the 1980s. When he does, he's in for a shock.

He will find that, over a 10 year period, everything changed.

The Hillier Parker Magazine [2]

While high-ranking public officials were celebrating the "urban renaissance" of the 1980s embodied in the grand new building complexes of London and New York, writers, academics, and community-based critics were condemning the pretensions and social impacts of the recently constructed projects. In a famous passage from his widely read book *Bonfire of the Vanities*, Tom Wolfe describes the scene on the trading floor of a New York City investment firm. His words capture both the physical setting of the great financial markets within these world cities and the social ambience they engendered:

It was a vast space, perhaps sixty by eighty feet. . . . It was an oppressive space with a ferocious glare, writhing silhouettes, and the roar. The glare came from a wall of plate glass that faced south, looking out over New York Harbor, the Statue of Liberty, Staten Island, and the Brooklyn and New Jersey shores. The writhing silhouettes were the arms and torsos of young men, few of them older than forty. They had their suit jackets off. They were moving about in an agitated manner and sweating early in the morning and shouting, which created the roar. It was the sound of well-educated young white men baying for money. (Wolfe, 1987, p. 57)

The real-estate investment market, while not quartered on a few trading floors like the stock and bond exchanges, formed a very significant part of the speculative milieu chronicled by Wolfe. It uniquely combined the intangible activity of risking other people's money with the extremely visible, physical endeavor of constructing the environment in which that activity took place. Property development belonged to the eighties financial boom as cause, effect, and symbol. Profits on large projects, huge tax benefits from real-estate syndication in the US,[3] and trading margins from mortgage securitization formed the basis for vast fortunes. As their wealth and visibility made them prominent actors in the cultural and social scene, the names of developers like Donald Trump, William Zeckendorf, Jr., and Mortimer Zuckerman in New York, or Stuart Lipton, Godfrey Bradman, and Trevor Osborne in London became widely publicized. Financial institutions that underwrote the property market likewise prospered. For example, the mortgage department of Salomon Brothers, under the leadership of Lewis Ranieri,[4] had made the bond-trading firm into the most profitable business on Wall Street:

> The wonderfully spontaneous mortgage department [of Salomon] was the place to be if your philosophy of life was: Ready, fire, aim. The payoff to the swashbuckling raiders, by the standards of the time, was shockingly large. In 1982 . . . Lewie Ranieri's mortgage department made $150 million. . . . Although there are no official numbers, it was widely accepted at Salomon that Ranieri's traders made $200 million in 1983, $175 million in 1984, and $275 million in 1985.[5] (Lewis, 1989, p. 108)

The burgeoning space needs of the expanding financial institutions, the businesses that provided them with services, and their suddenly wealthy employees produced a great surge in demand that was in part refueled by the office requirements of the development industry itself, its financial backers, and its service-providers. The steeply climbing curve of returns from real-estate investment prompted a stream of new development proposals which justified their costs with prognoses of ever-increasing earnings. The shiny skyscrapers housing the boisterous trading floors of the fabulously profitable investment banks, the high-rise condominiums and converted lofts affording havens for the young urban professionals, the renovated mansions and penthouses sheltering their bosses, and the glamorous marble-clad shopping malls, festive marketplaces, deluxe hotels, and opulent restaurants catering to their consumption whims constituted the symbolic setting for the excesses of the period.

In his keynote address to an international conference of planners, David Harvey declared that the two forces destroying New York City were drugs and the real-estate development industry.[6] Although Harvey's wholly negative assessment of developers might provoke disagreement, few would dispute that speculative property investment did indeed transform the functions and appearance of New York and London during the eighties; nor would they disagree that while the public purse helped finance physical change, private entrepreneurs using borrowed money were in charge. Since developers saw little profit in building factories or working-class housing, they confined their activities to producing offices and luxury residential units. The consequence of their development strategies was an economic and spatial restructuring of London and New York in the eighties that was dramatically uneven in its components.

Simultaneous investment and disinvestment created not just the juxtaposition of rich and poor, made obvious by the ubiquitous homeless within even the most affluent neighborhoods, but also sent whole communities on opposite trajectories. The growing numbers of relatively and absolutely impoverished city residents, displaced from factory jobs as a consequence of economic restructuring, dislodged from their homes by gentrification and financial catastrophe, or deinstitutionalized and suffering from disabilities, provided the counterpoint to good fortune. The symbolism of these contrasts was interpreted by the left as revealing the mordant injustice of privately led economic development programs and by the right as a moral lesson demonstrating the differential in rewards to the deserving and undeserving, the entrepreneurs and the wastrels.

For most of the eighties the constant fanfare trumpeting new development projects and the army of building cranes punctuating the London and New York skylines did appear to herald progress, whatever its imperfections. The visibility and hopefulness of new construction tended to override the caveats of critics. Community representatives who railed against the overwhelming effects of large projects on their neighborhoods were derided for standing in the way of progress. Despite soaring office vacancy rates in other American cities as the eighties progressed, New York developers continued to propose ever larger projects. And in London, memories of the property-market collapse of the mid-1970s faded, as banks ratcheted up their real-estate investments.

At the beginning of the decade it was by no means obvious that London and New York would witness such accelerated growth (see Buck and N. Fainstein, 1992). Employment and population had been declining in both cities; existing levels of development made land acquisition difficult and expensive; very high occupancy costs discouraged prospective commercial tenants; while planning restrictions combined with community opposition to create formidable obstacles to developers' ambitions. The fortunes of London and New York, however, reversed as world trade and global financial deals caused economic transactions within them to multiply exponentially during the 1980s.

This chapter examines, first, the heightened importance of global cities within the world economy during the 1980s. Second, it describes changes in the production of, and demand for, space. Finally, it analyzes the particular circumstances in London and New York that influenced their development. The following chapter investigates the causes of the subsequent property bust and the similarities and differences in the property development cycle that occurred in London and New York between 1980 and 1992.

THE INCREASED IMPORTANCE OF GLOBAL CITIES

Analyses of the rising importance of global cities[7] generally offer three reasons for the phenomenon: (1) the greater size and velocity of world capital flows; (2) the increased need for centralized command and control posts in a decentralized world economy; and (3) the extensive technical infrastructure needed by the finance and business services industries.

World capital flows

Several factors produced the explosion in the financial and advanced business services sector which fueled the economies of both London and New York in the 1980s and spurred their physical redevelopment. The internationalization of investment and the growth of international trade had greatly heightened the importance of the financial industry and financial markets. The restructuring of companies, the rapid expansion of mergers and acquisitions, and the restless search by corporations for low-cost production sites and marketing advantages accelerated the volatility of capital and thereby enlarged the role of firms that specialize in managing flows of capital. According to Sassen (1991, p. 19), transactions increasingly took place between firms located in financial centers rather than within the large American banks.[8] In other words, while the management of manufacturing and retail industries became more and more integrated *within* large corporations, ever greater financial flows were increasingly controlled through joint ventures, deals, and trades involving numerous actors.

The debt crisis that began in the 1970s had cut off third-world outlets for investment at the same time as financial institutions continued to acquire massive amounts of capital from pension and mutual funds. Moreover, this capital was increasingly lent directly to borrowers by investors, who purchased interest-bearing bonds, rather than by commercial banks (a process known as "disintermediation"). This shift greatly increased the activity level and profits of investment bankers, who were the underwriters and traders of these instruments, and investment banking firms accordingly added personnel and operational space.

A host of other financial "products" was invented, including "swaps"[9] – exchanges of debt holdings among institutions; junk bonds – high-yield notes that were rated below investment grade;[10] and index futures – agreements to purchase a group of stocks at a pre-established price at a later date. Globalization of investment and production increased the possibility of loss through currency devaluation or sudden, unforeseen market shifts, stimulating the development of new financial instruments as hedges against risk. The securitization of debt (initially mortgages and third-world debt, then consumer debt, including student loans) meant that banking institutions could "bundle" – that is, aggregate – their loans to businesses and individuals and convert them into paper instruments like bonds to be bought and sold. Banks were able to attain liquidity through selling their loans for an amount based on the present value of their expected returns.

The development of markets for all these novel financial products magnified the number of instruments traded within what had become an increasingly closed and volatile system of circulation of capital among the most developed countries. In the meantime, takeovers and leveraged buy-outs fueled the volume of new debt issues. Once-conservative investment institutions, ranging from university endowments to major insurance companies, sought the high rates of return offered by speculative financial instruments and became far more dynamic players in the hyperactive financial world.[11]

Deregulation of the financial industry combined with the various product innovations and huge increases in capital flows to heighten the frenetic trading activity and deal-making that characterized London and New York in the eighties. In the United States the Reagan administration's distaste for enforcing antitrust laws allowed the mergers and acquisitions and leveraged buyouts to involve more and more companies and greater and greater sums of money, along with ever larger phalanxes of legal and financial advisers. The relaxation of the barriers that existed between different types of financial institutions, such as investment, savings, and commercial banks,[12] further stimulated growth within the financial service industries.

The relationship between changes in the world financial system and in the financial district, known as the City or "the square mile,"[13] dominates explanations of London's economic and spatial restructuring:

> The City was to become the hub not of a culturally familiar, slow-paced, empire-oriented regime of trade finance but of a new fast-moving capitalism

in which the City itself was to become equally international. (Pryke, 1991, p. 210)

Response to foreign competition led to the weakening of restrictions on London's financial firms, culminating in the "Big Bang" of 1986. At the same time as fixed commissions on all domestic securities transactions were eliminated (a move that had taken place in the United States a decade earlier), membership on the Stock Exchange was opened to foreign institutions for the first time (Thrift et al., 1987). Not only did these changes directly result in greater business activity, but they attracted numerous foreign firms, which mainly sought space in the vicinity of the City of London. Many of the newcomers, however, ultimately found that the increase in financial activity did not meet their anticipations.

As corporate debt shifted from bank loans to direct borrowing, the major banks lost their previous dominance of financial transactions. Nonetheless, from the early 1970s onward, branches of foreign banks increased in number within both London and New York and continued to expand through much of the 1980s.[14] The growing volume of international trade, the greater presence of foreign subsidiaries in all economic sectors, the increasing numbers of executives from abroad in connection with this internationalized economic activity, and the end of fixed exchange rates all contributed to the demand for retail and commercial banking services. Growth in the real-estate industry itself stimulated bank expansion, since almost all construction loans emanated from the banking sector. Moreover, as large international banks like Barclay's and Citibank increasingly took on functions similar to those of investment banks by acting as financiers for corporate mergers and acquisitions, they too got caught up in the cycle of speculative growth within the corporate investment arena (Sassen, 1991, p. 78–83).

Transactions in the various securities took place mainly on trading floors within individual firms rather than through the exchanges. Nevertheless, the major investment banks and the headquarters of commercial banks felt it necessary to cluster close to the old markets. Because there is a very high level of interaction both among financial firms and between the financial sector and the concerns that provide it with legal, public relations, management consulting, and other services, this group of enterprises is led to settle only in those locations where an agglomeration of financial and advanced services firms already exist (see Amin and Thrift, 1992). Accountants, lawyers, tax consultants, and other advisers to the deal-makers also highly valued proximity to the investment bankers, since their presence at meetings of the various parties to a deal was frequently required. According to a recent study of the New York metropolitan area, large suburban firms continued to rely on Manhattan for most of their service needs (Schwartz, 1992). Thus, even firms headquartered outside the London and New York central business districts (CBDs) apparently found it more convenient to obtain business services within the supermarket of their dense advanced services agglomerations rather than closer to home.[15]

Proximity was crucially important for the participants in a major deal. For example, the account in *Barbarians at the Gate* (Burrough and Helyar, 1990) of the marathon negotiations in the buyout of RJR Nabisco shows that numerous investors, as well as virtually every significant law firm and investment bank in the country, took part. Although Nabisco's head-quarters was in Atlanta, Georgia, and its subsidiaries were scattered around the world, the action, which involved hundreds of corporate officers, investment bankers, lawyers, and financial advisers, took place in New York. On numerous occasions discussions lasted until dawn, and the presence of principals would suddenly be required at extremely odd hours. One cannot imagine where else but in Manhattan it would have been possible to assemble all the participants. Only the common location within a major financial center of the financial and legal firms involved permitted the necessary transactions.

As well as responding to the burgeoning demand for space to house the rapidly growing financial and business services sectors and their work force, property development activity was fueled by the ready supply of funds flowing into the real-estate industry. Property investment became interchangeable with other kinds of debt and equity commitment. Previously, because of its low liquidity and unique characteristics, property investment had been the province of a limited group of financial institutions and knowledgeable individuals. Now, however, greater opportunities for real-estate investment syndication, in which limited partners did not take an active role but received an income stream and could sell their interests in the project fairly easily, eliminated any reason but rate of return to prefer one type of investment over another. The prospect of high speculative gains attracted many to the property market. Moreover, the favorable tax treatment that real estate received in both the UK and the US, although especially the latter, often tipped the balance of investment decisions toward it, thereby increasing the flow of capital into the development industry.

Decentralization of production

In her discussion of the causes of global city formation, Sassen (1991) emphasizes the effect of the dispersal of manufacturing and of such routine business service functions as claims processing or monitoring of inventories.

Her argument is that spatial decentralization within the large corporation makes necessary the development of sophisticated managerial functions to maintain control over the disparate parts. These managerial control functions, she asserts, are physically concentrated: "The spatial dispersion of economic activity has brought about an expansion in central functions and in the growing stratum of specialized firms servicing such functions" (Sassen, 1991, p. 19).[16] Only a few cities offer a pool of sophisticated personnel, technological capabilities, and consultant services sufficient to enable the direction of such complicated organizations. Thus, the concentration of economic control within a small number of corporations makes necessary the existence of geographic centers to manage a dispersed production and marketing system.

Sassen's analysis is partly correct: the specialized firms that provide services to the management of multinational corporations are concentrated, as shown in the Schwartz study discussed above. Sassen does not, however, convincingly demonstrate that "central functions" occur in global cities. The out-migration of the corporate headquarters of manufacturing, transportation, and retail firms from New York indicates that no necessary connection exists between central management functions and geographic location (see Schwartz, 1992). The number of Fortune 500 manufacturing and mining headquarters in New York was more than halved between 1965 and 1976; it dropped by an additional 43 percent, from 84 to 48, or less than 10 percent of the total, in the next twelve years, even while the offices of financial firms were multiplying (Buck et al., 1992, p. 99).

In contrast, British industrial headquarters remain clustered in London, where they still comprise more than half of such offices in the country (Buck et al., 1992, p. 99). The commanding status of London, however, stems primarily from a combination of cultural factors and the political hegemony of the capital within a highly centralized state, rather than from purely economic causes (see Pryke, 1991; Harloe and S. Fainstein, 1992). In other words, other factors besides economic efficiency impel British corporations to establish their headquarters in London. And even in the United Kingdom, the importance of location in the capital for internal control of large corporations is diminishing.

Precisely because control over operations of their branches and subsidiaries is integrated within large firms, corporate headquarters do not receive great advantage from proximity to other firms. Small businesses lower their production costs by being close to suppliers, their distribution costs by being near to markets, and their personnel expenses by locating where there is an adequate skilled labor supply. Consequently we find clusters of specialized small businesses in industrial districts where they can maximize their overall situation, since they are not big enough to hive off parts of their enterprise to a variety of least-cost locations. Economists refer to the advantages of locating near to similar industries as agglomeration economies external to the firm.

Large multinational corporations, however, depend on networks of suppliers and distributors that are geographically dispersed, and their own offices, plants, and laboratories likewise span the globe. Thus, location of corporate headquarters in a global city would not bring them into proximity with the essential components of their operations. Moreover, these firms can easily purchase accounting, advertising, and legal services without being physically close to the providers. In short, while restructuring has increased the power of a small number of corporations over the worldwide production of goods and services, the headquarters of these firms have not flocked to global cities. Intensification of work within the headquarters still there, however, did probably add to the number of jobs and transactions taking place within London and New York. Moreover, many firms located outside these cities retain an agent or office within them, thereby further adding to economic activity.[17]

Technological factors

A number of contemporary theorists have stressed the importance of information, rather than natural resources or physical capital, to economic development. In the words of Manuel Castells (1989), contemporary capitalism is defined by the "informational mode of development." The impact of telecommunications and computer technology on the locational choices of firms cuts two ways. Even though new technologies foster decentralization by reducing the need for physical proximity among participants in a production process, they free those units which find advantages in city-center locations to seek out core areas, rather than staying with the routine processing sections of the enterprise. Thus headquarters can remain in London and New York after routine operations have departed, and firms headquartered elsewhere can maintain a presence within them.

Within the "space of flows," as Castells characterizes the new world economy, certain places stand out because they have the labor pools and technological structures to support the computer and telecommunications systems necessary for the management of the global economy. The recent enormous expansion in financial and advanced business services depended on the development of a technology adequate to handle the soaring volume of transactions. And, in a circular process, only relatively few centers have a sufficient density of transactions to support the necessary infrastructure (Castells, 1985; Moss, 1986; Sassen, 1991).

Nevertheless, according to a recent study by Coopers & Lybrand Deloitte (1991a) London and New York do not have an absolute advantage in these technologies. At least six other office centers (New Jersey, Chicago, Los Angeles, Paris, Tokyo, and Singapore) all offer a sufficient technological base.[18] The requirements for modern firms relying on information retrieval and processing include a heavily backed-up communications grid and a pool of technical personnel to operate and repair equipment. Modern office structures with building managers who continuously upgrade the information and telecommunications systems are also necessities (Daniels and Bobe, 1990). In 1980 many old buildings were not sufficiently adaptable for renovation to accommodate the demand for large trading floors and adquate space for cables and outlets. Business leaders and public officials in many cities, however, were aware of these needs and increasingly invested in their provision. The rapid installation of fiber-optics systems linking most large office centers further reduced the edge of London and New York, since a company no longer needed to be in these cities to tap into their facilities. In addition, their high level of congestion and histories of insufficient investment in transport (a non-high-tech but equally signficant part of the infrastructure) meant that both cities failed to provide easy physical access to their business districts. Thus, while the technological infrastructure of London and New York has been a necessary underpinning of their global city status, it does not guarantee their future dominance.

In summary, then, London and New York used their pre-eminence as the world's leading locations for securities and money markets to capture much of the growth in the financial and advanced services industries during the 1980s. They already possessed the critical mass of resources needed to direct the financial flows that energized the world economy, but they also needed to provide appropriate space for expansion. The requirement was provision of offices that met the technological demands of the computer age and development of luxury residential and high-end consumption facilities to cater to the needs of the leaders of the expanding industries. Although other cities competed vigorously to attract office-based industries, even the appeal of much lower operating costs elsewhere did not shake loose many of the firms anchored in London and New York. Their competitive edge, however, was threatened, and one of the factors driving policy during the period was fear that rivals could offer superior, less expensive space.

THE SPURT IN DEVELOPMENT

Comparisons with other cities manifest the pre-eminence of London and New York as office-based service centers during the 1980s (table 2.1). Worldwide only Tokyo and Paris are in the same league as measured by office space; within Britain and the United States their status is supreme.

Table 2.1   The office market in comparable cities

City	Sq. ft. of office stock 1990 (millions)[a]	Sq. ft. added, 1985-90 (millions)
New York	243.0	35.0
Tokyo	189.0	n.a.
Paris	171.7	6.3
London	154.7	26.0
Chicago	103.0	18.2
Frankfurt	82.8	8.6
Los Angeles	75.0	20.0

[a] Different sources disagree on the magnitude of these figures. Richard Ellis (1991) estimates the stock of Paris at 185 million sq. feet, of Frankfurt at 85.6 million square feet, and of Tokyo at 163.7 million square feet.

Source: Byrne and Shulman (1991).

In terms of capital value, central London contains an estimated 60 percent of the United Kingdom's entire office stock (Walls, 1991, p. 1). While New York's share of the national total is considerably less, it still approximates a dominating 21 percent (Byrne and Shulman, 1991, p. 13). Los Angeles, even after a major expansion in the 1980s and despite its overall economic and demographic competitiveness, has less than one-third the office space of New York. Chicago, the nearest challenger, possesses under half. The area closest to Manhattan in the size of its office stock is its own metropolitan periphery within New Jersey, southern Connecticut, and Westchester County; these adjacent locales contained 209 million square feet of space in 1990 (Byrne and Shulman, 1991).[19] Although other European and American cities added larger amounts of space in percentage terms at the peak of the development boom in the late eighties, none equalled the increment to London and New York in absolute numbers (table 2.1).[20]

Table 2.2 shows the magnitude of the office-development surge during the eighties. In both cities, but particularly in London, most new investment was in commercial rather than residential property (table 2.3).[21] London added nearly 30 percent to its office supply and New York

Table 2.2   Office stock and net additions, 1981–90

	London^a	New York^b
(1) Office stock, 1990 (millions of sq. ft.)	154.7^c	243.0
(2) Net addition, 1981–90 (millions of sq. ft.)	44.7	53.0
(3) (2) as % of (1)	29	22
(4) (1) as % of metropolitan area stock	61	54

^a Central London and Docklands only.
^b Manhattan only.
^c Richard Ellis gives the figure of 152 million square feet for central London not including Docklands. As of July 1990 an additional 2.7 million square feet had been completed in Docklands with another 6.9 million square feet under construction (Meuwissen, Daniels, and Bobe, 1991).

Other sources give larger numbers for both central London and Manhattan. Estimates of office stock vary according to whether they include government-owned and occupied offices, how the measure of net as opposed to gross space is calculated, whether buildings that were converted from other uses or are mixed-use structures are included, and in the case of London, where the boundaries of central London are drawn.

Sources: Byrne and Shulman (1991); Byrne and Kostin (1990); Real Estate Board of New York, unpublished data, 1991; Jones Lang Wootton Consulting and Research (1987); Richard Ellis (1991); Coopers & Lybrand Deloitte (1991).

more than 20 percent, almost all in redeveloped areas rather than on green-field (i.e. undeveloped) sites. This redevelopment took place either within the already developed CBDs or within nearby areas occupied by residences and small businesses. Some of it required the demolition of occupied structures, but the largest projects were placed on vacant land generated by the abandonment of obsolete transportation, manufacturing, wholesale market, and port facilities or created by landfill.[22]

Residential redevelopment expanded as well during the 1980s, although in neither city did it rival earlier peaks. When measured by the value of new orders obtained by contractors, annual private house-building activity within Greater London increased sixfold between 1980 and 1987 (UK Department of the Environment [DOE], 1991, table 1.3), with a net gain of 110,000 dwelling units during the period (UK DOE, 1991, table 9.1).[23] Within inner London the great bulk of the additions to the housing stock were attributable either to conversions, primarily within the inner London boroughs of Camden, Kensington, and Westminster, or to new construction on derelict land in the Docklands (Hamnett and Randolph, 1988; Harloe et al., 1992). In New York City between 1981 and 1987, there was a net gain of about 50,000 housing units, the first time in a

Table 2.3 New York City and Greater London: The value of residential, commercial, and industrial building construction compared during the peak years of the 1980s

	Total	Residential [a]	Commercial	Industrial	Commercial as % of total
London *(millions of £)*					
1987	3,541	699	2,599	243	73
1988	4,421	643	3,516	262	68
1989	3,371	451	2,699	221	80

	Total	Residential [a]	Commercial & industrial [b]	Commercial & industrial as % of total
New York *(millions of $)*				
1987	3,716	1,228	2,488	67
1988	2,348	924	1,424	61
1989	3,565	1,357	2,208	62

[a] For both cities figures on residential construction include both public and private housing. For London the figures on commercial and industrial construction exclude public facilities, while for New York public buildings are included.
[b] Figures for commercial and industrial construction are not available separately for New York. Commercial, however, constitutes by far the greatest amount of the total.

Sources: UK Department of the Environment (1991); Port Authority of New York and New Jersey (1991).

quarter of a century that the housing stock grew continuously for six consecutive years (Stegman, 1988, p. 199–200).[24] Between 1981 and 1987, 33,000 units were added to the city's housing stock as a consequence of either conversions from non-residential to residential use or conversions within the residential sector (Stegman, 1988, table 9.1). Almost all of these conversions took place in the gentrifying neighborhoods of Manhattan and Brooklyn. Moreover, the great bulk of new residential construction (better than 40 percent) occurred in Manhattan on previously utilized land (REBNY, 1985, 1990).

London

By the end of the eighties London was witnessing the largest office-building boom in its history. During the mid-seventies a rise in interest rates had meant that property companies were no longer able to meet their obligations based on current earnings; their shaky financial situation, following on a decade of speculative growth, had threatened many banks and required intervention by the Bank of England (Smyth, 1985, chapter 7; Ambrose and Colenutt, 1975). A decade afterwards, however, surplus space had been absorbed, and the anticipated advent of the Big Bang and, later, of European integration provoked high expectations of exploding demand and the seeming assurance of ever higher rates of return. The ensuing boom signalled the re-entry of banks into large-scale lending for property after the secondary bank crisis of the 1970s, although insurance companies and pension funds remained wary of risking their assets on the property market (Morley et al., 1989, chapter 1). A small number of development companies was behind most of the new speculative enterprises.[25]

The initiative for promoting redevelopment activity in London did not come from a local growth coalition of business leaders and governmental officials, as had been the case in many American cities (Mollenkopf, 1983). Rather the urgings of the national government, which incorporated Margaret Thatcher's views that private investors operating in a free market would create local economic growth, opened up London's once highly

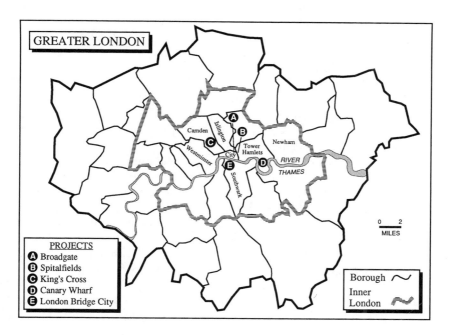

Figure 2.1 Greater London

regulated property development arena for speculative ventures (Harding, 1990, p. 10).

After the Thatcher government took office in 1979, it introduced a series of measures intended to spur private economic activity and diminish local-authority activism. In 1982 the capital gains tax was indexed to the rate of inflation, greatly increasing the potential profitability of property ownership; reduction of corporation taxes further encouraged activity by property companies. The Bank of England relaxed its requirement that primary banks must be located within the square mile around its building on Threadneedle Street, thereby opening up additional territory for office space to house banking operations (Pryke, 1991). The government's establishment of the London Docklands Development Corporation (LDDC) and of an enterprise zone in the Isle of Dogs portion of the Docklands attracted a massive influx of capital to that partially abandoned area (see chapter 9). In addition, the central government put considerable pressure on local authorities to relax planning regulations, sell property, and enter into joint ventures with the private sector. Through a series of circulars, legislation, and decisions by the Secretary of State for the Environment, it pressed local authorities to grant planning permission more readily. It capped (i.e., put a ceiling on) local-authority expenditure, forcing localities to look to the private sector for benefits that had previously been publicly financed. Centrally imposed limits on their revenue-raising capacity caused local authorities to regard sales of publicly owned land to property developers as a potential revenue source; central government interdictions on land-banking also stimulated localities to put land in the hands of developers.

The 33 local authorities that comprise Greater London each set its own development policy. Until the abolition of the Greater London Council (GLC) in 1986, London's boroughs nominally conformed to the Greater London Development Plan, which the GLC approved in 1969. This plan gave high priority to construction of council housing and stimulation of manufacturing employment. Lack of support for the plan by the Conservative central government, however, weakened its mandate well before its actual abrogation (see Thornley, 1991; Ambrose, 1986). Once the GLC was abolished, its plan had no status, and the Secretary of State for the Environment had the task of providing "strategic planning guidance" to the local authorities, each of which was required to formulate a development plan that would "facilitate development while protecting the local environment" (UK DoE, 1989, p. 5).

Developers avoided building in jurisdictions whose councils made life difficult for them.[26] Even though the British tax system recently stopped rewarding local authorities that attracted business enterprises, few authorities could afford to ignore the benefits of new investment in terms of increased employment and services.[27] Therefore they became increasingly competitive with one another, and even the more recalcitrant borough councils eventually assumed a pro-development posture.

Much of the new office construction went up on land that had been in the possession of public bodies, which they now released as a consequence of the central government's promptings. Local authorities had originally acquired large holdings in anticipation of building housing or other public facilities on them. Other governmental corporations, for example, British Rail and the London Port Authority, found themselves owning tracts on which the previous uses had become obsolete. Such vacant or derelict property became the sites for major construction projects.

Changes in technology had made the low ceilings and small floor areas of most existing office buildings obsolete. Potential tenants had begun to indicate a preference for high-quality space over a central location, which until then had been the *sine qua non* of site selection (Daniels and Bobe, 1990). This shift, combined with the early successes of fringe-area projects like Broadgate, which was located on the edge of the City of London, made feasible the development of property formerly considered unsuitable for offices.

The freeing up of developable sites, especially around London's numerous railroad stations, spurred many schemes. Developers, accustomed to the formidable barriers to planning permission that had long restricted new construction within London, responded quickly to their new opportunities. As one of Britain's most prominent speculative developers declared when asked about his siting criteria: "Projects went wherever people would let them."[28] Another head of a very large company commented: "Planning had been archaic, disorganized, unpredictable, fraught with pitfalls. You spent your time bargaining like a lunatic. It could take 20 years to get permission." The unaccustomed compliance of local authorities loosed a flood.[29]

Table 2.4 Net additions to office stock, Central London and Docklands, 1985-9 (thousands of square feet)

The City	16,500
West End	4,150
Midtown	960
Docklands	2,630

Source: Byrne and Kostin (1990).

The City

Nowhere did the Thatcher government's efforts to instigate local development activity have a greater effect than in the City of London (see table 2.4). Until 1983, concerns with historic preservation and the obduracy of the various guilds and titled families holding ancient freehold rights had blocked much potential development within the square mile.[30] Since the City did not harbor the antagonism to business evident in the Labour-dominated boroughs, however, once the economic benefits of restricting growth ended, attitudes toward physical change easily became more flexible and the commitment to tradition weakened.

For a long period financial firms that already possessed space adjacent to the Bank of England benefited from their monopoly position and had no motivation to favor expansionary policies. Financial deregulation and competition changed the stakes. Competitive office development in the nearby Docklands threatened the interests represented within the Corporation of the City of London.[31] If the City refused to accommodate expansion when deregulation was prompting accelerated financial-sector activity, firms already located there risked losing their locational advantage as the center of gravity shifted eastward. On the other hand, landowning interests within the Corporation stood to make considerable money through more intensive development of their holdings. Moreover, when the central government introduced a uniform national business tax, to be distributed to localities on a formula basis, it gave to the City of London alone the right to keep 15 percent of the business rate collected within its boundaries. Thus, the City's revenue position would continue to be significantly enhanced by increasing local commercial property values.

Once the determination to reverse the previous conservationist direction had been made, the City's officers embarked on an active promotional effort. The planning director solicited advice from firms concerning their space needs and encouraged developers to seek planning permission for buildings to accommodate them.[32] In addition, he identified new developable land, including space over highways and railroad tracks. In the process the local development plan was modified to raise floor area ratios ("plot ratios") sufficiently to permit an average 25 percent expansion in the size of buildings. While the local authority relaxed regulations and made discreet contacts with developers and potential tenants, it did not engage in an elaborate sales effort on the LDDC model (see chapter 9) nor deal-making in the frenzied New York City mode. Only in the case of the European Bank for Reconstruction and Development, which had been contemplating a site in the Docklands, was there an outright effort at enticing it to take a City location. An influential member of the governing body claimed that "it would be beneath us" to set up such an operation.

Rather, he said, "we create an atmosphere." He did note that the Lord Mayor possessed a trust fund allowing him to entertain foreign visitors, adding "we like to meet people and mix, but we do it in a private way."

Initially, either because of this subtle form of public relations or simply in response to availability of new, first-class space, tenants rushed to let the additions to the City's office stock. Of the new space that came on the market in the City between 1981 and mid-1987, virtually all of it had been occupied by the time of the October stock-market crash, 57 percent of it by banking and finance enterprises (Jones Lang Wootton, 1987, figures 14, 17). By far the largest single project adding to the stock during the latter part of the decade was Broadgate, a joint venture between the privately owned development firms of Stanhope and Rosehaugh and the publicly owned British Rail. Costing over £2 billion by 1991, this still ongoing enterprise has transformed derelict railroad yards adjacent to Liverpool Street Station into a mixed-use retail and office complex. Its siting in the City "fringe," adjacent to the low-income East London commercial and residential borough of Tower Hamlets, represented a distinctive break with tradition. As the development's fourteen buildings reached completion, initial success in attracting stellar tenants, even after the 1987 jolt to financial markets, seemed to augur unlimited possibilities for those

Figure 2.2 Broadgate

developers willing to invest in the most technologically advanced, luxuriously appointed projects. By 1990, however, the story had changed radically. As a result of sustained contraction in the financial industry and simultaneous continued large-scale property development, the City considerably exceeded the rest of central London in the amount of commercial space unoccupied.

Westminster

As home to Parliament, government departments, and prestigious private firms, as well as London's most exclusive residences and hotels, Westminster has always constituted an extremely attractive location for office development. During the eighties it trailed only the City in the the pace of office construction (table 2.4). Resembling Manhattan's East Side in its array of different land-uses,[33] Westminster likewise possessed residents who often found themselves at odds with developers and commercial occupants. A lengthy battle in the 1970s over the redevelopment of London's old wholesale food market in Covent

Figure 2.3 Covent Garden

Garden, located in the heart of Westminster by the theater district, mobilized numerous conservation groups and residents. The ultimate resolution of the original controversy was preservation of the old market buildings as a festive mall and the listing (i.e. protection as historic structures) of numerous surrounding buildings. The conflict left a legacy of mistrust which was reactivated during the 1980s in a still ongoing dispute over the intention of the Royal Opera House to erect an office building so as to finance renovation of its premises from the proceeds.[34]

The renovation of the market stimulated the subsequent transformation of the entire surrounding area to trendy retail and entertainment uses, featuring fashionable shops alongside cafes, restaurants, and bookstores. Changes within the market area occurred along with a general tendency toward the boutiquing of Westminster's commercial sector and its orientation toward tourism rather than services for residents. Like South Street Seaport, its counterpart project in New York, the rehabilitated Covent Garden satisfied those historic preservationists whose aims were limited to the conservation of architecture, demonstrated that property developers could prosper equally from renovation and new construction, and continued to provoke disdain from community organizations representing low-income groups and preservationists devoted to authenticity.

Whereas in the City of London the governing body relaxed its planning controls, Westminster's council, despite its Conservative majority and close ties to the central government, moved in the opposite direction. Intensified development threatened the substantial public amenities of the area[35] and rising land prices squeezed out residents.[36] Increasingly the council came to regard its mandate as protection of its residents rather than promoting business expansion (Westminster, 1988), especially once it became apparent that, under the uniform business tax, ratepayers would gain no advantage from commercial growth. The Westminster council, unlike the City of London Corporation, served only a residential constituency that had little economic interest in further development. Consequently it subjected development proposals to ever stricter examination, and its chief planner committed himself to extracting as much planning gain[37] as possible from development schemes. The slower pace of building in Westminster than in the City left it with higher rents and a lower vacancy rate at the end of the decade.

Labour-controlled boroughs

Despite the preference of developers for operating within congenial Tory boroughs, several large projects and many smaller ones were planned or built during the 1980s in the inner-London, Labour-controlled boroughs of Southwark, Camden, and Islington.[38] The redevelopment of the Surrey Docks, south of the Thames in Southwark, was largely completed by the end of the decade and represented the first major crossing of the river by up-scale development. The most important project there, London Bridge City, was owned by the Bank of Kuwait. Containing one million square feet of an office and retail complex on land adjacent to London Bridge Station, it is one tube stop away from the City and is the terminus of rail lines to the wealthy commuter areas surrounding the metropolitan area ("the home counties"). This complex succeeded in attracting the routine operations ("back offices") of many foreign and domestic banks, including Citicorp, the Banque Arabe et International, and Lloyds. Another million square feet was built nearby to accommodate the *Daily Mail,* which had joined many of London's other newspapers in deserting Fleet Street in the City for the more spacious Docklands. Furthermore, by mid-1988, when the housing market had begun to crash, 5,000 units of housing, of which almost 90 percent was intended for owner occupation, were either completed or under construction in the Surrey Docks area.[39]

Intense community resistance within this working-class borough has had little effect on these projects. The new developments are unrelated to their surroundings. The park and shops are not used by local people; 80 percent of the housing has been sold to outsiders; and relatively few of the new jobs have been taken by local residents. The council, which at the start of the decade consisted of traditional Labour politicians, was initially extremely unsympathetic to the community-based radicalism that fought the projects. As a result, it reflexively dismissed the proposals put forth by community organizations that were seeking alternative modes of development (Goss, 1988, p. 92). Interestingly, the old trade-union based Labour organization in which this council was rooted did not feel threatened by the functional conversion that new development would bring. Rather, the councillors believed that office construction would revitalize the borough's economy and that the sons and daughters of working-class residents would find work in the white-collar enterprises quartered in the new structures (Goss, 1988, p. 101).[40]

The expulsion of the old Labour leadership, however, did not change the course of development. At mid-decade, the previously excluded radicals gained control of the party machine, but planning powers over the area now belonged to the LDDC, and its strategy of market-driven property investment prevailed over council antagonism. Eventually the council's new political leadership succumbed to the pressures emanating from the central government, and five years after its ascendance, the borough was actively seeking planning deals with private developers, including the trading of land for concessions of housing, amenities, and job-training schemes.

In the borough of Camden experienced community groups were prepared to mount strong resistance to the initiatives of developers (Edwards, forthcoming).[41] Nevertheless, British Rail saw another opportunity to exploit its landholdings proximate to a major station at King's Cross, and developers immediately showed strong interest in the project (see the detailed discussion of the King's Cross project in chapter 6). Ultimately the council, feeling that it had no alternative course, agreed to negotiate with the developers. Similarly, in Islington the Labour local authority became active in negotiations with developers despite considerable community dissent. Although gentrification had proceeded throughout the eighties in this borough, large-scale developer interest was more recent. In both Camden and Islington, however, the real-estate slump of the nineties halted implementation of the proposed efforts. Thus, while the Labour-controlled boroughs did finally acquiesce in the strategy of property-led regeneration, by the time they did so the development boom had passed. As a consequence, except in the sections under LDDC control, these boroughs received relatively little property investment.

New York

Economic recovery began in New York in 1977. The city's decline in the preceding years had been sharper than London's; likewise its revival was more dramatic (Buck et al., 1992). By 1981 office construction began climbing rapidly, rivalling, although never equalling, the pace of the early 1970s.

Perhaps because of the global scope of their interests, New York's business leaders have not worked as vigorously as those in other American cities to frame an agenda for their metropolis. Even the business press has noted the reluctance of corporate heads to become involved with city issues:

> They view themselves as running worldwide enterprises that just happen to be located in New York. . . . It's almost provincial to be concerned and involved in what happens here; that kind of local focus is for the quaint burghers out in Chicago and Atlanta. *(Crain's New York Business,* March 23, 1992, p. 11)

New York's elite is philanthropically active, ornamenting the boards of the city's numerous cultural institutions and contributing generously to them. A number of upper-class, good government groups, some dating back to the start of the century, reliably testify at hearings concerning major land-use proposals. Yet, with the exception of the Downtown Lower Manhattan

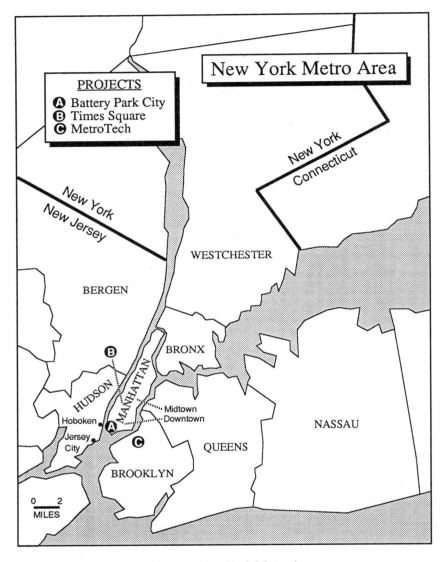

Figure 2.4 New York Metro Area

Association, which as its name implies has focused on only a part of the city, New York, like London, has had no business-led growth coalition to formulate a citywide planning strategy. During the 1975 fiscal crisis, New York's business elite actively promoted its conservative response to the budgetary shortfall;[42] more recently it has lobbied extensively against taxes, and throughout the Koch years it supported public-sector redevelopment initiatives. It did not, however, participate actively in redevelopment planning. Rather, particular elements of business, especially developers and securities firms, influenced politicians directly through heavy contributions to political campaigns.[43] The approach of these political influentials was not to press for comprehensive solutions to New York's problems but to seek specific benefits like tax abatements and zoning variances.

Public programs

Spending on major capital projects had virtually halted during the years following the fiscal crisis and private-sector recession of the mid-seventies (see N. Fainstein and S. Fainstein, 1988). After 1981, however, increased local revenues arising from the city's economic revival combined with state and federal subsidies for economic development to launch a number of major development projects. Chief among these were South Street Seaport, Battery Park City, the Javits Convention Center, and the Times Square Marriott and Grand Hyatt Hotels, all located in midtown or downtown Manhattan. The city paid for supporting infrastructure and granted tax subsidies; it also used federal Urban Development Action Grants (UDAGs) to subsidize the Seaport, developer Donald J. Trump's Grand Hyatt – his first major enterprise, which adjoined Grand Central Station – and the massive Marriott, located in the heart of Times Square. The Urban Development Corporation (UDC), a semi-independent agency of the State of New York with the mission of promoting economic development, was revived from bankruptcy by the infusion of new state funds; it managed the construction of the convention center and the planning and infrastructure for Battery Park City. The UDC's legal powers, exercised through separately incorporated subsidiaries for each project (the Convention Center Development Corporation, the Battery Park City Authority), freed it from oversight requirements that affected city-sponsored efforts: it did not need to go through the normal process of community consultation for project approval; it did not have to request a variance[44] if it did not conform to the zoning law; and the city's governing bodies had no authority over it.

Besides participating in those major projects where public authorities took the initiative, private developers took advantage of tax-subsidy programs for new construction. Since under New York law all local revenue measures must be enacted by the state government, these programs were products of state legislative action; nevertheless, they applied to local property levies rather than state tax liabilities. The Industrial and Commercial Incentives Board (ICIB), which administered a tax incentive program for businesses, participated in office-building, hotel, and retail projects, initially almost all in Manhattan. Although the initial purpose of ICIB had been to revive New York's manufacturing base, it quickly turned into a real-estate development program, and the construction of new speculative office buildings became equated with economic growth in the views of the program's sponsors. Two tax subsidy programs for residential development – 421a for new construction and J-51 for rehabilitation[45] – were also heavily used to assist luxury housing in Manhattan. On the East Side, always New York's wealthiest district, publicly subsidized projects included Donald Trump's Hyatt Hotel and his famous Trump Tower luxury retail and condominium residence, as well as the AT&T (now Sony) Building, designed by Phillip Johnson as a postmodern statement, and across from it, the IBM building. In 1981 and 1982 alone, twelve office buildings, comprising more than 7 million net square feet, were completed on Manhattan's already very densely developed midtown East Side. Although restrictions were eventually placed on the tax incentive programs to direct them to less affluent parts of the city, before these limits were imposed late in the decade, almost every building intended for wealthy business or residential occupants made use of such subsidies.

Media responses

The New York press largely acted as a reliable booster of real-estate development. Although the architecture critics of the *Times* frequently found fault with particular buildings for their bulk and occasionally delivered broadsides against the city's unplanned physical development, the media largely did not question the basic equation of real-estate development with economic growth.[46] In particular Donald Trump, New York's best-known (although by no means biggest) developer of the eighties, adeptly used the media to promote his glamorous skyscrapers (see Barrett, 1992)[47] and, by inference, the whole ambiance of Upper East-Side luxury that surrounded them. Trump was not only man but metaphor. *New York* magazine (November 16, 1987, p. 50), in the preface to an excerpt from his autobiography, declared: "Donald Trump is one of the most remarkable figures of the roaring eighties – a true creature of the age. More than a New York real-estate developer and deal-maker, Trump has become the personification of hustle and chutzpa." *Newsweek* (September 28, 1987, p. 52), which featured him on its cover, marvelled:

> Donald John Trump – real-estate developer, casino operator, corporate raider and perhaps future politician – is a symbol of an era. He is the man with the Midas fist. For better or worse, in the 1980s it is OK to be fiercely

ambitious, staggeringly rich and utterly at ease in bragging about it. . . . For the new rich, says a New York real-estate broker, the name [Trump on a building] is synonymous with "status."

The failure of the mainstream media to offer a general assessment of the city's redevelopment priorities meant that conflicts over particular schemes took the form of local skirmishes rather than contributing to a citywide debate over appropriate economic strategies.

Intensity of development

New York, unlike London, possessed a unified, centralized city government and a department of city planning; it nevertheless lacked a citywide development plan. Development proceeded on a project-by-project basis as developers assembled a site, raised financing, and exploited available subsidies. If they did not require zoning variances or seek zoning bonuses,[48] they did not need planning permission at all and could build as of right. The zoning code already offered a floor area ratio (FAR) of 12:1 (i.e. twelve square feet of floor space for every square foot of the total site) on most lots that were zoned for office use. It granted bonuses to developers who provided public amenities like plazas or subway station improvements; typically such awards raised the FAR to 15:1, three times the level of London. Developers could also purchase the air rights[49] from adjacent buildings, pyramiding these allowances on top of their bonuses, thus building even higher.[50]

Throughout the decade the city government largely refrained from developing plans that would specify its priorities as to kinds of structures, preferred locations, or desired amount of space. When influential civic groups, led by the Muncipal Art Society, protested about over-building on the East Side, the City Planning Commission (NYCPC, 1981) responded with a report recommending restrictions on East-Side development and more permissive zoning on the Midtown West Side so as "to move development westward." By the following year, however, when the proposal was implemented, hardly a buildable site remained on the East Side that was not already in process of development (table 2.5). Under the stimulation of this "new midtown zoning," which raised the allowable floor area ratio on the West Side from 15:1 to 18:1, many millions more square feet of office space were constructed even without the prospect of tax abatement.[51]

New residential construction, almost all for the luxury market until 1987,[52] continued unabated wherever potential sites were not protected by historic district status. Extremely strong demand for residential space in the heart of the city allowed developers to obtain extraordinarily high returns

Table 2.5   Net additions to Manhattan office stock, 1985–9 (thousands of square feet)

Midtown East Side	5,371
Midtown West Side	7,792
Downtown	17,670

Source: Calculated from data supplied by the Real Estate Board of New York.

on their investments. Nevertheless, the city continued to provide tax benefits for luxury residential development under the 421a program until 1986. When the city government finally decided to end subsidies for buildings in central Manhattan, developers rushed to put foundations in the ground so as to take advantage of the tax benefits before they disappeared.[53]

The high level of development activity during the boom years of the eighties markedly changed the appearance of Manhattan. The midtown and downtown office cores expanded and became much more dense. A number of large apartment buildings replaced low-rise structures on the Upper West Side and filled in the gaps remaining in the West Side Urban Renewal Program dating from the 1960s. Battery Park City, to the west of Wall Street, and Tribeca, an old industrial area just north of the financial district, gained thousands of housing units, producing a residential community in a part of New York that had been devoted wholly to business for well over a century. Huge new residential structures lined the East Side between the East River and Third Avenue. Almost all the new construction in Manhattan required the demolition of existing buildings.

The spin-off effects of the Manhattan boom were mainly felt across the Hudson River in New Jersey, where a number of new, large commercial and residential projects lined the waterfront; although New York City's boroughs felt some residential pressure, their business districts remained mostly untouched. Only one major project, MetroTech in downtown Brooklyn, represented a serious attempt to decentralize office construction to New York City's boroughs (see chapter 7).[54] A proposal to build a large-scale development at Hunters Point in Queens, directly across the East River from midtown, hung fire for a decade, due to lack of developer interest (N. Fainstein and S. Fainstein, 1987). Even at the time when real-estate activity was at its height, planners had been unable to identify a market for first-class office space in Queens. Most recently they have been seeking to interest several United Nations agencies that have been contemplating moving to Germany in the site. Intended as a joint venture between the city, the Port Authority, and private developers, the project, like King's Cross in London, remained in the planning stages at the end of the boom market.

THE END OF THE BOOM

Suddenly, a few years after the cave-in of financial markets in October 1987, the construction boom foundered, and the enthusiastic portrayal of a prosperous future for London and New York as global cities faded along with it. The newspaper business pages presented a staccato of defaults and bankruptcies where formerly they had published the press releases of the deal-makers. The cranes disappeared, and in their stead empty office buildings and vacant flats eerily recalled previous optimism. As the job gains of the decade vanished, little else remained to mark the flush times besides the millions of square feet of space that had been created. Both London and New York suffered disproportionately from the recessions affecting their nations. Worst of all, the very industries that during the eighties had been the object of their economic strategies, the source of their growth, and the symbol of their accomplishments lost the most employment. In London, jobs in the financial and business services sector fell by 90,000 between 1990 and 1992, wiping out all the employment gains within the sector of the preceding five years (SERPLAN, 1992, p. 3). During the three years 1989–91, New York sustained comparable losses, as finance and business service employment dropped by 91,000, returning the city's job level to the lowest figure since 1983 (PANYNJ, 1992, pp. 6–8). And, although the boom proved short-lived, the impoverishment that had grown alongside it swelled ever larger. Chapter 3 explores the causes and consequences of this abrupt decline.

NOTES

1 Linda Davidoff is executive director of the Parks Council, a civic group active in New York City. The quotation appears in "Senator Ohrenstein Reports to Manhattan," a 1992 newsletter to his constituents from State Senator Manfred Ohrenstein.
2 No date (1990?), p. 17. This glossy, expensively produced magazine is published by one of Britain's largest and most internationalized firms of chartered surveyors.
3 The 1981 Tax Act shortened the period for computing depreciation on real-estate investments to fifteen years from a range between 22 and 40 years, thereby stimulating an explosion in real-estate syndication operations. Passive investors in a real-estate project could deduct huge paper losses from their taxes on the basis of a relatively small investment in the project; therefore, they

invested in real estate (i.e. became part of a syndicate developing or owning a property) not because of its potential profits but because of its effect on their tax return. The syndicators received large fees, the investors gained major tax benefits, and the developers did not have to promise a positive rate of return in order to attract funds (Downs, 1985, chapter 6).

4   In 1992 Ranieri joined with Paul Reichmann in an unsuccessful bid to take the Canary Wharf project in London's Docklands out of bankruptcy administration.

5   The spectacular profits achieved by Ranieri did not involve direct investment in new construction but rather the provision of a facility by which the deregulated savings and loan industry could acquire liquid capital through unloading disastrous real-estate loans and simultaneously purchase mortgage bonds underwritten by Salomon, representing the non-performing loans of other thrift institutions. Since the federal government guaranteed the mortgages and also insured depositors, it bore the final cost of the wave of real-estate and banking defaults that eventually swept over the country at the end of the 1980s. (See Lewis, 1989, chapter 6.)

6   Keynote address to the joint conference of the American Collegiate Schools of Planning (ACSP) and the Association of European Schools of Planning (AESOP), Oxford, United Kingdom, July 1991.

7   See Sassen (1991); Leyshon et al. (1987); Thrift et al. (1987); Thrift and Leyshon (1990); Pryke (1991); Castells (1989, chapter 6); Beauregard (1991); Healey, 1990.

8   Castells (1989), like Sassen, devotes most of his discussion of the New York economy to an analysis of capital markets. See also Buck et al. (1992).

9   Leyshon et al. (1987, p. 19) define a swap as "the exchange of debt obligations between two counter-parties which is designed to take advantage of differing interest rates or currency opportunities that each can obtain." Thrift et al. (1987) characterize the swap market as the most important new market and credit it with bringing about an increasingly integrated world financial system.

10   While there had always been high-yield bonds, it was Michael Milkin, of the investment banking firm Drexel, Burnham, Lambert, who gave them the sobriquet "junk" and transformed what had been a minuscule sector of the financial markets into what became their largest and most profitable sector during the height of the boom (see Bruck, 1989). Ultimately Milkin was convicted for securities fraud.

11   In the United States, for commercial banks and savings and loans (S & L's) that were paying interest rates to depositors higher than the returns they were receiving from mortgages, and for insurance companies that were forced to lend money against life insurance policies at rates lower than the price of new funds to them, solvency depended on finding highly profitable investments. Mortgage securitization allowed banks to liquefy their old loans at a discount to their face value and invest the funds released in potentially more remunerative offerings. S & L's, which had been freed from restrictions limiting their investments to home mortgages, were most affected by mortgage securitization and used their sudden liquidity to become most involved with

high-risk instruments. They were particularly impelled to do so because of the asset loss resulting from the write-downs on their mortgage loans, although the pain of this loss was partially compensated for by a tax break allowing them to offset their losses against any taxes paid over the previous ten years (Lewis, 1989, p. 103–4). The subsequent collapse of the junk-bond and real-estate markets produced the ensuing wave of bank and S & L failures.

12 In the UK, building societies are roughly equivalent to US savings banks (also called thrift institutions) and the major commercial banks are referred to as clearing banks.

13 The City, which surrounds the Bank of England, is London's traditional financial district and is comparable in its occupancy characteristics to downtown Manhattan.

14 Between 1977 and 1986 the number of employees of foreign banks and security houses in London more than doubled, from 24,294 to 53,833 (Thrift et al., 1987, table 5); in New York City foreign bank employment alone (excluding securities houses) grew by 25 percent, from 125,000 to 149,000 between 1979 and 1988, expanding from 15 to 24 percent of all bank employment (Byrne and Shulman, 1991, figure 4). In 1990 there were 450 foreign banks in London and 392 in New York (Port Authority of New York and New Jersey [PANYNJ], 1991, figure 20).

15 The study found that, of the suburban-based *Fortune* 1000 industrial companies for which data are available, all use Manhattan-based investment bankers, 89% use Manhattan-based law firms and commercial banks, 59% use Manhattan-based auditors, and 43% use Manhattan-based actuarial consultants (Schwartz, 1992, p. 15).

16 Castells (1989, p. 343), who acknowledges the influence of Sassen's work on his own, likewise attributes spatial concentration to the functional need for control over dispersed production networks:

> What explains this striking paradox of the increasing concentration of global flows of information, controlling global flows of capital, in a few congested blocks of one particular city? Several elements seem to be at work. The first is the concentration there of high-level directional corporate activity in the US economy.

17 Bruck (1989) tells the story of the move of the headquarters of Triangle Industries, an industrial firm in New Brunswick, NJ, into Manhattan. Although seemingly contradictory to my argument, it actually illustrates it. The move was not occasioned by the needs of the firm's tiny wire-manufacturing operation but by the personal desires of its owner, who, using junk bonds arranged by Drexel Burnham, transformed it into a shell for the purposes of taking over the National Can Corporation. National Can itself remained in Chicago, and Triangle's wire-manufacturing enterprise ultimately folded. Thus, while Triangle Industries was nominally a manufacturing firm when it moved into Manhattan, in fact it was really a financial holding company.

18 Although New York is considered to be even with New Jersey and to have technological superiority over Chicago and Los Angeles (although not over

Tokyo and Singapore), the study finds it inferior to all three American competitors in terms of occupancy costs. London is considered technologically inferior to New York, New Jersey, Paris, Tokyo, and Singapore, and also either inferior or at best equal to all the other cities surveyed in occupancy costs.

19   Other things being equal, real-estate investors prefer to put their resources into already large markets because of the greater possibility they offer for selling assets and thus for providing liquidity (Dijkstra, 1991).

20   Figures available for Tokyo are so extremely discrepant that I have not shown any estimate.

21   The figures for commercial building include retail and hotel as well as office construction. While most investment was in office space, there was considerable hotel construction, especially in Manhattan, where the number of rooms in major hotels increased by 32 percent, from 45,000 in 1980 to 57,301 in 1990 (Real Estate Board of New York [REBNY], 1987, p. 10; 1990, p. MMP-14). In both London and New York much of the office development was for mixed use, involving retailing on the ground floor.

22   The construction of Battery Park City in New York on landfill adjacent to Wall Street technically constitutes new development rather than redevelopment. Its absolutely central location, however, implies that even though there had been no pre-existing use, it involved a restructuring of the core.

23   In terms of contribution to the value of new housing construction, the public sector constituted about one-third over the 1980–7 period. While public exceeded private investment in 1980, the private share steadily increased and was 3.7 times the public's in 1987 (UK Department of the Environment, 1991, table 1.3).

24   London's net gain in units exceeded New York's because of a much lower rate of demolition and abandonment, not because of greater new construction.
    Between 1985 and 1990, 46,178 new units were constructed in Manhattan; of these almost half were in condominium or cooperative forms of ownership (REBNY, 1990).

25   In an interview, Rupert Nabarro, managing director of the Investment Property Databank, estimated that 50 percent of the property developed in the boom years had been produced by five development companies: Olympia and York, Speyhawk, Stanhope, Greycoat, and Rosehaugh.

26   The developers I interviewed indicated that they bypassed boroughs (usually Labour-led but also Tory environmentalist) which they regarded as uncooperative.

27   Before the introduction of the uniform business rate in 1990, local authorities lacking business ratepayers received a compensating central government grant. Once the uniform rate was in place, no locality could increase its revenues through attracting business.

28   Where published sources are not cited, material is drawn from interviews conducted by the author in London between 1990 and 1992 and in New York between 1989 and 1992.

29 Because of the differing policies of the various local authorities, the presentation of London includes separate depictions of parts of central London as well as an analysis of the whole.

30 In 1981 22 conservation areas, affecting 28 percent of the land area in the City, were designated.

31 The City is governed by a Corporation, consisting of 159 common councilmen and 26 aldermen. Unlike the borough councils, whose members are selected only by residents, members of the Corporation are chosen by business firms as well as the small resident population. Approximately 14,000 voters, the majority of whom are not residents, elect the members of the Corporation.

32 Until the 1980s the City did not have a planning officer but only an architect who concerned himself with design approvals.

33 Although the East Side cannot lay claim to residents as illustrious as the Queen and the Prime Minister or buildings as exalted as Westminster Abbey and Buckingham Palace, it does contain the United Nations and its associated embassies, as well as the city's most desirable residential addresses.

34 The current real-estate market has undermined the potential profitability of the office building and the project is in abeyance.

35 In 1990 Westminster contained 12,000 listed (i.e. protected) buildings.

36 In addition to commercial pressures on the housing stock, demand for short-term lets by business visitors inflated prices beyond the reach of prospective permanent residents.

37 Planning gain refers to the benefits obtained from developers in return for planning permission. The term "exactions" is usually used in the United States.

38 Additional discussion of Labour-dominated areas in which planning is under the control of the LDDC is contained in chapter 9.

39 Information supplied by LDDC, January 1989.

40 In contrast, the Coin Street area, situated near the National Theater and straddling the Lambeth-Southwark boundary, was preserved from large-scale redevelopment by community opposition and became the site of a community-developed plan.

41 Peter Hall chronicles the controversy over the siting of Britain's new National Library within Camden. He comments on the original plan, which involved extensive demolition within the Bloomsbury section of the borough: "few decisions can ever have excited such instant obloquy from the British establishment" (Hall, 1980, p. 177). Somewhat similar to New York's West Side in social composition, home to several colleges of the University of London and numerous cultural institutions, Camden housed many highly articulate citizens who, as on the West Side, made common cause with working-class neighbors on development issues.

42 In the new fiscal crisis that began in 1989, business leaders, with the exception of Felix Rohaytn, partner in Lazard Frères and head of the Municipal Assistance Corporation, have largely withdrawn from a prominent role. It has been alleged that the reason for their previous assiduousness and present

passivity is that, whereas in the mid-seventies New York banks had invested heavily in New York's bonds, this time they had ensured that they would not be seriously at risk.

43 See Sleeper (1987); Newfield and DuBrul (1981); Barrett (1992). According to the *New York Times*, Mayor Koch in his 1985 re-election campaign raised more than $4 million, almost all in contributions of more than $10,000 from real estate, law, and financial firms.

44 A zoning variance refers to permission exempting a developer from a regulation contained in the zoning code. The zoning code specifies the type of use (e.g. office, manufacturing, etc.) to which a parcel of land may be put, the height, bulk, and density of the structure, its relationship to the street, the presence of curb cuts, etc.

45 The numbers refer to sections of the governing statute.

46 A lengthy piece by Jason Epstein (1992) in the influential *New York Review of Books* made the city's failure to support manufacturing and its heavy support of real-estate growth the cornerstone of its argument concerning the reasons for the deterioration of New York. Written in 1992, however, within the context of a completely dead real-estate market, it represented a rather belated response.

47 Barrett (1992, p. 311) characterizes a Sunday *New York Times Magazine* profile of Trump as "fawning."

48 A zoning bonus refers to permission to exceed the space limits contained in the zoning law.

49 Air rights existed when a building did not take full advantage of the "envelope" allowed it in the zoning ordinance. Essentially a building owner who did not use up the entire envelope could sell the unused portion to the developer of an adjacent site in the form of rights to that amount of space.

50 A study of a sample of buildings that received bonus floor area in exchange for the provision of amenities estimated that the market value of the benefits received by the developers was $108 million, while the cost of the amenities they provided was about $5 million (New York State Office of the State Deputy Controller, 1988, p. MS-3).

51 This was intended as a temporary inducement that would exist for only six years. Consequently developers hastened to beat the deadline, constructing eight buildings, comprising 4.5 million square feet of space, in the last year of the program. (Information supplied by the Real Estate Board of New York.)

52 In 1986 Mayor Koch introduced the Ten Year Housing Plan, aimed at producing, preserving, and rehabilitating 252,000 affordable housing units between 1987 and 1996 (see chapter 5). By the end of the decade the program had produced about 3,500 new subsidized apartments in formerly abandoned buildings; another 13,000 were under construction (*New York Times*, March 18, 1990, Section 4).

53 Over 12,000 units of expensive housing, more than twice the previous year's amount, were started in 1985, the last year of the program (REBNY, 1990, MMP 21).

54 Even people who live in the Bronx, Brooklyn, Queens, and Staten Island refer to Manhattan as "the city" and their own location as "the boroughs." In London the usual distinction is between central London, comprising the area formerly within the jurisdiction of the London County Council, and "the outer boroughs." Most of the outer boroughs more closely resemble New York's suburban area rather than its boroughs. The area beyond the London green belt is called "the outer metropolitan area"; it roughly corresponds with New York's peripheral suburban area

3

Markets, Decision-Makers, and the Real-Estate Cycle

The downfall of the property markets in London and New York trailed the October 1987 stock market crash by about two years. Once in motion, however, the loss in value of property was both swift and steep. The failure of most observers to predict the end of the boom magnified its abruptness. Experienced property market analysts had shown a remarkable lack of prescience concerning the future of the market. In a book written earlier but whose publication coincided with free-fall property values, members of a London property consultancy began their chapter on prospects for the industry by commenting: "1987 and 1988 have marked a clear turning point for the property industry. In our view, these years represent the final emergence of property from the long backwash of two major recessions in the last fifteen years" (Key et al., 1990, p. 17). While noting some potential instability, they (1990, p. 40) went on to say:

> Property companies, indeed, might stand as a model of the Thatcherite economy: a freer market, a rash of new enterprises growing rapidly on the back of readily available loan and equity finance – and a crop of new property millionaires to provide an example to the rest of us.

Similarly Jones Lang Wootton Consulting and Research (1987, p. 3) claimed that their 1987 study of office demand "has provided yet further evidence of the strength of the Central London Office Market."

On the other side of the Atlantic analysts expressed only slightly less optimism. In a report about the New York economy written the year after the stock market plummeted, the Port Authority's research arm showed some caution but nevertheless prophesied: "We would expect that some proposed projects will be postponed or canceled. This is a moderating picture: the Manhattan real estate market is not generally considered to be overbuilt and will remain one of the strongest ones in the U.S." (PANYNJ, 1988, p. 6).

THE PROPERTY BUST

The lagged effect of continued investor confidence in 1988 and 1989 meant that millions of square feet of new space were becoming available just when demand was dropping precipitously. Figures depicting average rents and vacancy rates indicate the steepness of the decline in real-estate values that ensued just after the boom peaked. Table 3.1 records the sudden downward movement of the office market;[1] steep as the drop shown is, however, rental figures are misleadingly high, as they show rents paid by primary tenants who may have sublet their space at a loss.[2] In many cases the values of buildings fell considerably below the amount of principal outstanding on their mortgages.

The collapse in real-estate values quickly rippled through the entire financial sector; in turn troubles in financial institutions holding large real-estate investments aggravated the property situation as their own needs for office accommodation shrank. According to the *Economist* (May 12, 1990, p. 82), in the first five months of 1990 the shares of half the property companies listed on the London stock market lost more than one-quarter of their market value;[3] for more than 25 percent of the 80 such firms listed, debt exceeded equity and interest payments were more than twice their rent receipts.[4]

The weakness in the property market, resulting in non-performing loans, undermined the asset base of major banks. In the years 1987–90, banks had increased their property lending in Britain from £10 billion to £34 billion, or about 8 percent of total loans. However, since approximately 40 percent of these loans came from overseas banks, the impact of falling property values on the British banking system was less severe than in the United States. Moreover, foreign, especially Japanese, involvement was greater than that of British lenders in London's more risky ventures, as British banks restricted their participation mainly to less speculative endeavors (Byrne and Kostin, 1990).

In New York the real-estate exposure of two of its largest banks, Chemical and Manufacturers Hanover, led them to a merger in 1991, which itself resulted in a major contraction of their space requirements and a consequent further weakening of the market (S. Fainstein, 1992).[5]

Table 3.1   Average office rents and vacancy rates

London (pounds per net buildable square foot)

	The City		West End		Docklands	
	Average rent	Vacancy rate	Average rent	Vacancy rate	Average rent	Vacancy rate
1986	30	3.5	25	4.0	15	n.a.
1988	55	4.0	50	3.0	25	n.a.
1990	50	15.0	55	7.0	24	n.a.
1991	44	17.1	52	10.0	24	n.a.[a]

New York – Manhattan (dollars per net buildable square foot)

	Midtown		Downtown	
	Average rent	Vacancy rate	Average rent	Vacancy rate
1980	22.9	2.1	13.3	5.1
1982	40.1	4.2	28.0	2.1
1984	39.6	5.4	31.3	6.4
1986	41.0	8.9	31.5	11.6
1988	41.2	10.7	35.3	12.6
1990	39.2	14.5	31.6	17.6
1991 (Mar.)	37.7	16.7	29.6	19.4
1991 (Sept)	36.4	17.1	28.3	20.4

[a]In 1992 when the first major phase of Canary Wharf opened, an estimated 40 percent of the project remained unlet (*Time*, April 6, 1992, p. 50).

Sources: Byrne and Kostin (1990); *Economist* (May 5, 1990); Walls (1991); *Financial Times* (April 30, 1992); information supplied by Real Estate Board of New York, 1992.

Chemical Bank planned to vacate its 800,000 square foot headquarters building on Park Avenue and its 1.2 million square foot data processing facility downtown; the two banks were also to give up an additional 750,000 square feet of office space elsewhere in the city; and 70–80 branches were to be closed (*Crain's New York Business*, July 22, 1991).[6]

As the real-estate crisis worsened, major developers found themselves in increasing difficulty. In New York the icon of the eighties, Donald Trump, underwent a complicated workout of his monumental indebtedness, estimated at over a billion dollars (Barrett, 1992). Although Trump did not formally declare bankruptcy, he essentially turned over control of his assets to his creditors.[7] Similarly in London, Godfrey Bradman of Rosehaugh PLC, another celebrity developer who had also symbolized the seeming triumphs of the times, defaulted on his loans. Bradman was forced to give up his leadership of the firm, which had a net indebtedness of £310 million (*Financial Times*, December 7–8, 1991). Most serious of all was the crumbling of the empire of Olympia & York Developments Ltd. (O & Y), the world's largest development firm. Developer of Battery Park City in New York and Canary Wharf in London (see chapter 9), it was New York City's biggest office property owner (controlling nearly 22 million square feet)[8] as well as a major force in central London.[9] O & Y owed more than $18 billion, exceeding the indebtedness of most third-world nations.[10] Its tangle of debts created a symbiosis between the markets of the two cities, as it used its older New York buildings as collateral to finance its equity contribution to London's Canary Wharf.

Like the other developers in trouble, O & Y could not refinance its loans, as investors cut off lending to the property sector. Since all construction loans are short-term and intended to be refinanced through long-term mortgages when construction is finished, withdrawal of mortgage money from the market destroyed the viability of developers whose buildings were approaching completion. Firms like O & Y, which had issued short-term bonds backed by occupied buildings as collateral so as to finance further growth, were in the especially unenviable situation of needing to either pay off or roll over the bonds on a quarterly or even monthly basis.

The real-estate slump was not restricted to commercial development; in fact, residential properties had felt the downturn in the market before offices. While serious housing shortages at low and moderate price levels persisted in both London and New York, the shock of the 1987 stock-market crash set off a crisis in the luxury market. Thousands of new units in Docklands, intended for the rising stars of the City of London, and multitudes of new dwellings in Manhattan, created in time to beat the elimination of the 421a tax subsidy, flooded a shrinking market.

In New York the problem for developers of co-ops and condominiums was exacerbated by the 1986 federal Tax Reform Act, which eliminated passive losses for individual real-estate investors, thereby converting paper losses into real ones. Because the size of the tax loss, which was derived from a depreciation formula, was based on the value of the property rather than the individual investor's actual contribution, over the years its worth in taxes foregone by the government greatly exceeded the investor's stake. Once the tax advantages were lost, investors could no longer sustain underutilized structures, and a theoretical oversupply became real (Feagin and Parker, 1990, p. 84). Since thousands of apartments had been purchased for tax purposes,[11] the termination of these tax advantages dealt a heavy blow to the upper end of the market.

Continued demand for *affordable* housing, on the other hand, did not elicit increased production by the public sector in either London or New York, and activity by non-profit entities only somewhat compensated for governmental withdrawal. In Greater London local-authority production of dwellings shrank from over 16,000 units in 1980 to 1,260 in 1987, rising only slightly to 1,818 in 1990, while non-profit housing associations produced an approximately equal number of units (UK Department of the Environment, 1991, table 6.4).[12] In New York by the early 1990s most housing construction involved publicly subsidized affordable housing built by community non-profit housing development corporations. The cuts in the city's capital budget resulting from the newest fiscal crisis, however, translated into serious reductions in support for these groups.[13] Plans for 1992 involved ending all major housing production programs, including new housing for moderate to middle-income households and major rehabilitation of vacant buildings, thus limiting activity to moderate rehabilitation of occupied buildings (*New York Times*, April 5, 1992).

At the same time the general economic recession that marked the end of the decade in Britain and the United States dampened retail sales. Consequently vacancies glutted the market for retail space, and in New York returns on store rentals dropped precipitously. Developers, who had based their optimistic revenue forecasts for mixed-use, office-retail, and residential-retail buildings on the very high earnings projected for street-level stores, never realized their rosy predictions. In London retail rents moved down only slightly, despite the rising level of vacancies. In Manhattan, however, the last three years of the decade saw rents in prime Upper East Side areas slipping from a range of $150–$300 per square foot to $90–$225 per square foot (REBNY, 1987; REBNY, 1990). The silver lining on the retail side, which kept the vacancy level from reaching the same proportions as in offices, was the continuing demand for space at some price. Whereas office use was simply contracting, many prospective retailers previously frozen out of the market stood ready to take advantage of bargains. Consequently, after Manhattan retail vacancies shot up by about 75 percent between 1988 and 1990, they began to decline in 1991 (*Crain's New York Business*, October 21, 1991).[14] Although the return from many of these establishments was insufficient to cover the owner's carrying costs, it was in no one's interest to let the property remain vacant. Thus, in Manhattan the fall in retail rents stimulated a minor resurgence in marginal service establishments, like coffeehouses and bookstores, that had been driven out in the eighties; X-rated video outlets, odd-lot retailers, and suburban chain stores also moved in to fill the gap.

WHY DID IT HAPPEN?

The swings in the real-estate market can be understood in various ways. Real estate has always conformed to highly cyclical trends, and there are a number of theoretical analyses that seek to explain this trait.[15] My discussion attempts to identify the factors underlying the boom and bust that occurred in London and New York in the 1980–92 period. Some of these elements characterize the industry generally, while others were specific to its dynamics within these global cities in this historical period.

Oversupply

The standard explanation for overproduction of real estate is that projects take so long to come to fruition that investors cannot easily foresee the market at the time of completion. Just as farmers must plant their fields long before they can know the market for their crops, developers cannot easily adjust their inventory to current demand. In this respect, real-estate investment is by definition speculative.

The structure of the industry also contributes to its strong cyclical tendencies. Like the agricultural sector, and for many of the same reasons, the property industry tends to overproduce. While the real-estate industry is less competitive than agribusiness, no small group of firms dominates the market sufficiently to control overall supply;[16] thus, even when developers anticipate oversupply, they cannot put a cap on the total amount built. New York developers have sought to reduce risk by preleasing buildings prior to construction, and often financial institutions will not lend without an assurance of an anchor tenant.[17] In London, Olympia & York, as we shall see in chapter 9, through buying into other development firms, was following a deliberate, although ultimately unsuccessful policy of seeking to control the market.

By 1987 it was becoming fairly obvious that already planned projects in London and New York could meet all likely demand. Moreover, prospective investors in these two cities could look to numerous other locations, especially in the US sunbelt, for examples of vastly overbuilt office markets. As early as 1986, *Fortune* magazine had called the period "the worst of times for real estate" (Taylor, 1986, p. 29), noting that more than a fifth of US office space was empty. In places like Denver, Miami, and Dallas, the vacancy rate throughout the eighties had hovered at above 18 percent, bearing witness to the enthusiasm of builders who had responded to earlier service-industry expansion by constructing millions of square feet of space in excess of demand.[18] A little prudence would have identified the same factors at work in London and New York as well. Nevertheless, developers continued to dream up ever bigger projects; banks increased their lending; property analysts persisted in advising their clients to continue investing in real estate; and governmental authorities kept on turning to property-led development as the remedy for fiscal and employment shortfalls.

The pressure to build

When I asked leading developers, officers of lending institutions, property consultants, and public officials why project commitments had continued in the face of mounting evidence of their fragility, they responded fairly unanimously that there had been a herd instinct at work. ("They're all like sheep, these fund managers," snapped one company director.) The CEO of one of Britain's largest firms, who claimed to have started selling off property steadily since 1986 and thus to be relatively undamaged by the slump, declared: "It came from stupidity. Most people in the business have a pretty impoverished level of intellectual capacity. Most lenders are uneducated, not well trained." In virtually the same words a partner in a famous investment firm remarked: "Banks have a herd mentality. They didn't learn the lessons of 1974. They are not run by the very intelligent." Another London CEO proclaimed: "The market is not driven by experience or technology but by emotion."

Americans in the industry came to similar conclusions. In the words of one observer who had held a number of high-level public- and private-sector positions, "Financial institutions had a lot of money. They never learn." A consultant stated:

> Real estate was where everyone wanted to be. There was a tremendous bias toward real estate. In the seventies a momentum began to be built up. In the eighties it exploded. The projections were all rosy. People were unwilling to see when saturation would occur. And there was optimism that "my project was best" along with an explosion of available cash.

Many observers echoed the explanation that individual developers managed to persuade themselves – and investors – that their project would work even if others would not. Another popular interpretation of rash commitments was the "greater fool" theory; under this hypothesis it was always possible to rid oneself of a poorly performing property.[19]

Knowledgeable analysts agreed that the availability of financing drove the market, that developers would build as long as someone was willing to provide the necessary funds. In the words of one developer: "There is a belief that bankers finance what builders build. In fact, the opposite is true. Money is the *sine qua non*. If you have money you will build." Because developers needed to put so little of their own equity into a project, they had little motivation for caution. As another developer commented, "Every property man loves to build. They forget the risk. They're not using their own money. It's lovely building with other people's money." Even if developers foresaw problems, they could avoid personal jeopardy – most development firms received non-recourse financing, in which the loan was collateralized by the building and the builder was not further liable in case of default.[20] Developers were further encouraged by political leaders expecting that new development would generate employment and tax revenue.

Moreover, without a stream of new projects, developers could not keep their organizations going and their own salaries paid. One developer compared his operation to a movie production, wherein he was the impresario who brought together the cast of architects, contractors, lawyers, accountants, financial consultants, investors, construction workers, etc. who created and financed a building project. Although the core staff employed by the development firm itself was small, any reduction of its size made future productions difficult and undermined the personal relations that undergirded this type of entrepreneurial organization.

Bankers seemingly had stronger incentives than developers to scrutinize risks. But, as another CEO remarked: "Banks competed to get deals rather than doing an overall assessment." One investment banker saw himself in virtually the same position as a developer: "Investment bankers are just intermediaries. They will underwrite if there are buyers [of the bonds]." Commercial banks appeared to be in a different position from investment institutions since they bore direct responsibility for the loan and therefore presumably had reason to be more careful (although even they could pass off some of their risk through syndication). They, however, lacked other outlets for loans, and in addition received payments for services connected with the granting of funds. The vice-president of a leading American pension fund that invested heavily in property mused: "Commercial banks have been the largest source of money for property. They are driven by the desire for fees. They saw very high returns at the time relative to other lines of business."

The director of a very big, quite conservative, property investment company in the United Kingdom reflected on the pressures that had operated on him in the eighties: "I'm on a public company treadmill. All these analysts are sniping at you all the time." Because his company's assets were not fully leveraged, his firm was a tempting takeover target, and he had been forced to devote considerable energy to defeating such a maneuver. Although in 1991 he could pride himself on the stability of his firm, he remained defensive about the obloquy he had sustained during the expansionary years: "They accused us of being too dozy." In the hyperactive, deal-making world of 1980s finance, sleepiness seemed the most embarrassing insult of all.

In fact, the pressure to make deals did not simply arise out of faddism or the spirit of a go-go age. While the long-term interests of firms might depend on wise investing practices, the immediate rewards for individuals seeking bonuses, promotions, and rising equity depended on increasing the firm's business. For publicly held enterprises, stock prices depended on growth. Within the banks and other investment institutions, which for much of the eighties were paying out high interest rates to investors and depositors, there was a desperate search for highly remunerative outlets (Downs, 1985, chapter 10). Past successful experience with using real estate as a hedge against inflation further bolstered the view among investors that property represented a wise investment choice.

Advice and research

Real-estate developers and property investors need two types of information when contemplating an enterprise: first, what is the likely overall market situation when the development is completed; and second, what type of project on which site is most likely to produce the greatest return. In my investigation of the industry I sought to discover the sources of such information and its effect on investment decisions.

As in any other major industry, property-investment and development firms use both in-house staff and outside consultants for advice and research. The training of people who fill these roles differs between London and New York. Within the United Kingdom the profession of chartered surveyor encompasses a group of individuals who, through a combination of formal education and apprenticeship, study all aspects of property, from construction techniques to financing methods to valuation. A number of the officers of major development firms had such training, as do many planning officers of local authorities; in addition, firms of chartered surveyors offer consulting services to both the public and private sector (see Leyshon, Thrift, and Daniels, 1990). In the United States no comparable professional category exists, and its functions are divided among planners, lawyers, real-estate brokers, and business-school graduates. Consequently, in the United States strategic analyses tend to be more fragmented and impressionistic. Although the similar conditions of the London and New York property markets apparently belied the advantages of the expertise provided by chartered surveyors, the fact that large speculative risks were taken by only a small number of bankers and developers in London might support the hypothesis that adequate analysis was available to those who sought it.

Few development firms in either London or New York boasted in-house research units; those that did primarily investigated consumer satisfaction with their earlier developments and sought to identify amenities that would help sell future projects. Heads of development firms on both sides of the Atlantic indicated that they had little faith in the utility of formal research endeavors. The CEO of a very large London firm commented: "We've got various marketing research advisors. They do research. But they get it [the market] wrong." The chairman of a major firm currently teetering on the edge of bankruptcy asserted during better times: "We don't do a lot of research. We know the market. A feel for the market is the most important thing." The head of a huge British property corporation declared: "We don't have a real research department. The research is in my head. I talk to people in the [financial] markets every day. . . . We have a sort of circle." A leading New York developer similarly declared: "Most developers sense intuitively where there is an opportunity. They don't rely on economic studies. . . . As a practical matter you are guessing ahead – so the past does not tell you what you need to know." Another New York CEO likewise dismissed the usefulness of research results: "It's today's wisdom extrapolated into the future." One of the few women in the development business observed: "You smell things, touch them."

Serendipity and connections are apparently the principal basis on which the industry operates. Several developers indicated that they relied on tips and chance encounters when identifying a site on which to build. According to one New York developer:

> I picked one site by seeing a sign on a building. I knew the area was good, so I followed it up. I get calls from brokers all the time – some of them pay off. Lawyers make significant introductions.

A real-estate lawyer upheld this commentary:

> If you're in this business you get phone calls – from brokers, friends, clients, others who are just knowledgeable, hoping for a brokerage fee. They will call me [i.e. a lawyer] instead of a client because they know that this way a number of clients are potential buyers. At this stage you're not an attorney, you're just a facilitator.

Even in financial institutions, personal relationships underlie judgments concerning developments that officers are willing to back. A director of the pension fund with the largest real-estate holdings in the US, who managed its New York City portfolio, indicated that her investment decisions depended fundamentally on who was the developer:

> We build up great familiarity with the major players. Our investments are almost always with developers with whom we have experience. We must trust the developer, share his philosophy. We do not work with a large staff, and therefore we must depend on the developer's decisionmaking.

A managing partner in a British investment firm stated that "we would get involved in a real-estate deal because we believe in the man first, the market second, and the location third."

Developers primarily seek advice when they have very specific questions. They turn to trade organizations like the British Property Federation and the Real Estate Board of New York (REBNY) for information on tax law, landlord-tenant legislation, and building regulations. They consult planners and attorneys for assistance on planning permission and zoning matters once they have identified a site that they wish to develop. Their research is primarily directed at the likely prospects for the individual property that they are developing; the assumption is that present overall trends will continue, and the forces shaping the broad contours of the market are not usually the subject of investigation. Only retail developers do much market research, but their focus is mainly on demographic projections rather than on the likely actions of their competitors – that is, they predict changes in demand not supply.

Institutional investors usually rely much more on market data when making their decisions than do developers (see McNamara, 1990). Various financial advisory firms, including Salomon Brothers, Jones Lang Wootton, Landauer Associates, and the Investment Property Databank provide regular market updates to their clients. According to the managing director of such a firm:

> Within London, financial institutions that looked carefully at the market used the boom to unload properties. The people who built the buildings were speculators, not users of research, not long-term thinkers. Most of the money came from non-traditional sources, especially Japanese banks.

In New York it is more difficult to make such a clear-cut distinction between the types of institutions that relied on research to guide them to withdraw from the market before it peaked and those that were willing to finance speculative real-estate development. Many major US domestic banks and insurance companies made substantial real-estate commitments at the end of the boom period; greater caution was a function of individual management rather than being associated with general categories of firms.

Even if developers and investors had relied less on their intuition and more on professional advice, very likely they would have acted little differently. As one chartered surveyor admitted wryly: "It was not to the advantage of consultants to tell everyone to pull back when the future was beginning to worsen." Among the lawyers, chartered surveyors, brokers, and other advisers to the property industry, there were virtually no disadvantages to promoting further construction projects. Large consultancy fees depended on a commitment being made; the only penalty for bad advice was loss of reputation – and since everyone was encouraging property investment, it was unlikely that any firm would be singled out for culpability.

The role of government

Not only did governing bodies in both London and New York forgo their earlier predilection to regulate growth, they instead devoted themselves to reinforcing expansionary tendencies (see chapter 4). The various specific benefits given to developers, including the provision of infrastructure, low-priced land, grants, loans, and regulatory and local tax relief, further induced activity. Combined with encouragement of private-market strategies for economic growth at the level of the national government and biases in favor of real-estate investment in the tax codes of both countries, these local efforts had the effect of loosening the remaining constraints on supply.

In Britain, where the Treasury resists the use of tax incentives, governmental encouragement of real-estate development mostly arose from the relaxation of restraints. Some British developers now lament the lack of an overall planning authority for London and feel that the industry would have benefited from more coordinated and limited development. The chairman of a firm that was among the most active in London during the eighties remarked at the end of the decade:

> It is socially and economically harmful to be overbuilt. . . . I am [now] urging for restraint through planning. It has been too easy to get permission. All you have to do is buy them [the local authorities] with planning gain. Market-led development has turned out not to be as great as we expected. Without tension between restraint and entrepreneurship there is no balance.

In contrast, no New York real-estate leader that I interviewed wished to see governmental constraint. When the head of one firm, who had formerly directed a city agency, was asked whether the city would have been better off if it had restricted development, he responded typically:

"Why should government worry about oversupply? Government shouldn't protect the market." Nevertheless, New York developers, somewhat surreptitiously, attempted to restrict the amount of development by funding environmental groups that were opposing projects of other developers. Thus, community opponents of 42nd Street redevelopment had substantial sums at their disposal, provided by unidentified sources; and the developer Seymour Durst, a property owner in the Times Square area, openly supported attempts at blocking the development of four large office towers there. Donald Trump, in an effort to prevent construction of a competing building across Fifth Avenue from Trump Tower, paid the $50,000 legal fee of an attorney representing the Municipal Art Society, a civic group fighting the project (Barrett, 1992, p. 320).

Government officials in both London and New York rejected the view that it was their role to guide the market. One London borough council leader commented: "I always find it extraordinary that developers, who are proponents of the free market system, should want planning. No one forces developers to overbuild." A councillor in the City of London remarked:

> There has not been overbuilding. More availability is good from the tenant's point of view. The choice of whether to build is one of the owner not the planner – planning permission does not mandate construction. Planners should not predict the marketplace; they are not qualified to make that judgment.

A New York development agency head asked, "Did we overbuild or did we just lose an awful lot of jobs? Today's surplus is the result of decisions made four or five years ago." He argued that "government could not have accurately predicted the current situation." Interestingly, in San Francisco, public officials and business interests fiercely resisted a citizens' ballot initiative to restrict office development to under a million square feet a year. Restrictions, however, were adopted, and the vacancy rate, as a consequence of the controls on new construction, dropped from 18 percent in 1986 to 12 percent in 1991 despite the recession (REBNY, 1987; Colliers International Property Consultants, 1991). Evidently governmental controls have the potential to stabilize the industry despite itself.

LONDON AND NEW YORK COMPARED

Although London and New York followed similar trajectories during the 1980s and early nineties, there remain differences between the two cities, which make the character of decision-making somewhat dissimilar and might cause their paths once again to diverge. London's development firms are mainly publicly held, and heads of firms usually proceed up through the ranks as in other business organizations. In New York, on the other hand, many major firms are not only privately held but are run by groups of relatives: the LeFraks, the Roses, the Rudins, the Tishmans, and the Trumps are among New York's leading real-estate families with firms bearing their names. In a number of cases the present CEO is the son of the founder. The culture of New York's firms tends to be more personalistic than that of their London counterparts, and relations with governmental officials are closer.

In the New York property world, the clubbiness of the City of London, where relationships are often based on implicit understandings rather than formal rules, is replaced by an equally informal but more explicit quid pro quo. Favoritism is not a product of club memberships and old school ties. Instead developers contribute heavily to political campaigns and expect consideration in return (see Newfield and Barrett, 1988). Construction unions and contractors are notoriously crooked and politically influential; developers routinely pay the costs associated with inflated labor charges and kick-backs. In the words of one insider:

> The political system in . . . [New York] City and State is thoroughly corrupt and psychologically geared to a time when corporations had to be in the city. The system was devised to divide up action that was assumed to be there. In the eighties the money was there again for a little while. But the political system increases the costs of doing business, and businesses no longer have to stay. There is a significant massive indirect tax levied by a corrupt political system.

In contrast, even the most virulent critics of London's property firms do not believe that personal payoffs significantly warp the dealings between government and development interests. The CEO of a British firm with assets of £2 billion commented that his firm would no longer work in New York because of the level of corruption there. He did not believe that maintaining close contact with politicians would be useful in London and claimed that he did not contribute to political campaigns.

London firms borrow to cover virtually all development costs and usually build without commitments from tenants. Although on the face of it their operations appear more speculative than those of their New York counterparts, office developers in London in fact have operated within a more predictable market. Although the system has begun to break down because of weak demand, office tenants typically hold 25-year leases, which are subject to five-year, upward-only rent reviews performed by firms of chartered surveyors. The owner and the tenant each has a surveyor who represents their interests; if they cannot reach agreement, an arbitrator makes the final decision. Since relatively few leases expire in a single year, this system assures that during downturns in the market tenants cannot easily search out bargains; for those whose leases still have many years to run, buying out their leases is a very expensive proposition. In New York the plunge in the market has allowed many large tenants to assiduously pursue deals with their landlords, effectively pushing the average price down much more quickly than in London (see table 3.1).

London's tenants have fewer alternatives than New York's, as no other city within the United Kingdom seriously competes with London for financial and advanced services firms. Whereas in the US a central-city location does not carry particular prestige, within the United Kingdom considerable prejudice remains against locations outside central London (Pryke, 1991; Meuwissen et al., 1991). While this situation is changing as the southeast of England becomes increasingly polynodal, for the medium term traditional preferences remain a significant factor in maintaining London's strength as against the rest of Great Britain. In contrast, New York's pre-eminence is threatened not only by other major US financial centers, like Los Angeles and Chicago, but also by its own suburban

Table 3.2   Effective class A office rent,[a] July 1991

	$ per square foot
Tokyo	216
London	94
Paris	60
Hong Kong	52
Glasgow	42
Frankfurt	41
Birmingham	39
NY – midtown	37
Toronto	36
Washington, DC	34
Los Angeles	29
Chicago	28
Minneapolis	22
Brussels	21
Northern New Jersey	18

[a]Effective rent is defined as average annual effective rental costs per square foot, including base rent, operating expenses and taxes less an amount equal to the amortized value of landlord concessions of free rent and/or cash contributions but does not include landlord contributions for tenant improvements.

Source: Colliers International Property Consultants (1991).

hinterland. Within this metropolitan periphery a number of locations like Princeton, New Jersey, and Stamford, Connecticut, carry equal, if not more, cachet to Manhattan. In the future, competition from continental Europe will challenge London's importance, but Paris, Frankfurt, and Brussels are unlikely to dislodge London from its dominant position in financial markets nor to overcome the advantages of English-speaking service firms within the world market more generally.

Relative to all other cities except Tokyo, London has exceptionally high occupancy costs. These result from several factors, including the leasing arrangements described above, its long history of strict planning controls, and the monopolistic position of landowners. A 1991 survey of office rents for class A (highest quality) space, adjusted for differences in the kinds of services (like renovations and utilities) included in the basic rental agreement, showed London's rates are more than 1.5 times those of Paris, and 2.5 times those of midtown Manhattan's (table 3.2). While this situation protects owners of occupied buildings and the banks and financial institutions that lend to them, it injures London's competitive position within the world and generally inflates prices within the metropolis. In simple terms, it benefits the property industry relative to all other British industries.

THE CONSEQUENCES OF THE PROPERTY CYCLE

Despite market differences, developers in both London and New York made similar types of calculations during the real-estate boom. The large office or multi-use structure comprised the principal investment object. In both cities property analysts stressed the need of financial firms for large trading floors that could not be accommodated in older buildings. The total number of financial institutions requiring such facilities, however, is quite small, and even within firms with large staffs of traders, the technological necessity for keeping them within shouting distance of each other has never been wholly clear and is diminishing with the development of advanced computer networks.[21]

Whereas residential market structures used to be very different in London and New York, they became much more alike during the eighties. Public-sector housing production in Britain dwindled to a near halt during the eighties, while, in a striking turnaround, New York's commitment to publicly subsidized affordable housing considerably exceeded London's by the end of the decade. Private developers in both cities built almost exclusively for the luxury market in condominium forms of ownership; they found that the number of households that could afford their product was limited and, once recession struck, almost nonexistent.

In both cities the property-led strategy for economic development has meant that public resources that might have been used elsewhere became embedded in real estate. If the true purpose of this investment was to attract firms, and therefore employment, through lowering occupancy costs, then the alternatives to subsidizing construction would have been to invest directly in those enterprises – by providing training for their labor forces, by offering loans and grants for equipment and start-up costs, or by taking an equity interest. In reality public subsidy represented a taxpayer investment in a leading industry – the property industry itself; ironically, the failure of the public sector to moderate expansion destabilized the sector.

Defenders of recent public policies argue that empty office buildings do no harm, that the new buildings will eventually be filled while the old ones deserve abandonment, and that by bringing down prices, vacancies will encourage economic growth. Governmental stimulation of large-scale commercial development, however, incurs major public costs: it involves heavy public staffing expenses; it often relies on the sale of publicly owned land at below market prices; it requires considerable expenditure on infrastructure; it crowds out alternative uses of land and contributes to gentrification; it causes a focus on the central business district at the expense of neighborhood development; and its impact on the quality of the urban environment has been at best mixed.

Initially public intervention was intended to prevent inflation in land prices from making property unaffordable to businesses and residents. Rather than moderating price increases, however, it first inflamed speculation that produced leaps in land values greatly exceeding the average rise in living costs; eventually it contributed to the oversupply that caused rapid and damaging devaluation and a corresponding reduction in the value of the public's investment.[22] Even if the price of property in 1992 were the same as would have prevailed if, instead of boom and bust, there had been moderate yearly price increases, the social consequences are quite different. Moderately profitable businesses of all sorts lost their premises, causing the break-up of established patterns of patronage; business and residential communities dissolved and cannot be reconstituted. The bargains currently available may eventually regenerate some of the old vitality of diverse business districts and mixed residential neighborhoods, but at the cost of great disruption in the lives and fortunes of those who were driven out.

We do not know yet whether London and New York are in the process of continuing the descent that preceded the eighties or are simply in a routine cyclical trough from which renewed demand will lift them, causing today's white elephants to prove a reserve of opportunity for tomorrow's growth. Whatever the outcome, however, certain lessons are apparent from the last decade's experience: promoting real-estate development is not identical with fostering stable economic growth; and the opposition by the industry to regulation is not even in its own long-term interest.

NOTES

1 In New York assessed values declined by 8.6 percent in fiscal year 1992 from the previous year (New York State OSDC, 1991, p. 12).

2 American Telephone and Telegraph subleased its Upper East Side world headquarters to Sony at a reported price of $20 per square foot, barely more than half the ostensible average rent for the area (*Barron's*, July 22, 1991, p. 10). It was also reported that the Bank of Nova Scotia sublet some of its downtown space to a financial firm for $12 a square foot after a one-year rent-free period (*Crain's New York Business*, March 23, 1992).

   Rental figures also fail to reflect the deals – for example, free provision of fixtures, buyouts of current leases, etc. – that most developers have had to offer to attract tenants.

3 During the 1974 UK property crash, when prices dropped by 40 percent, the vacancy rate was only 11 percent (*Economist*, May 12, 1990, p. 82).

4 Comparable statistical information is not available for New York, where development firms are privately held and thus not subject to the disclosure requirements of public corporations.

5 In 1991 these two banks together held $4.1 billion in outstanding real-estate loans, $1 billion in foreclosed property, and $6.7 billion in foreclosed and problem loans. In even more serious trouble was Citicorp, New York's largest bank, which held $7 billion in outstanding loans, $2 billion in foreclosed property, and $14 billion in foreclosed and problem loans (*Barron's*, July 22, 1991). These loans, of course, were not restricted to New York City

6 In addition to its direct effects on jobs and the use of space within the restructured banking organization, the merger has caused the downsizing of a number of firms that provided services to its predecessors. For example, Price Waterhouse received $7 million per year in fees for auditing Chemical while KPMG Peat Marwick received $4.9 million for its services to Manufacturers Hanover; in the losing accounting firm 40-50 professionals plus their support staffs were to lose their jobs. Similar competition exists for legal and advertising accounts and a host of smaller services ranging from couriers to car services to florists (*Crain's New York Business*, July 22, 1991).

7 More than 60 banks, many of them foreign, had participated in syndicates underwriting the Trump properties. Peter Kalikow, another of New York's best known speculative developers, sought bankruptcy protection in mid-1991. His more than $1 billion in debts was owed primarily to New York banks. He also owed the city more than $1 million in real-estate taxes (*New York Times*, August 21, 1991).

8 In order to induce tenants to move into its two large new developments, O & Y bought out their existing leases. Consequently, in addition to owning a

number of older buildings in the two cities, it held the leasehold of many more blocs of space.

9   Complicating depiction of its London holdings is its participation in the equity of other large development firms, including Stanhope, of which it owned 20 percent.

10 Of 66 third-world debtors, at the peak of the third-world debt crisis in 1987, the bank debt of only four (Argentina, Brazil, Mexico, and Venezuela) exceeded $18 billion (US Bureau of the Census, 1991, table 1486).

11 The tax benefits were such that investors could rent out apartments at a price less than their carrying charges yet make a profit as a consequence of their tax situation. They achieved this because they could claim the rapid depreciation of the entire cost of the unit as a deduction on their personal income tax, even while they had borrowed most of this cost.

12 Housing associations receive a subsidy from the central government's Housing Corporation, but they operate autonomously and are responsible to private boards.

13 The city had initially planned to spend $1.34 billion between 1992 and 1996 on subsidies for affordable housing; a reduction of nearly 38 percent ($510 million) was proposed (*New York Times*, March 24, 1992).

14 In the office sector, despite continuing contraction, lower rents did succeed in forestalling moves to the suburbs that had previously been contemplated by Manhattan firms (*Crain's New York Business*, March 23, 1992).

15 See, for example, Lichtenberger (1991), who presents an institutionalist analysis; Mills (1980), Markusen and Scheffman (1978), and Sweeney (1977), who examine market determinants using econometric modelling techniques; and Weiss (1991), who looks into the political influence and objectives of the industry at various points in the cycle.

16 The real-estate literature emphasizes the ease of entry into the industry and pictures it as a highly competitive arena. While this depiction is partly accurate, it really does not apply to large-scale projects where access to major amounts of credit is essential. Only a handful of firms are capable of raising hundreds of millions of dollars for a project.

17 As the case of 7 World Trade Center in New York indicates, such assurances do not necessarily hold. This nearly 2 million square-foot building had been intended to house Drexel Burnham Lambert; that firm, however, had declared bankruptcy by the time the building was completed and did not occupy it.

18 In 1986 Manhattan had the lowest vacancy rate of any major US office market, being one of only three cities with rates below 10 percent. Fourteen of the 21 major office markets had vacancy rates exceeding 14 percent; Denver with the highest had a rate of 26 percent (Real Estate Board of New York, 1987, p. 8).

19 Barrett (1992) notes that Donald Trump always assumed he could unload his holdings on a greater fool.

20 Many of Donald Trump's troubles arose because he pledged his personal credit on a number of his projects.

21 The fashion in office buildings has already changed. Demand now is for slimmer structures that offer many private offices with windows.

22 I owe thanks to Patsy Healey for her clarification of this point to me.

4

Policy and Politics[*]

London and New York have quite different political structures, resulting in important dissimilarities in local autonomy, political expression, and planning. London is the national capital; it is directly subordinate to the central government; a programmatic, nationally controlled, multiparty system structures its mode of political representation; and its municipal government is decentralized to 33 local authorities. In contrast, New York is neither its nation's capital nor even that of its own state; it has powers of home rule; its politics is dominated by a single, locally based party; and it possesses a centralized, general-purpose government.[1]

Despite these differences the policy histories of London and New York passed through a similar, although not precisely synchronous, set of stages in the postwar years. During the 1950s and 1960s, reconstruction of war-damaged property and large-scale housing programs transformed the appearance of London. The public sector bore direct responsibility for building many of the new housing estates itself. It also played a strongly interventionist role in shaping private development, both in limiting developable sites and in specifying desirable types of projects. Simultaneously New York, under the leadership of Robert Moses,[2] an appointed

[*] Parts of this chapter are drawn from a work that I co-authored with Ken Young (Fainstein and Young, 1992). I wish to acknowledge his contribution to some sections of the writing. I owe him thanks as well for acquainting me with some of the themes developed.

official who during his 44-year career controlled its parks, urban renewal, public housing, and highway programs, underwent major physical changes as expressways and massive low- and middle-income housing projects remade the city. In London nothing was built to compare with the enormous highway system that Moses imposed on New York; on the other hand, investment in public transit continued, with both the modernization and extension of underground and commuter rail lines.

For much of the postwar period New York City government invested heavily in infrastructure, housing, and welfare institutions, including public hospitals, social-service centers, and recreational facilities. As well as using federal subventions, it had access to substantial funding from the State of New York for its construction programs. A series of liberal mayors, strongly supported by trade-union organizations, led the city until the late 1970s (see Buck and N. Fainstein, 1992). John Lindsay, first elected as a Republican then as an independent, held office for eight years during the politically turbulent period starting in the late 1960s. His regime's policies, which shifted emphasis from the concerns of the white working class to the black and Hispanic poor, stimulated a realignment of political forces and set the stage for the divisions that defined New York during the following decade. Although the Lindsay administration's economic strategies encouraged continued investment in the Manhattan central business district, it used federal funds to target the poorest areas of the city for housing and community development programs. Lindsay did not take the strong ideological positions of London's Labour leadership, but he did incorporate minorities into his regime and raise the level of social spending. Lindsay's administration was supplanted by the caretaker government of Abraham Beame, whose lackluster response to the 1975 fiscal crisis quickly brought his mayoralty into disrepute; in 1978 Edward I. Koch replaced Beame as mayor and committed himself to restoring economic prosperity.

During the 1970s the British Labour government mounted an inner-city strategy modeled on the War on Poverty and Model Cities programs that had begun and ended earlier in New York (Lawless, 1989). Under the leadership of Ken Livingstone, the Greater London Council (GLC) of the 1980s sought to fuse an industry-based economic development strategy with political radicalism (Mackintosh and Wainwright, 1987). Although comparable to the Lindsay regime of the previous decade in New York, the GLC went much further in seeking to combine elaborate social-service programs with community participation and economic revitalization strategies built on a "bottom-up" rather than a "trickle-down" approach. To this end, it established the Greater London Enterprise Board (GLEB) as its principal instrument. In the Docklands it sought to foster manufacturing, in contrast to the later emphasis of the London

Docklands Development Corporation (LDDC) on office construction (Marris, 1987). Labour-dominated borough councils similarly stressed small-scale development and continued provision of social housing. GLC activism, however, stimulated the wrath of the Thatcher government, which brought about the GLC's abolition in 1986, thereby bringing both its own directly administered programs and its support for Labour boroughs to a halt.

Since the sharp economic downturn of the mid-seventies, the governing regimes of London and New York have both actively sought to promote growth in economic activity and employment. Their dedication to social amelioration and community participation over the same time-span has been less certain. During the 1980s New York's mayoral administration and the British ministry with responsibility for London displayed strikingly similar social philosophies (Barnekov, Boyle, and Rich, 1989). As well as defining governmental planning and regulation as inimical to economic vitality, these regimes used real estate development (in contrast to job training or infrastructure investment) as their primary strategy for stimulating expansion. They identified global city status as the hallmark of their economic advantage and fostered those forms of development – especially first-class office space and luxury housing – which responded to the needs of the upper echelons of the financial and advanced service industries participating in world economic coordination.

The two regimes also resembled each other in confronting conflicting political agendas at subordinate levels of government and in operating within a region fragmented by numerous uncoordinated governing bodies. New York, however, as well as lacking London's dominating position within the national economy and governmental system, faced serious challenges even within its own region. Its economic primacy extended only to finance and advanced services, and its political influence within both the state and national governments was weak. Adjacent municipalities on the New Jersey waterfront and in suburban Westchester (New York) and Fairfield (Connecticut) Counties competed to capture the generators of growth and to exclude those populations and facilities that imposed financial, social, or environmental costs without commensurate benefits (Danielson and Doig, 1982).

INSTITUTIONAL STRUCTURES

Differences in the governance of London and New York stem fundamentally from national differences between the United States and the United Kingdom. In the United States a federalist, presidential system creates checks and balances that prevent any branch of government from dominating the others. Cabinet government in the United Kingdom can produce much more sudden reversals in policy than occur in the United States, where divided government provides a considerable flywheel effect. The abrupt change in British policy, which made it much more like the United States, reflects this institutional difference and implies that their orientations could rapidly diverge once again.

In the United States home rule (i.e. the devolution of authority to municipalities by state governments) has traditionally strengthened local representation and made it easier than in the UK for urban regimes to adopt policies opposed by the national party in power.[3] The non-programmatic nature of political parties and territorial divisions within metropolitan areas, however, prevent the adoption of broadly redistributive strategies at the local level. In contrast, centralized parliamentary government has consistently limited the autonomy of local government within the United Kingdom (Loughlin, Gelfand, and Young, 1985; Hambleton, 1989). The principles of cabinet rule and party control make national party programs dominant both through the mechanism of parliamentary supremacy and, for the national opposition parties, through the party machinery. Final responsibility for local planning rests with the cabinet minister who heads the Department of the Environment (DoE), and the power of the central government to curtail the level of local taxation and expenditure further constrains local authorities.

Local governance

London

The absence of a municipal administration to govern the urban core area puts London sharply at variance with New York. Even when the GLC, established in 1965 as a metropolitan government, reigned over both central London[4] and the outer boroughs, it did not possess as much authority as the government of New York City. The central government could always overrule the GLC's decisions, and the borough authorities retained control of most housing provision, land-use planning, and housekeeping functions like street-cleaning and firefighting. Moreover, the leader of the GLC did not have the dominant position in framing the city's agenda possessed by the mayor of New York. Once London lost its metropolitan government in 1986, overall executive authority shifted to the DoE (and ultimately the Prime Minister), but the DoE's London office has never devised a policy for the city comparable in scope or detail to the program of a New York mayor. Nor, of course, is it specifically responsible to London's electorate.

Responsibility for day-to-day government in London rests with 33 elected local authorities.[5] Although relatively weak compared to local governing bodies in the rest of the United Kingdom, they have far more power than New York's subsidiary jurisdictions (boroughs and community districts). Organized like the national Parliament, local councils are run by the majority party with an executive group consisting of a leader and chairs of the various functional areas for which the council is responsible (e.g., education, housing, social services, finance, planning, and transportation). Councillors are elected by ward; the number of councillors for each borough varies but in all cases exceeds the 51 that constitute the membership of New York's newly enlarged city council, which has jurisdiction over the entire city. Under London's governmental system, not only does a representative body operate at a level far closer to the neighborhood than in New York, but the location of administrative offices in every borough allows its citizens to carry out their transactions with government much closer to home than their New York counterparts. As well as dispensing a full range of municipal services, local authorities were until recently the principal suppliers of shelter for low- and moderate-income households.

Local authorities raise most of their funds themselves – until recently rates (i.e. property taxes on households and businesses) along with miscellaneous fees, rents, and property sales were their principal sources of revenue. In 1990 rates were supplanted by the community charge or "poll tax," which required each adult householder within a locality to contribute the same amount, regardless of income or property holdings. In 1993 a new form of local taxation called the "council tax" reintroduced a levy based on property values. In addition a grant from the central government supplements local government revenues, with the amount received by each local authority varying according to its resources and level of need (Travers, 1986). The partial equalization resulting from the central government grant means that local authorities do not need to engage in the intense competition for tax base that afflicts American municipalities; the termination of the locally paid business rate in 1990 and its replacement by a uniform national business tax removed all incentives to attract business simply for its revenue-enhancing potential.

New York

New York City, like most other large American metropolises, has its governing powers divided between a mayor, who possesses executive authority, and a council with legislative powers.[6] The council is elected by district, and the mayor is chosen at large. Until 1990, however, New York also possessed a unique body called the Board of Estimate. With final authority over all land use and contract matters, it wielded extraordinary influence over the city's affairs and caused the council to play a relatively minor role.[7] After the elimination of the Board of Estimate, the council assumed its powers. Although the 1990 City Charter revision improved its staffing, it continued to lack a sufficiently unified organizational structure to enable it to wield coherent authority.

The borough presidents, who formerly exercised legislative power when sitting on the Board of Estimate, also hold some executive power within their own boroughs; there is not, however, a corresponding borough legislative body. The establishment in 1977 of 59 community boards allows for some decentralization within the city government, but far less than is the case for the London boroughs (Marcuse, 1987). Community board members, who are appointed by the borough presidents and the city council members from their districts, exercise advisory power over land use and capital budget matters but have no executive authority,

New York, like all American cities, must depend primarily on tax revenues generated within its own boundaries;[8] in 1988 federal aid to New York City comprised only about 11 percent of its total revenue (Krauskopf, 1989). The tri-state division of the New York region, moreover, allows the creation of tax differentials much greater than those that typify other US metropolitan areas.[9] The city government, which cannot share in the tax base of its suburban ring, must forever strive to keep revenue-generating people and industries within its borders in order to stay fiscally solvent. Even if, from a regional standpoint, economic rationality justifies moving manufacturing, back-office, and warehouse facilities outside the city limits, New York's fiscal situation forces its government to oppose such moves.

Planning

London

Patrick Abercrombie's plan for postwar London, updated by the Greater London Development Plan of 1968, set forth the principles of green-belt preservation, peripheral manufacturing, and population deconcentration, thereby providing a framework for development that had no New York counterpart (Clawson and Hall, 1973; Foley, 1972). Planning officials emphasized clustered development around town centers and a sharp demarcation between city and country; regulation was much stricter than in New York; and the preservation of the green belt around Greater London constituted a cardinal principle. Preservationist concerns played a much greater role in limiting and directing development in London than in the New York region throughout the 1980s.[10] London still has more restrictions on the right to build than New York, and each local authority within the region produces development plans to guide growth within its jurisdiction.[11]

Until the 1970s British public policy aimed at decentralizing population and economic activity out of London (Buck et al., 1986, chapter 2). The policy of deconcentration, however, was eventually reversed, as London began to lose industry along with population at an unanticipated rate, causing a weakening of the city's economy. With the encouragement of the Labour government of the mid-seventies, central London's planners began seeking to retain population and industry in the city, and throughout the eighties planners in London increasingly shared the same economic development goals as their New York counterparts.

Even though British planners remained more active than their American counterparts in prescribing land uses, Prime Minister Margaret Thatcher's emphasis on using the market to allocate investment meant a notable relaxation of planning controls during her time in office. The end of the GLC meant the elimination of any authoritative planning body for the London region as a whole and the fulfillment of the Thatcher government's planning philosophy, which was expressed as follows:

> London's future depends on the initiative and energy of the private sector and individual citizens and effective co-operation between the public and private sectors, not on the imposition of a master plan. The role of the land-use planning process is to facilitate development while protecting the local environment. (UK DoE, 1989, p. 5)

In the absence of a planning authority for the metropolis, the London Planning Advisory Committee (LPAC) was installed to give planning advice concerning London to the central government. Consisting of a small staff that reported to a joint committee of thirty-three members drawn from all London's boroughs, it had to achieve a consensus among Conservative and Labour constituencies for its recommendations.[12] LPAC's *Strategic Planning Advice* (1988) did reflect a surprising degree of agreement and went sufficiently beyond total non-intervention to irritate the DoE London office. Its advice, however, remained just that – and neither the boroughs nor central government paid heed to it unless they so desired. Likewise, the agency with an even broader geographical mandate, the Southeast Regional Planning Council (SERPLAN) was reduced to ineffectuality by its lack of either political or administrative authority.

When asked about the effect of central government control of strategic planning for London, a local authority planning director responded:

> LPAC is toothless. They don't even know what's going on any more. DoE studies are crap. They propose a recipe for disaster in land use planning and transport. The borough associations [of which there are two, one of Conservative and one of Labour authorities] can be unified – they are now

on traffic and transport. But central government doesn't listen to local government.[13]

Although the DoE was responsible for planning the metropolitan region, it did not interpret its mission as the aggressive coordination of local initiatives or the preparation of a detailed comprehensive plan. It acted primarily as an appeals body, frequently overturning lower-level decisions that had denied planning permission to developers. Borough councils became more and more inhibited from blocking development proposals for fear of having to defend their decisions on appeal to the Secretary of State for the Environment, and, if they lost, being required to pay the developer's costs as well as their own. In addition, the Secretary of State also had the power to "call in" a proposal if he so chose, thereby removing it from the jurisdiction of the local authority even without an appeal. Thus, while avoiding a formative role for itself in shaping the region, the central government also limited planning by local authorities.

Perhaps the most important recent planning decision made by the central government involved the routing of the railroad connecting London to the Channel Tunnel. Its approach to this issue manifested its general aversion to detailed planning. The government had to decide whether to bring the train directly to King's Cross Station in central London or to divert it to Stratford in East London. The former location would have benefited the proposed development on the King's Cross railroad yards, in which British Rail had a major financial interest (see chapter 6); it was, however, strongly opposed on environmental grounds by the borough of Camden, in which the station is located. The latter alternative, which had the support of virtually all professional planners, would have assisted nearby Docklands development and spared the extensive demolition of structures necessary to bring the right-of-way to King's Cross. British Rail chose the King's Cross location, but eventually, under great pressure and after considerable vacillation, the government overruled its selection. Altercation over the site consumed years and produced great uncertainty for all the enterprises that would be affected by the decision. The government, moreover, never committed itself to an overall strategic transportation plan for the region, did not set forth its siting criteria, and made no effort to integrate land use and transportation planning.

New York

Outside the city itself few institutional mechanisms provide a framework for regional planning or the resolution of territorial inequities. The Port Authority of New York and New Jersey has responsibilities on both sides of the Hudson, but its mandate is limited to transportation and some development activities. It operates autonomously and gives first priority to maintaining the fiscal soundness of its investments. The principal democratic check on its operations is the requirement that the minutes of its board meetings (and therefore any decisions it might take) be approved by the governors of New York and New Jersey. The Metropolitan Transportation Authority plans and operates public transit in the New York State suburbs as well as the city. Its purview, however, does not extend to either Connecticut or New Jersey.

Despite their proximity,[14] New Jersey and New York City not only do not coordinate their activities but engage in active competition with each other. A 1991 pledge by the governments of New York City and State and New Jersey not to raid each other for business investment quickly broke down. In retaliation for New Jersey's subsidies to firms leaving New York City for New Jersey locations, Vincent Tese, New York State's director of economic development, vowed: "We will be targeting New Jersey firms that for whatever reason are looking to change locations. . . . Then New Jersey will wind up spending money keeping firms they've got, and it's not going to be a pleasant situation for them" (Prokesch, 1992a). New York officials were further enraged when a furniture store located within a New Jersey enterprise zone close to New York City took out full-page newspaper ads to inform customers they could save 5 percent on their sales tax by shopping there.[15]

Overall, peripheral expansion has continued unchecked.[16] The most egregious example is rapid commercial growth along the Jersey side of the Hudson River – the principal recipient of overspill development from the Manhattan business district during the boom period of the eighties. Each of the numerous municipalities that line the Jersey waterfront has virtually total responsibility for construction within its borders.[17] Millions of square feet of offices sprang up in the narrow band between the river and the palisades behind it during the 1980s; altogether northern New Jersey offers nearly 120 million square feet of space, almost all of it comprising modern structures capable of meeting the needs of computer-reliant firms. Despite enormous problems of transportation access from the suburban hinterland on the New Jersey side, each riverfront locality continues to accept further development, in part to increase tax revenues, but also because of the pervasive influence of real-estate interests within municipal governing bodies. The proximity to Manhattan and lower costs offered by New Jersey comprise the principal justification for the generous assistance offered by New York City's government to firms threatening to leave its jurisdiction. And, indeed, the absolute absence of any regional policy for targeting office development leaves the city constantly vulnerable to raids on its economic base by its neighbors.

POLITICS AND IDEOLOGY

Although New York in the 1970s surpassed other US cities in its commitment to social welfare policies, London still presented a model of greater state intervention. By the mid-eighties, however, there was a remarkable convergence between the two cities in both the content of public policy and its justification. In an article written more than a decade ago, Norman Fainstein and I (1978, pp. 139–42) attributed the government's more active and redistributional role in London than in New York at that time to three factors within the British socio-political system: (1) the political capacity of the state to establish a sphere of autonomy for itself; (2) the existence of a dominant class of capitalists that construed its interests collectively and held a paternalistic vision of its role in society; and (3) the political capacity of subordinate classes to influence state policy in their own interests. The two cities continued to differ on the first of these three dimensions throughout the eighties. But the state autonomy that formerly allowed British bureaucratic personnel to take the initiative in augmenting universalistic welfare programs permitted the Thatcher regime to reverse direction more abruptly than could a government under greater constraint.

Differences along the latter two dimensions have narrowed in Britain (Jenkins, 1988). Under pressure from competition abroad, responding to ideological transformation at home, and changing in composition because of displacement within their ranks, British business leaders have increasingly emulated the individualistic, entrepreneurial style of their American counterparts. In both the US and the UK, conservative national regimes reinforced the position of those business groups that supported their electoral successes; in turn, business managers as a group responded to the ideological currents emanating from the governing regimes and moved in a more conservative direction. At the same time the working class became increasingly stressed and fragmented by the consequences of economic and spatial restructuring, as processes of increasing income inequality, massive commercial development, and gentrification occurred (Rees and Lambert, 1985; Buck et al., 1986; Townsend, 1987). The increased assertiveness of management in the workplace and the lack of sympathy of the national government to community-based demands for housing and social-service programs contributed to the accelerating weakness of subordinate classes. Neither the major opposition parties nor community-based movements were able to develop an effective counter-program that impressed electoral majorities as containing a strategy for economic growth as well as social equity (Krieger, 1986). Nevertheless, while national currents thus fundamentally affected politics in the two cities, local conflicts and events also played a role, to which I now turn.

London

Despite the historic and increasing influence of the central government on London, local interests have continued to affect London's fate during the Thatcher-Major era. Labour control of about half the boroughs meant that opponents of Conservative policies could shape local-authority agendas and use them as bases of resistance to the initiatives of developers. Whereas white, male, trade-union leaders had previously dominated the Labour councils, by the time the Thatcher government came into power their composition had changed considerably. Throughout the 1970s intense political struggles went on within the Labour Party between liberal-left, largely home-owning, university graduates and still-dominant, right-wing, manual workers. At the start of the eighties the former group had largely triumphed, although the closed regimes of the eastern London boroughs continued to distribute patronage to their supporters and to exclude middle-class constituents for half a decade longer. Based on tiny ward organizations and self-selection for office, these local political machines were finally forced to yield power when the challengers took over the ward parties and expelled sitting councillors from their candidacies (Goss, 1988). The new activists focused on different kinds of issues from their predecessors and were, on the whole, less favorable to development proposals.

Ethnicity and gender

Blacks and feminists also successfully challenged the white male dominance of Labour strongholds in east and south London. But, even though Asians and Afro-Caribbeans increasingly achieved representation on councils in boroughs with large minority populations, and women also gained additional council seats, class still defined the major fissures in London society and politics. Whites remain the majority group in every London borough;[18] although immigration into London continues, its scale is dwarfed by the influx of immigrants to New York.[19] Hence the racial-ethnic competition for jobs and living space that underlies New York's politics displays itself only weakly in London. Moreover, there is no history within London of urban redevelopment programs having been widely used as a method of racial relocation (as happened in the 1950s and sixties in New York, where they left a significant residue of mistrust). While the Bengali community regards expansion of office uses on the eastern fringe of the City of London as a threat to its continued residence there, development politics is rarely more generally construed in racial-ethnic terms, as often occurs in New York.

Fiscal issues

London like New York has suffered from fiscal stress in the last two decades, although less as a result of local conditions. Even Labour, when it controlled the central government in the 1970s, sought to deal with national budget deficits by reducing grants to local governments; under Margaret Thatcher this necessity became a principle (Glassberg, 1981; Parkinson, 1987, p. 2–7; Pickvance, 1988). Consequently the London authorities – like most other municipal governments throughout the United Kingdom – have confronted social deterioration with diminished revenues and reduced staffs. The central government has restricted local-authority budgets through "rate-capping" (i.e., centrally imposed limits on local taxation) and a requirement that half the proceeds from land sales must be turned over to the Treasury. As a result, even greatly heightened prosperity, while it would reduce demands on the public fisc, would not allow London's local authorities to use locally generated revenues to increase their spending dramatically.

British tax policy has not permitted local governments to offer tax breaks to firms threatening to depart from their environs.[20] Thus, London has mainly avoided New York's controversies over tax giveaways to the rich. The one exception to this policy lay in the tax incentives provided within the Isle of Dogs enterprise zone in the Docklands, where all entering firms received a five-year tax holiday. This system, however, differed from New York's in that every investor received the same deal, preventing the development authority from entering into bidding wars. Docklands developers also benefited from cheap land sales offered by the LDDC. Political opponents of Docklands development seized on these advantages given to business interests while investment was simultaneously withdrawn from social housing, contending that these policies demonstrated class bias.

Ideological constraints

The conflict over the abolition of the GLC had importance beyond its immediate implications for planning and administration. Under Ken Livingstone the GLC had become a significant political force in opposition to Thatcherism; its commitment to low transit fares, manufacturing investment, social housing, and "fringe" cultural institutions brought upon it the wrath of the Conservative central government. During the six-year period from 1978 to 1984, its current expenditures increased in real terms by 65 percent (Smallwood, 1984, p. 4). Its abolition took place in 1986 under the rubric of administrative efficiency, despite a referendum showing support for its continuation by an overwhelming majority of Londoners. Its elimination was widely and correctly interpreted as an attack on municipal radicalism and local autonomy (Mackintosh and Wainwright, 1987; O'Leary, 1987).

Conservative success in terminating the GLC subdued opponents of the central government's free-market ideology, undermining the institutional and ideological support that had previously legitimated redistributional policies (D. King, 1989). With GLC support gone, local authorities opposing the central government's market-led policies lost access to resources that had assisted them in steering a more independent course. A further consequence was to produce a kind of local political paralysis: the ease with which the Conservatives simply wiped out a whole level of government inhibited local-government activism as it seemed to show that local deviation from central government policy would have little chance of success.

By the end of the 1980s local-authority politicians and officers who had once opposed central government policies had largely given up. Although they lacked enthusiasm for market-led development, they acquiesced in its inevitability. One planning director of a Labour-controlled borough viewed as "difficult" by developers described the situation succinctly: "We have embraced the new realism. I have no enthusiasm but little choice." Another Labour-borough planning director told me that the central government's fears of local authorities deviating from its policies had become wholly unfounded:

> The DoE has completely lost touch [with the boroughs]. Authorities like this, which used to be very anti-private sector, have changed. We recognize the need for private investment. There are a lot of good public-private partnerships. People like Pelling [head of the DoE London office] don't actually understand what happens on the ground. . . . Government has won. It has steamrolled places like this. But they are incapable of recognizing this and continue to intervene.

Bob Colenutt, a Docklands activist and long-time critic of "the property machine," observed to me that the Tories were divided between those who favored more planning and community service ("the Heseltine view") and those who would "let the market do its business and get the public sector out of the whole thing" ("the Ridley view").[21] But, he went on, "all are ideologically pleased that they have smashed Labour, destroyed local authorities, and [in their terms] regenerated the inner city. Many senior Labour politicians would admit they have no real alternatives. They are critical but they have no other agenda."

New York

The Democratic Party has dominated postwar electoral politics within New York City.[22] It is, however, divided into "reform" and "regular" wings, with the regulars devoting themselves almost entirely to the allocation of nominations and patronage. Whereas in the 1960s the Reform Democrats had strong, liberal policy positions, their influence and ideology alike have waned during the ensuing decades. In general, the party system exists primarily for the purpose of contesting elections rather than for exercising programmatic control, and it has therefore largely failed as a vehicle for representing neighborhood or minority interests (Mollenkopf, 1988). It is not possible to describe a party program on economic development for the simple reason that there is none. Hence, in contrasting New York and London, one cannot compare Democrats with Labour supporters or Republicans with Conservatives, on either this dimension or on the evolution of ideologically based internal party divisions.

During the 1980s real-estate boom, district-based representatives, including both state legislators and city councillors, frequently played ombudsman roles in city affairs and lobbied for neighborhood concerns. Lacking formal responsibility for land-use decisions, however, the most such officials could do in this crucial arena was to put pressure on the citywide elected officials and borough presidents who made up the Board of Estimate. These policy-makers usually responded to more highly organized and wealthier constituencies and almost uniformly supported large development projects.[23] The dominant role played by the Board of Estimate in the governance of a city of over 7 million people made it extremely difficult for community-based representatives to build their reputations and attain sufficient financing to seek higher office.[24]

Ethnic divisions

Mobilization by low-income minority groups in the late sixties strained the alliance between New York's working-class communities, labor organizations, and progressive, elite, civic associations that had previously sustained governmental activism. As the city's population became increasingly non-white, its extensive array of social services failed to adapt sufficiently to the demands of their new clients and began to suffer crises of financing and legitimacy. The city, partly because its urban-renewal program had eliminated pockets of black population scattered throughout Manhattan, and partly because white flight emptied many formerly middle-class neighborhoods in the boroughs, became increasingly segregated. Demands by racial and ethnic minorities for school desegregation, the ending of job discrimination, and improved services met resistance from the predominantly white city bureaucracy. The various subsidized housing programs foundered over the racial issue, as white voters refused to support programs that they saw as primarily benefiting minorities.

By 1968 minority groups had switched from demanding the desegregation of housing and schools to pressing for community control in areas where population composition was homogeneously black and Hispanic. During the crisis over community control of schools, which pitted black parents against white principals and teachers and resulted in that year's three-month-long school strike, lines were drawn that were never subsequently overcome. In particular, the public service unions, which had formerly joined forces with their clienteles to press for the enlargement of social programs, now regarded their vociferous clients as hostile and vice versa. The unions continued to make successful demands for salary and pension improvements, but the ostensible beneficiaries of their activities no longer saw themselves as gaining from budget increases for salaried city workers.

Fiscal distress

New York's fiscal crisis of 1975 marked the demise of a governing regime incorporating labor and minority interests. As with the abrogation of the GLC, the resolution of the fiscal crisis proved a traumatic event in the political history of New York. The immediate cause of the city's 1975 revenue shortfall was the refusal of banks to refinance New York's short-term debt once the city lost its approval by the principal investment bond-rating firms. Unlike the nation, New York had still not recovered from the recession at the beginning of the decade; as a consequence its revenues were falling, but its financial commitments went on rising. The city government increasingly borrowed to fund current expenditure, backing its bonds with mythical or previously committed anticipated revenues. Once the banks refused to continue lending, New York City had no alternative source of financing by which to meet its obligations.

Essentially the fiscal crisis resulted inevitably from the effort to sustain a strongly interventionist public sector within a situation of economic contraction without greater support from the national and state governments. Interventionism comprised both large subsidies to capital, in the form of infrastructure investment to support new development, and major guarantees of social welfare. The costs of government were further expanded by relatively high total compensation for municipal employees.[25] With no new revenues and inexorable pressures to spend, the crisis could not be averted.

The two years after the 1975 crisis marked an interregnum in New York's political life. Negotiations to provide new capital and keep the city from formally declaring bankruptcy caused the New York State government to create a number of business-dominated bodies to oversee future spending. Control of public policy shifted from the office of Mayor Abraham Beame to these new agencies – the Municipal Assistance Corporation (MAC), the Financial Control Board (FCB), and the Office of the State Deputy Controller (OSDC) for New York City (Shefter, 1985; Morris, 1980). The semi-autonomous MAC had been guaranteed a revenue stream against which to borrow and was entrusted with the job of restoring the city's credit. The FCB, which was an agency of New York State, oversaw and had veto power over the city's financial plan, while the deputy controller acted as its staff, auditor, and research component. Businessmen chaired the MAC board and the FCB, which consisted of public officials and business and civic leaders; the MAC board had one black member while the FCB included no members of minority groups.

The criterion these boards used for evaluating city policies was their effect on the balance sheet. Even after the 1977 election of Mayor Edward I. Koch and the subsequent return to a more assertive city government, these agencies strongly influenced the city's budgetary priorities in a fiscally conservative direction. Under their direction the city cut thousands of municipal jobs, drastically curtailed services, halted all major capital programs ranging from school to subway building, froze civil service salaries and public assistance levels, introduced tuition fees in the City University, and deferred routine infrastructure maintenance. The municipal unions, whose strikes and strike threats had enabled them to wring billions of dollars of concessions from the Wagner and Lindsay administrations, grudgingly agreed to purchase the MAC bonds that no one else showed much interest in buying. Their leadership began to meet regularly with bank executives in order to work out mutually acceptable strategies for city expenditures.

During the bleak years following New York's near bankruptcy, almost the only investment activity that took place within the city involved the renovation and conversion of existing residential and factory buildings into middle- and upper-income homes. These projects took advantage of tax-subsidy programs which substantially reduced costs to new occupants and resulted in the gentrification of parts of Manhattan and Brooklyn where working-class people had inhabited architecturally appealing buildings (Sternlieb, Roistacher, and Hughes, 1976; Zukin, 1982; Tobier, 1979; Hudson, 1987). The single major effort to provide low-income housing consisted of the *in rem* program, which used federal Community Development Block Grant funds for maintenance and rehabilitation of buildings seized for tax delinquency. At the same time large numbers of units dropped out of the housing stock as a consequence of landlord abandonment, condemnation, and fire.

Ideological transformation

Koch's electoral victory signalled the empowerment of a regime with little practical or symbolic commitment to low-income minorities, and which, once prosperity returned in the mid-eighties, continued to emphasize economic development rather than social welfare activities (Mollenkopf, 1992). The mayor summed up his attitude as follows: "I speak out for the middle class. You know why? Because they pay the taxes; they provide jobs for the poor people" (Koch, 1984, p. 221).

The period 1975–80 was one in which New York City appeared hostage to financial institutions and economic forces well beyond its control (Tabb, 1982; Alcaly and Mermelstein, 1976). It was also a time in which, contrary to many predictions, retrenchment led low-income groups to moderate their claims rather than threaten the legitimacy of the government. Even before the conservative tide swept over the US national government after the Reagan election of 1980, New York City's regime expressed its determination to control governmental extravagance, which was interpreted as providing for the poor rather than offering incentives for investors and services for the middle class. Whereas in the late 1960s and early 1970s groups rooted in New York's poor neighborhoods mobilized strongly in favor of programs to improve their communities and brought protestors out onto the streets when they opposed a program, the post-fiscal crisis policy switch met with acquiescence.

After the economy began to turn around in the early 1980s, the resolution of the fiscal crisis through the creation of new institutions to ensure solvency on terms set by business provided the context for the development politics of the next decade. Ideologically these new institutions – combined with widespread popular belief attributing fiscal demise to the squandering of resources on the undeserving (and predominantly black and Hispanic) poor – undermined the city government's traditional role in assuaging the frictions between classes and ethnic groups through patronage and welfare provision.[26] The achievement of economic growth and fiscal solvency was substituted for service provision as the test of governmental legitimacy.

The establishment of a group of institutions to guide New York City's fiscal policy constituted a parallel event to the elimination of the GLC and the parcelling out of its functions to higher and lower levels of government. They were rooted in different causes and took on contrasting institutional forms. Their effects, however, were similar: they weakened the power of local elected officials; they delegitimated redistributional local policies; and they strengthened the ideological onslaught in favor of market-led economic development programs. The variance that had previously existed in both cities between national and local policy directions, wherein the municipal regime followed a more radical course, was consequently substantially reduced.

NOTES

1 The population of Greater London is about 6,775,000; of New York, 7,323,000 (see appendix B). New York's borough populations are: Staten Island: 371,000; the Bronx: 1,173; Manhattan: 1,456; Queens: 1,911; Brooklyn: 2,301,000 (Fainstein, Gordon, and Harloe, 1992, p. 24, 27). London's borough populations range from about 175,000 to 225,000; New York City's community districts are somewhat smaller.

2 Robert Moses held public office from 1924 to 1968. During that time he possessed a number of titles, none of which gives a full indication of his power. The most important was as head of the Triborough Bridge and Tunnel Authority. Lewis Mumford contended that: "In the twentieth century, the influence of Robert Moses on the cities of America was greater than that of any other person" (quoted in Caro, 1974, p. 12).

3 A prime example of this capacity is New York City's system of rent regulation. Anathema to the national Republican administration, it nevertheless endured despite, under the Reagan presidency, efforts to cut off federal aid to cities that controlled private-sector rents. These efforts never got very far, primarily because they would have constituted federal intervention in a local matter and thus strongly contravened federalist principles whereby cities are creatures of state rather than national government.

   While federalism has enhanced the capacity of local regimes to enact policies different from those of the national government, it has typically protected private enclaves of power from national regulation and limited the development of the national welfare state (Robertson and Judd, 1989).

4 This area was governed by the London County Council until the formation of the GLC.

5 Whereas in the United States the term "authority" refers to a non-elected body with the power to issue revenue bonds, in the United Kingdom it is used to denote both elected and non-elected bodies with governing powers.

6 New York City has a "strong mayor" system, meaning the mayor has the power to hire and fire the heads of city departments. Although the city council is nominally co-equal to the mayor, in reality it is a much weaker entity.

7 The Board of Estimate consisted of the mayor, with three votes, the city council president and controller with two each, and the borough presidents with one vote apiece. It was declared an unconstitutional violation of the principle of one person one vote by the US Supreme Court in 1989. The equal voting power possessed by the borough presidents had given the same representation to Brooklyn with its 770,000 registered voters as Staten Island

with 170,000.

8 In 1985, 47 percent of general revenue for New Jersey and 28 percent for New York state municipalities derived from local property taxes. Only about 5 percent of total municipal revenue in these states came from the federal government, while about one third derived from state aid. The remainder derived from income taxes, fees, and miscellaneous sources (Advisory Commission on Intergovernmental Relations, 1987).

9 Until 1990 New Jersey's income tax was considerably lower than New York State's. Connecticut had no income tax at all. New York City has its own income tax on top of the state's; residents of suburban municipalities typically pay no local income tax although they must pay state income taxes, as well as an earnings tax if they work in New York City. There is wide variation in property tax rates, licenses and users' fees, and nuisance and sales taxes among municipalities and between the states. In 1991 Connecticut introduced an income tax, and New Jersey raised its tax rates. Nevertheless, residents and businesses in New York City still pay a higher proportion of their income and revenues in taxes than do similar groups outside the city.

10 The United States and New York State and City do have more elaborate regulations concerning the environmental impacts of all kinds of projects than does the United Kingdom, and unlike London, New York requires mitigation of negative environmental effects.

11 Each London local authority is required to produce a "unitary development plan." In contrast, New York's community boards have been empowered to develop local plans only since the 1990 Charter revision. The formulation of such plans is, however, optional, and only some boards have actually started the process.

12 During the late 1980s borough control was equally divided between the two parties, with the single Liberal Democratic borough of Tower Hamlets holding the balance.

13 Unless otherwise indicated, quotations are drawn from my interviews. This interview took place in 1989.

14 To reach Hoboken or Jersey City, two of the municipalities on the Hudson waterfront, requires only a four-minute ride from the World Trade Center in downtown Manhattan via the Port Authority-owned PATH train.

15 Although the normal New Jersey sales tax was 6 percent, only two points below New York City's, operation in an enterprise zone allowed a firm to reduce it by half. For purchases of major items like furniture, the 5 percent differential was sufficient to justify a trip.

16 Hoboken voters in a 1992 referendum did defeat a Port Authority proposal to develop an enormous mixed-use project on their waterfront just across the Hudson from downtown Manhattan, despite enthusiastic support by their elected officials. They objected to the density of the complex and its effect on the character of their community.

17 New Jersey has two important state planning endeavors that guide new development: the Meadowlands Authority and the state plan. The Meadowlands Authority wields planning powers over a swampy area a few miles west

of Manhattan, which had remained partially undeveloped for much of the century; the area under its control includes parts of a number of communities. It has succeeded in promoting large-scale commercial and residential development as well as a major sports complex, despite friction with subordinate municipalities. Governmental units within its boundaries share the tax revenues from new development.

The state land use plan seeks to channel growth within certain municipalities while restricting development elsewhere. While protecting rural parts of the state, it does not limit development within the already dense cities that lie between the palisades, a rocky ridge to the east of the Meadowlands, and Manhattan.

18 Estimates for 1996 indicate that fourteen boroughs will by then have ethnic minority populations of about 20 percent or greater (Cross and Waldinger, 1992: 159).

19 In 1981 approximately 18 percent of the population of Greater London was born in the New Commonwealth and Pakistan; the proportion of people of color in the population did not increase considerably in the following decade, due to the United Kingdom's strict immigration laws. In contrast, 39 percent of New York City's population was classified as nonwhite in 1980, and the proportion increased to 48 percent in 1990. Groups not included by the Census in the "white" population are blacks, native Americans, Asian/Pacific Islanders, and "others" (Fainstein and Harloe, 1992, p. 24, 27).

20 At the time the community charge was established as the principal form of local taxation, the Conservative government exempted businesses from local taxation and instead set up a national business tax, effective in 1991, that would go directly to the national treasury then be dispersed to local authorities on a formula basis. Local authorities that had previously benefited from the presence of industry within their boundaries were held harmless by this policy – that is, the amount they received under the previous system could not be diminished – and thus the policy did not sacrifice the future revenue streams of the affected boroughs. The tax had the effect of reducing incentives among jurisdictions to compete for industry.

21 Michael Heseltine and Nicholas Ridley both served as Secretary of State for the Environment during the Thatcher years.

22 John Lindsay's victory as a liberal Republican in 1969 marked the last time a Republican won the mayoralty, although Rudolph Giuliani, the Republican nominee in 1989, lost the election by a close margin. The city council is overwhelmingly Democratic.

23 A study by State Senator Franz Leichter's office showed that campaign contributions to Board of Estimate members in 1984 and 1985 came predominately from real-estate interests and financial institutions. Of the total $8.5 million raised, 166 large contributors were responsible for half; of that amount, real-estate interests accounted for $3 million, while $1.2 million came from financial institutions. Much of this money was donated while the contributors had major items before the Board of Estimate (Mollenkopf, 1992, p. 95).

24   So far the transfer of decision-making authority from the Board of Estimate to the city council has not cut into the ability of developers to obtain approval for their plans in the face of community opposition. Thus, in 1993 the council voted to approve Donald Trump's application for his huge Riverside South development on Manhattan's Upper West Side and also assented to a plan to build a garbage-burning incinerator in Brooklyn (Dunlap, 1993).

25   McCormick, O'Cleireacain, and Dickson (1980), after comparing twelve large cities, concluded that New York City paid neither the highest nor the lowest, although in examining seven job categories they found New York's employees predominantly within the upper half.

26   Interpretations of the 1975 fiscal crisis have been heavily contested. Radical critics blamed the city's plight on overspending for capital accumulation and the rapacity of banks and political insiders. They argued that the crisis was deliberately provoked so as to discipline the city's government (see Tabb, 1982; Marcuse, 1981).

Liberal defenders pointed to obligations like higher education, public hospitals and welfare borne by the city government for which higher levels of government took responsibility elsewhere. They contended that the crisis would not have happened if New York State had shouldered its appropriate burden (Morris, 1980). Within the electoral arena, however, the interpretation of excessive attention to the poor at the expense of the middle class prevailed with the election and successive re-elections of Edward Koch.

5

Economic Development Planning Strategies

For much of this century urban planning in both London and New York concentrated on controlling and improving the physical environment. Planners engaged primarily in determining land uses and proposing public investments in infrastructure, amenities, and housing. To be sure, infrastructure planners have always sought to improve economic function, and inner-city redevelopment planning has throughout the postwar period aimed at eliciting private investment. The premise of these types of planning, however, was essentially physically determinist – planners assumed that changes in the physical environment would yield an economic response. Holding a supply-oriented view of urban space, planners expected that private investors would avail themselves of adequately serviced, centrally located land without further incentives.

Until the 1970s, urban planning's justification lay in comprehensiveness, an orientation to the long term, protection of the environment, and preservation of the public interest through orderly development and attention to the interests of all social groups. Numerous critics have argued that these goals were never attained, that planning always primarily benefited business interests, and that economic advantage has perennially constituted the real objective of city planning.[1] Nevertheless, even if planning has always aimed at producing private economic gain, both the rhetoric surrounding its attainment and the *modus operandi* of planners have changed. Moreover, the earlier construction of urban problems as defined by poverty and inner-city decline has been reconstituted in terms of competitiveness and fiscal solvency.

The discourse of planning

The discourse in which planners in London and New York interpret the world and communicate their intentions has shifted from long-term concerns with environmental quality to an emphasis on short-term accomplishments. Much of planning theory during the 1960s and 1970s had focused on the specification of the rational model, by which planners generated a possible range of actions to reach previously designated goals (see Dror, 1968; Faludi, 1986, 1987). Only shortly after this effort to portray a universal approach to planning had triumphed in the theoretical literature, however, a quite different but broadly generalizable planning mode was emerging in practice. Modelled on the methods of the corporation rather than the laboratory, this planning strategy deviates considerably from the formulaic norm of the rational model. Rather than framing and testing an exhaustive and abstractly constructed set of alternatives, planners concerned with maintaining neighborhoods or bringing new investment into the central business district aim at discerning targets of opportunity. Instead of picturing an end state and elaborating means to arrive at it, they establish narrow goals and grab for that mixture of devices which will permit at least some forward progress.[2]

Even planners working for government or non-profit groups who do focus on distributional effects are absorbed into the discourse of business negotiations and a single-minded concentration on the deal at hand (Teitz, 1989). Their goals, which center on employment for unskilled or displaced workers, low-cost housing, and neighborhood economic development, likewise are met piecemeal through the funding of individual projects. Without national government support for comprehensive neighborhood programs, which were briefly attempted under the Model Cities program in the US and the Community Development Project in the UK, community-based planners had few choices but to seek support in whatever quarter they could find it.

Whereas the vocabularies of architecture and the law once permeated their discussions (Boyer, 1983), planners now speak in the same language as investment bankers, property brokers, and budget analysts. The old arguments for planning had been comprehensiveness and reducing negative externalities – that is, preventing development from harming the environment around it (Klosterman, 1985). The new claims are competitiveness and efficiency. The debate over the utility of the rational model becomes meaningless when planners spend their time negotiating with private investors rather than devising plans. Whereas planning was previously seen by both its supporters and its right-wing critics as antithetical to markets, it is now directed at achieving marketability of its product – urban space (Levy, 1990). (By this term I mean not just territory but the set of development rights and financial capabilities associated with a piece of land.)

Many planners continue to work at traditional planning functions like establishing zoning regulations or transportation programs. The new discourse of planning affects them relatively little. For planners concerned with economic development, however, the focus has changed dramatically, regardless of the particular scheme to which they devote their time. Projects on which planners work vary from the grand scale of mega-developments like Battery Park City and Canary Wharf to the small scope of shopping-strip revitalization or Neighborhood Housing Services. The *style* of local economic development planning behavior, however, varies less than the types of projects. At various scales, regardless of whether the project is an office development, a high-tech manufacturing center, or a low-income housing cooperative, planners perform a mediating function, bringing together private investors and public sponsors, interceding between utility companies and energy-using businesses, dealing with outraged members of the public, and cajoling developers for exactions. Negotiation rather than plan-making has become the planner's most important activity. The director of planning of London's City of Westminster remarked to me that nothing in his training as a planner fortified him for his role as a deal negotiator: "Education won't prepare you for the experience of having a megamillion pound individual sitting across from you who will break your legs!"

The resulting landscape reflects the piecemeal, accommodationist mode in which planning today is carried out. Most office projects and upper-income condominiums, which once would have formed part of a larger development program, are now single-site efforts uncoordinated with their surroundings, contributing to the postmodern vista of checker-board development, unmatching architecture, uncontrolled congestion, and sharp juxtaposition of rich and poor. Low-income housing, unlike the large public-housing complexes of yesteryear, is now almost always placed opportunistically, wherever a site can be found or a private developer can be enticed. In both London and New York planners seek to persuade private developers to build mixed-income projects in which market-rate units subsidize the much smaller percentage of low-income ones. Planning in both cities has become interstitial rather than comprehensive.

In an important critique David Harvey (1978) depicted planning as the coordination of the interests of business. Although an accurate portrayal of the activities of most economic development planners in London and New York, his analysis fails to explain why the scope of planners is limited to facilitating specific projects rather than extended comprehensively to the relationships of projects to each other and to the housing and transit systems. While certain business groups, especially property developers, use local government to advance their positions, business elites have largely not attempted to deploy governmental power more broadly to plan for their long-term interests in an efficient urban system (N. Fainstein and S. Fainstein, 1985).

The independent deal-making associated with each project and the efforts by individual developers and separate communities to gain the most advantage for themselves reinforce the fragmentation already created by the local governmental system. Within Harvey's terms the particular interests of individual capitalists triumph over their combined interest in strategic management. This outcome results not just from the preferences of capitalists for individual autonomy but also from democratic and institutional factors. To understand the constraints on comprehensive planning, one must examine the role played by community groups and politicians and understand the location of planning agencies within the governmental structure.

The democratic contradiction

While under the influence of business interests, planning is also subject to what Foglesong (1986) calls the democratic contradiction: governments depend on capital for their resources but they remain accountable to electorates. Institutional devices for popular representation and legal challenge are insufficient to give voters a determinative role in development planning, but they do offer them channels sufficient for considerable veto power.

Citizens in London and New York have few avenues for taking planning initiatives, but a variety of requirements for public hearings – and, in New York, considerable opportunity for litigation – allow them to delay and sometimes block projects completely. In London, despite the pressure from the central government for project approval, local authorities often continue to side with community opposition and demand project modifications and community benefits. Likewise, the New York community boards provide a forum for critics and a location for trading concessions between developers and neighborhood groups. While New York state legislators and city councillors until recently had no official role in development approvals, they too provided a route for opposing projects or negotiating changes. Most major development proposals therefore involve a good deal of bargaining between the parties.

In New York landmarks and environmental legislation present the grounds for lawsuits, even though the basis on which they are brought often has little to do with the real objections to a project. Thus, for example, plans for Westway, a federally funded expressway along the

Hudson in Manhattan, foundered when a judge ruled that the road would endanger the spawning grounds for striped bass. The contest over the highway actually revolved around the desire of public officials and developers to create acres of developable property on landfill above and next to the road and the intense opposition by West Siders to increased density, road traffic, and the effects of ten years of construction.

The role of politicians

The orientation of local elected officials in both London and New York has also shifted away from a focus on government-sponsored programs to concern with benefits generated by the private sector. In both cities the influence of local politicians increased in relation to department and agency heads who previously had an expanding flow of funds coming from the national government at their disposal. In London during the 1980s a number of Conservative councillors switched their emphasis from environmental quality and service delivery to attracting business enterprises. In particular, the chairs of planning in the Cities of London and Westminster took the lead in overcoming opposition to large commercial projects within their jurisdiction. Thus, Michael Cassidy, the City of London planning chair, declared to me that his purpose was to preserve the City as a financial center when its dominance was threatened by Docklands development. He considered that before his time the corporation had maintained a "curious attitude" in which coucillors did not concern themselves with attracting desirable businesses. He took pride in having been instrumental in changing the City's stance toward development and streamlining its process for applications for planning permission. Similarly, David Weeks, the planning chair of Westminster, while somewhat worried about the possibility of overdevelopment, described to me his efforts to overcome community opposition to projects he thought desirable. He recounted his assistance to the Royal Opera House, which needed planning permission to build an office building adjacent to its Covent Garden site so as to fund expansion: "I had to push it through. It required being rough and aggressive."

On the other side of the political fence, Labour councillors interested themselves in improving retail districts and – without much success – attracting light manufacturing to their areas. They saw financial deals with developers as the only path to community improvement. One Labour council leader, who had previously held a high position in the GLC and who called himself a "participatory socialist," indicated that he tried to hire "entrepreneurial" officers to head departments. He described with pride one deal by which a developer built a park over an old gravel pit in return for the right to develop an office, and another under which the council collected a percentage of the rents from a shopping mall built on the site of the old town hall. He differed from the Conservative councillors to whom I spoke, however, in being highly committed to community participation in formulating development schemes.

In New York, where the previous generation of politicians prided themselves on the size of the grants they could obtain from Washington, the current group expends its energy on making the city attractive to business. Mayor Koch pioneered the system of negotiating with firms to keep them from leaving the city and Mayor Dinkins has continued this effort. Like the Labour councillors in London, New York's more progressive politicians emphasize assistance to manufacturing, non-profit organizations, and small business rather than large corporations, but they also affirm the system of providing private-sector incentives. Thus, for example, Ruth Messinger, the borough president of Manhattan and a long-time opponent of giveaways to developers, has lobbied for inducements to manufacturers to operate in central Manhattan, which currently is excluded from the city's Industrial and Commercial Incentives Program. She also supported the granting of subsidies to the commodities exchanges for construction of a building in downtown Manhattan and sponsored a study to recommend assistance intended to keep the diamond industry in Manhattan. In an interview she indicated to me that: "There are ways out of oversubsidizing developers, but we must give subsidies. We have to assume that the New Jersey threat is real." She, however, wished to place a number of conditions on assistance to developers: subsidies would only be provided for "smart" buildings incoporating technological advances; tax abatement would only be available when a building was 60 percent rented; and special abatements would be granted to landlords who rented to non-profit organizations.

The situation of planning agencies

The present operating style of planning agencies reflects both the expectations of politicians that they will act as negotiating agents and the institutional framework that prevents comprehensiveness. Because the development process does not take place under the aegis of a powerful metropolitan planning body in either city, the very structure of government causes both geographical and functional fragmentation. The division of London into boroughs, and of New York into much larger boroughs and somewhat smaller community districts, means that each development proposal follows a different path to approval and must be framed in relation to localized situations. The allocation of primary responsibility for infrastructure and facilities planning to a variety of agencies (roads, public transit, ports, parks, education, etc.) with distinct

lines of authority means that Herculean efforts are required to coordinate
their intentions. Since, in addition, these agencies report to different levels
of government, or are semi-autonomous, the problem is exacerbated. In
the UK the Secretary of State for the Environment theoretically has the
power to impose unity on the various levels, but he is ideologically opposed
to exercising it; in New York no elected official has authority over all the
agencies that plan the city, much less the region.[3]

Written plans

The last comprehensive development plan for either London or New York
was formulated at the end of the 1960s. At present, when planners for
these cities do produce a written plan, they no longer try to create a
blueprint for development. Instead they view themselves as providing a
framework for mediation that places only the broadest limits on public-
and private-sector activities. Two recent planning documents, one from
London and one from New York, indicate how even traditional master
planning has changed. In 1989 the United Kingdom Department of the
Environment (DoE) developed a general framework to guide the London
boroughs in their planning activities (UK DoE, 1989),[4] and the City of
New York produced a general plan for the development of affordable
housing (New York City DHPD, 1989). These documents were especially
notable because they represented the increasingly rare effort to formulate
broad goals and strategies in the form of a written report. Both plans arose
within a context of political controversy, and both were characterized by
extreme brevity; the first is only 23 pages long, the latter eleven.

London's Strategic Planning Guidance

This document was intended to guide London's 33 borough authorities in
constructing development plans that meshed with each other and worked
toward citywide goals. Produced by the DoE, it replaced the planning
framework previously supplied by the Greater London Council (GLC).

The *Strategic Planning Guidance* called for a significant reversal of the pro-
manufacturing and social-housing orientation contained in the Greater
London Development Plan. In the new document the DoE summarized its
overall stance toward development planning as follows:

> London's economy has undergone significant changes in recent years and
> will continue to do so. . . . It will be important to maintain and strengthen
> London's international competitiveness. London is well placed to benefit
> from further advances in information technology, developments such as the

of. Matte p.
indig nt3.

Channel Tunnel and the creation of the single market within the European Community in 1992. *It is vital that these opportunities should not be lost because of unnecessary planning restrictions. (United Kingdom DoE, 1989, p. 7; italics added)*

One of the ways in which the DoE sought to inhibit "unnecessary planning restrictions" was by limiting the powers of borough authorities to negotiate for planning gain[5] by requiring that any such agreement had to be directly related to the project's impact; it declared that "a local planning authority is not entitled to treat a developer's application for planning permission as an opportunity to obtain some extraneous benefit . . . for the benefit of the whole community" (UK DoE, 1989, p. 9).

Otherwise the report contained few specific prescriptions. Beyond setting borough targets for new dwelling units, it outlined no breakdown of the types of housing to be provided, by either price or density. In its discussion of planning for business and industry it urged local planners to identify "well-serviced, accessible sites of job-creating development." It noted that "this practical approach is likely to be more effective than policies aimed at confining development to limited 'growth points'." It declared, in addition, that local plans "should reflect the changing needs of industry . . . and should not seek to distinguish between light industrial and other business uses" (UK DoE, 1989, p. 9). In other words boroughs should not attempt to preserve land for manufacturing enterprises when office sites were in demand.

LONDON
planners
remove
restrictions

The planning advice offered to London's local authorities was mainly hortatory, urging them to do all they could to provide space for private market initiatives. It eschewed concepts of managed growth and restricting development to specified parts of the city. The underlying idea was that local authorities could best foster development through removing barriers that might inhibit investors rather than through governmental direction. When in 1989 I queried the author of the DoE report concerning the potential for a glut of office space within London, he replied that the market would take care of the problem and that private investors would not risk their money without a strong likelihood of return.

New York's housing plan

During the 1980s the shortage of all but luxury housing in New York City became increasingly acute (N. Fainstein and S. Fainstein, 1987). Indicators of the crisis were rapidly growing homelessness, a vacancy rate below 2.5 percent overall and below 1 percent in low-income housing in 1987, and soaring housing costs (Stegman, 1988, p. 45, 47). Despite the salience of the problem and rising political pressure from middle-class constituents as well as advocates for the poor, the administration of Mayor Edward Koch directed most of its attention to attracting private commercial development. Only in 1988 did the mayor specify the housing program he had announced in 1986. He proposed to use city funds directly to finance construction and rehabilitation of low-income units on city-owned property, as well as to assist private developers willing to construct additional affordable units for low- and middle-income households.

The introduction to the revised published plan states:

> The Plan does not designate specific projects or allocate funds to specific neighborhoods. However, it does provide a general outline as to the kinds of programs which will operate over the next ten years and the proportion of the total funding which will be devoted to these programs. (New York City DHPD, 1989, p. 1)

In other words, the document does not contain a plan at all. Rather its contents, set in quarter-inch bold type surrounded by much blank space, are as follows: a set of targets (e.g. rehabilitation of every occupied city-owned building); the presentation of a funding goal of $5.1 billion total; a gross breakdown of proposed expenditures into five categories (e.g. rebuilding of vacant city-owned buildings – $2.4 billion); a schedule of intended beneficiaries by income group, consisting of low, moderate, and middle; a listing of sources of funding (e.g., capital budget – $3.2 billion) without specification of either new revenue streams or reallocations of old ones that might provide the additional funding required; a categorization of the types of housing units to be created (e.g. 15,000 for the homeless); and finally some comparisons with past performance. Left to be worked out on an *ad hoc* basis were: the location of new housing production; the size and composition of individual projects; the order of priority of units to be rehabilitated; the method for selecting tenants; the particular funding arrangements to be used for each endeavor; the projects that would involve private participation and the concessions to be awarded in return; and the infrastructure and social-service needs that would be created by the projected 84,000 new units to be produced. Although the plan announced a major commitment of public funds, it depended on private for-profit and non-profit developers for much of its implementation. Rather than stipulating what activities it expected private actors to perform, the Koch administration largely chose to await their proposals in order to identify the projects and locations that would receive public subsidies.

The "Ten Year Housing Plan" indicated in general the method by which the city government expected to provide housing. It offered a context in which housing officials could support projects. It did not, however, provide any of the information required to ascertain the city's specific intentions in regard to, for example, the rehabilitation of residential neighborhoods in the South Bronx or the housing of Manhattan's homeless. In sharp distinction to typical redevelopment plans, it contained no maps and named no projects. Essentially it freed the hands of the implementing agencies to pursue individual projects as they saw fit, to whatever extent community support would allow.

PUBLIC-PRIVATE PARTNERSHIPS

The definition of planning as the process by which the government enables the private sector to invest profitably in urban space is at odds with the prevalent conservative perspective that views government as antagonistic to business. The common interest of both government and developers in maximizing the potential return on a site allows the flourishing of public-private partnerships. Most of these arrangements involve joint public-private participation in major commercial projects, but some agencies assisting low-income households and neighborhood businesses, as well as some Labour-dominated borough authorities, have also resorted to this method of resource mobilization.

The revised relationship between the public and private sectors that began to characterize planning in the mid-1970s has its roots in those changes in global relations that transformed urban economies and increased interurban competition. As investment, financial management, communications, and information-providing activities burgeoned and manufacturing shrank, pressures for reconfiguration of the existing built environment grew and became the basis on which the governing regimes of London and New York built their growth strategies. Within an extraordinarily fluid space economy, land development offered private investors opportunities for enormous profit; facilitating such development gave planners leverage over the private sector at the same time as nationally provided resources that formerly supported regeneration programs were withdrawn. Governmental agencies had largely abdicated their earlier direct role in urban regeneration, whereby they acquired and serviced land and built public facilities.[6] But government could use its tax and borrowing authority to lower development costs and thereby make projects more attractive to the investors on which the development industry depended without incurring the high front-end expenditures entailed by the previous approach. Moreover, the large scale of the most profitable projects meant that almost none qualified for governmental approval without the relaxation of regulation, nor could they be developed without the provision of infrastructure. This need for governmental intervention created the opening for bargaining, in which public officials traded governmental approval or capital spending for private contributions to housing or public facilities.

The trading of public and private benefits, implemented through planning gain and exactions (see below), together with the melding of public and private powers into development corporations, constituted the principal vehicles by which the urban redevelopment process proceeded in London and New York during the 1980s. These arrangements took a variety of forms, including, among others, the trading of planning permission in return for the construction of affordable housing; the collaboration of public agencies with community organizations in low-income neighborhoods to form local development corporations; and the granting of tax holidays to private investors within enterprise zones in the hope of employment expansion.

[handwritten margin note: public/private arrangement]

PLANNING GAIN AND EXACTIONS

Public officials in London and New York have expanded the concept of exactions beyond its original meaning. Initially developers were called upon to satisfy infrastructure needs created by their undertakings (e.g., streets and sewers) or to provide compensation (impact fees) for the negative effects of a project (Alterman and Kayden, 1988). More recently, however, planners have made developers contribute to off-site improvements, including affordable housing and daycare centers, as a condition for approval of their proposals. Developers anxious to get their projects moving will frequently offer a range of concessions in order to elicit cooperation from planners; planners who can no longer look to higher levels of government for substantial capital assistance see negotiations with developers as their principal opportunity for obtaining community benefits.[7] The package of public permissions and developer obligations becomes incorporated into a development agreement.

Because British local authorities have great discretion in the granting of planning permission, London local-authority planners occupy a potentially dominating position in the quest for planning gain. Central government has attempted to limit what it and many developers regard as blackmail by instructing local authorities to require the developer to provide benefits directly related to the project's impacts (Rosslyn Research Limited, 1990). Nevertheless, deals continue to be struck since developers often prefer to reach agreement rather than go through the lengthy and uncertain process of appealing their cases at the DoE. One planning director indicated that, since the government prohibits local authorities from requiring developers to provide housing units in exchange for permission to build offices, he merely "suggests" associated

residential development. Since his borough plan limits office development, developers desiring to overcome the presumption against them
incorporated within the plan frequently accede to his suggestions.
Another planning director described a typical deal in which, in return for
being allowed to build offices on a two-acre publicly owned site, a
developer agreed to build 50 industrial units and a hostel for the
homeless, as well as contributing to improvements in the local tube
station.[8] In the London borough of Islington planners managed to
negotiate an arrangement, now in abeyance, whereby the local authority,
the Thames Water Corporation, and the Sadler's Wells Company would
jointly build an office complex and a new theater as part of a mixed-use
development; the theater constituted an unprofitable addition that would
provide a community amenity and vistor attraction. Within the
Spitalfields Market development area (see chapter 7) the development
consortium donated twelve acres to a community land trust so as to elicit
cooperation from neighborhood groups; the community is further
bargaining for a commitment of £40 million for community development efforts, 127 units of housing, and a job-training scheme.

Similarly in New York, even though developers do not need to seek
planning permission if their project conforms to existing zoning, most are
willing to engage in bargaining that permits them to build a bigger
project than would be permissable under the zoning statute. Other deals
are made in order to gain public subsidies. Office developers
participating in the 42nd Street Redevelopment Project agreed to
contribute to rebuilding the subway station and to renovating the
theaters along 42nd Street as a condition for designation as the recipient
of the tax benefits associated with the scheme (see chapter 6). Developer
William Zeckendorf, Jr., has built hundreds of units of affordable housing
in return for permission to construct two large developments over
neighborhood objections. In an unusual bargaining arrangement that
occurred before the project entered the public approval process,[9] Donald
Trump negotiated with West Side community groups concerning the
configuration and contents of his huge proposed project on old railroad
yards. The developer agreed to donate land to the city for a rerouted
West Side Highway, to build a park, and to construct affordable housing;
in return the civic organizations acceded to the scale and density of the
plan for this long-contested site (Bagli, 1991).[10]

In addition to negotiated exchanges, developers in New York can tap
into a set of regularized rewards to which they are entitled if they
undertake certain actions viewed as providing community benefits.
Thus, they receive tax benefits for working outside Manhattan under the
Industrial and Commercial Incentives Program (ICIP); they can obtain
the right to build additional space if they construct specified public

amenities under the zoning bonus system; and, under the "80–20" housing program, residential developers receive various subsidies and regulatory relief if 20 percent of their units are affordable housing.

URBAN DEVELOPMENT CORPORATIONS AND OTHER PUBLIC-PRIVATE ORGANIZATIONS

While development agreements represent *ad hoc* relationships between the public and private sectors, the urban development corporation (UDC) is a formal vehicle through which government entices private developers to participate in fulfilling its economic development objectives. UDCs retain many of the governmental powers of their participating public agencies while not being subject to the normal requirements, such as holding open public meetings, filing extensive reports of their activities, providing avenues for community participation, and conforming to civil-service rules, to which the public sector is subject. While ultimately responsible to public elected officials, UDCs operate much like private firms, employing the entrepreneurial styles and professional image-building techniques more customary in the corporate than in the governmental world (see Lassar, 1990; Squires, 1989).

British approaches

The beginnings of a new approach to redevelopment in Great Britain appeared in the Labour Government's Inner Urban Areas Act of 1978, which gave urban partnerships (comprising central government, certain local authorities, private business, and local voluntary organizations) powers to encourage industrial and commercial development (Rees and Lambert, 1985). Under this program, as well as providing site improvements and supporting infrastructure, local authorities could offer loans and grants to private firms. After the Conservative triumph of 1979 made Margaret Thatcher Prime Minister, stimulation of private-sector investment became much more central to urban policy-making than previously, and UDCs became the centerpiece of its effort. The central government designates and finances UDCs, which are directly accountable to it but not to the local planning authorities in the areas in which they operate (Parkinson and Evans, 1990). Although British UDCs resemble New York's development corporations in many respects, they differ in that the American entities have considerable autonomy from all levels of government and have no connection at all with the national government.

The London Docklands Development Corporation

The London Docklands Development Corporation (LDDC), established by Parliament in 1981 as the planning and development agency for 8.5 miles of territory in East London, was the most prominent partnership agency in London throughout the 1980s (a more detailed analysis of it appears in chapter 9). It encompassed within its jurisdiction parts of the boroughs of Tower Hamlets, Newham, and Southwark, superseding their planning authority in the area along the Thames. Throughout the 1970s these three local authorities (along with the adjacent borough of Greenwich) had sought to implement an overall planning strategy for the Docklands that emphasized industrial and public-housing uses. When the Conservative government took power in 1979, however, although progress had been made in infrastructure preparation and the demolition of derelict structures, little new investment had been obtained (Marris, 1987; Brindley et al., 1989).

The LDDC received title to much of the vacant land in the redevelopment area and sold it cheaply to private developers. Public contributions consisted of an enormous infrastructure program, overall planning and management, tax breaks within the enterprise zone that had been established on the Isle of Dogs, and a sales and public-relations effort. Except for infrastructure planning, most of the energy of LDDC personnel went into selling the enterprise to potential investors, and it mounted an extremely sophisticated and elaborate public-relations and sales effort to do so.

The intended scope of Docklands redevelopment was vast and included within it a variety of separate projects. Proposals for the area included offices, housing, schools, retailing, recreational space, a sports arena, and some manufacturing and warehousing (LDDC, 1988a). The largest office complex, Canary Wharf, located within the Isle of Dogs Enterprise Zone, was to be developed by Olympia & York (O & Y) on an order of magnitude even greater than O & Y's World Financial Center within New York's Battery Park City (see chapter 8); ultimately the venture was to encompass 12.5 million square feet of commercial space.

During the peak of London's property development boom, the LDDC was wildly successful in attracting private investment; in the first eight months of 1988 alone, £4.4 billion ($7.5 billion) of private money had been committed (*Guardian*, August 24, 1988). In March 1992 the LDDC estimated the total private-sector commitment at £9.1 billion ($16.4 billion) and the cumulative government grant for the same period at £1.37 billion ($2.47 billion) (LDDC, 1992). By that time, however, the future of O & Y's Canary Wharf investment had become doubtful, and many other Docklands projects were in serious trouble or even bankruptcy.

The LDDC has been heavily attacked for its emphasis on roads at the expense of transit, its encouragement of development in such an inaccessible area, its causing a bias in the entire transportation investment program of the United Kingdom toward the Docklands, and its neglect of the area's original residents.[11] Its emphasis on office development meant that few new jobs would match the skills of existing residents, although it should be noted that while the service industries moving into the office complexes offered little employment for displaced dockers, they did provide clerical jobs for local women. Its residential strategy of selling land to for-profit housing developers meant that local residents could not afford the new units. During the late eighties the LDDC did increase its emphasis on job training and social programs to benefit long-time occupants. Once the property slump set in at the end of the decade and a number of developers could no longer meet their financial obligations, however, it backed away from its social commitments and again began to concentrate single-mindedly on maintaining private investment in the area. Further-more, the UDC mechanism, under the control of a board appointed by the central government, excluded residents from the planning process (Lawless, 1987; Church, 1988a,b). Bob Colenutt, director of the Docklands Consultative Committee, commented to me: "Power in Docklands lies outside the people we represent. It's with the big developers, the LDDC. The local authorities have very little power, and where they do, they don't use it."

City Challenge

Another major regeneration effort sponsored by the central government also lay adjacent to the City of London. In response to a request for proposals, the Tower Hamlets council applied for a City Challenge grant for Bethnal Green, one of its neighborhoods. It received the grant in 1992 for a community-oriented effort at achieving redevelopment under the auspices of a public-private partnership (see chapter 7). Here, while large developers were still regarded as the main source of development capital, greater provision was made for community participation in planning for the area, program goals included housing construction and the provision of business premises for the original occupants, and the East London Partnership, which acted as the coordinating agency, did not have the special powers of the LDDC.

City Challenge, while much more responsive to local communities than the UDC approach, still represented the new mode of planning whereby decision-making rested in an agency outside the regular governmental structure. The government contribution was intended to leverage private-sector commitments, and community organizations were supposed to assist small-scale entrepreneurship. The City Challenge grant program was intended to stimulate activity by the kinds of elite corporate entities and community development groups long active in American inner cities, but not yet very visible within the United Kingdom. Because, historically, local authorities had both taken the initiative and provided the funding for community-based economic and housing activity, these kinds of intermediate organizations had been rare in London, although community advocacy associations were plentiful.

Housing associations

Housing associations are the closest British equivalent to American housing development corporations. They have a long history within London, stretching back to the philanthropic and church-based organizations that sponsored improved housing for slum-dwellers in the nineteenth century. While a subset of these associations are neighborhood-based cooperatives, the great majority are run by boards drawn from outside the communities in which they operate and function as charities rather than community organizations. Most are simply landlords, but many of them also develop housing.

The central government's Housing Corporation is the principal financial underwriter of housing-association construction and has become the main conduit of central government funds into low-income housing construction. British tax law does not provide special incentives for corporations to invest in low-income housing and therefore there is no comparable source of funding to that provided by the Local Initiatives Support Corporation (LISC) in the United States (see below). Housing associations increasingly also raise money in the private credit market, but with some difficulty. Britain has no equivalent to the American Community Reinvestment Act, which requires banks to invest in their service areas; the government does not offer loan guarantees to defray risks to private lenders; until recently housing associations did not keep their accounts in the same way as private corporations and thus banks had difficulty in assessing their cash flow; and neither the housing associations nor lending officers were accustomed to dealing with each other. Although many housing associations specialize in building housing for special populations (e.g. the handicapped or single people), others have been active within particular communities, especially within the East End, or have addressed the problems of immigrant populations and the homeless. Throughout the decade of the eighties they produced an average of about 1,500 housing units per year in Greater London, equalling or exceeding public production in the latter five years (UK DoE, 1991, table 6.5). They have stepped up their production considerably in the 1990s as the government increased its grant by more than 100 percent in 1992.[12]

As resources available to local authorities for council-housing production have shrunk to almost nil, they have come increasingly to rely on the housing associations to take up the slack. Although many housing associations are highly professional, experienced, and flexible, the limited funds at their disposal keep them from greatly enlarging the pool of housing available to low- and moderate-income households. At the same time the sale of council housing is causing a large reduction in the number of units affordable by such households.

US approaches

Within the United States, public-private cooperation has always formed the touchstone for urban redevelopment policy. Local government never played the major role of British local authorities in housing provision and industrial development. Elite, business-dominated groups like Pittsburgh's Allegheny Conference, Boston's "Vault," and San Francisco's SPUR had long acted as quasi-official planning agencies for their municipalities. A series of federal housing and development programs, beginning with the Housing and Urban Renewal Act of 1949, have relied primarily on private developers to rebuild blighted areas by using public subsidies to stimulate private investment. During the 1970s, however, a detectable shift took place in the character of US programs, as the federal government reduced its financial support and withdrew from its oversight role.

The contraction in federal subsidies forced localities to turn to the private sector for start-up funds for major projects. In 1974 Congress terminated the Urban Renewal and Model Cities programs and substituted the Community Development Block Grant (CDBG), which, as well as reducing the amount of subsidy received by big cities, switched the emphasis from large-scale redevelopment efforts requiring compre-hensive planning to individual projects and housing rehabilitation (S. Fainstein et al., 1986, chapter 1).[13] Urban Development Action Grants (UDAGs), introduced in 1977, made federal support for a project contingent on the leveraging of private funds, with local governments acting as intermediaries. Although the Bush administration eventually terminated this program, it set a precedent for future activities under local auspices (and was imitated by the British government, which continues its program under the rubric City Grant). Local governments became increasingly entrepreneurial in attempting to stimulate private investment (Eisinger, 1988), actively promoting their available sites and hawking a range of subsidies, training programs, and expedited procedures designed to facilitate business operations. The break with the past lay not in the priority given to private-sector desires, but in the heightened level of local-government initiative in enticing private-sector involvement.

The Public Development Corporation (PDC)

In New York an array of development corporations provided the structure through which the city worked with private firms to foster physical development. The PDC, renamed the Economic Development Corpora-tion (EDC) in 1991, acted as the lead agency in collaboration with the private sector (N. Fainstein et al., 1989). Established as a quasi-independent local development corporation with a board of prominent business people, the PDC played an entrepreneurial role in spurring construction during the eighties. Unlike the LDDC it did not have a limited geographical jurisdiction; rather its boundaries were co-extensive with the city's. When New York real-estate investment was at its peak, the PDC was active in every borough; during 1987 it was involved with 200 projects, worth $13 billion (*New York Observer*, February 15, 1988). As reconstituted, EDC's responsibilities include the development, marketing, selling, and managing of city-owned land; funding of commercial, industrial, and waterfront projects, including markets and some transport facilities; working to retain private businesses in the city; and obtaining loans and financial assistance for developers. With an annual capital budget of $67 million obtained through a contract with the city, the EDC, like its predecessor agency, acts primarily as a financial intermediary, putting together packages of land improvements, tax abatements, and funding for specific development sites (Lin, 1991).[14] The Department of City Planning, which technically has responsibility for land-use planning, largely deferred to the PDC/EDC's definition of the city's development strategy.[15]

For its larger projects the PDC worked together with New York State's Urban Development Corporation (UDC). The two agencies spun off separate development corporations to operate particular projects, including the construction of the Javits Convention Center and the 42nd Street Redevelopment Project (see chapter 6). In addition, the Battery Park City Authority (BPCA), which planned and developed a large mixed-used project on landfill adjacent to Wall Street (see chapter 8), was a semi-autonomous UDC subsidiary. Originally established to develop housing

EDC:
from
housing to
economic
growth

for low- and moderate-income groups, the UDC was reborn as an economic development agency. Within New York City it retained its original power to override local zoning and citizen participation requirements. Its involvement in development projects, therefore, permitted a streamlined process of regulatory approvals.

Community Development Corporations (CDCs)

Non-profit community (housing and commercial) and industrial development corporations have become increasingly important non-governmental actors outside the Manhattan business district.[16] Once incorporated, CDCs are free to seek financing from public and private lenders and grantors. Sources of funding are quite varied, including state and local governments, religious organizations, private philanthropists, and constituent businesses and housing groups. Two national groups – the Local Initiatives Support Corporation and the Enterprise Foundation[17] – funnel money to CDCs, primarily in support of housing construction and rehabilitation, but also for business development in low-income neighborhoods. As of 1990 these two organizations had participated in the construction or rehabilitation of nearly 2,000 housing units within New York, which has received considerably more funding from them than any other city. LISC has also established a secondary market (LIMAC – Low Income Mortgage Assistance Corporation) wherein community development loans can be traded. Furthermore, a number of banks have set up autonomous development corporations which lend money in low-income neighborhoods. These subsidiaries, which are expected to make a profit, generally participate only in projects in which some part of the costs is subsidized.

Except for renovation work on some of its own properties, the city has relied on non-profit development corporations to implement its affordable housing program. Housing development corporations (HDCs) have built or rehabilitated many thousands of units of housing throughout New York; typically an HDC will mix grants, loans, and revenues from several sources in any single project. The Brooklyn Ecumenical Council, for example, consisting of 25 churches throughout Brooklyn, sponsors an HDC. This organization had 1,800 units of *in rem* housing[18] committed to it by the city, which it was rehabilitating using funding from LISC, the Roman Catholic Archdiocese, and the city. By renting some of the units at market rates, it was able to use proceeds from the more expensive dwellings to cross-subsidize those for low-income households. Although HDCs resemble British housing associations in their non-profit status and freedom to choose their projects, they differ in their funding sources, their community base, and their more entrepreneurial organization.

Housing programs

For most of his time in office Mayor Koch had no program to address the city's low-income housing crisis. When he did finally introduce the ten-year program for affordable housing described earlier in this chapter, he tilted it toward assistance to moderate and middle-income projects; under Mayor Dinkins it has shifted more toward housing low-income and homeless people but still retains a middle-class component. The initial commitment to new construction for middle-income ($32,000 – $53,000 per year) households generated considerable controversy. Between 1981 and 1991, the nonprofit Housing Partnership received public subsidy for the construction of more than 5,000 units for owner-occupants.[19] Many community advocates castigated the Partnership for its top-down planning style and its targeting of the relatively affluent. Its suburban-looking, one- and two-family, detached homes combined a 20 percent city and state contribution with market-level loans from commercial banks. Defenders contend that the program retains a middle-class population in the inner city that would otherwise move to the suburbs; that 85 percent of the buyers are minorities; and that three-quarters either live or work in the neighborhoods where they invest (Mittlebach, 1991).

The fiscal crisis of the early 1990s caused major cutbacks in the entire New York City housing program. In 1989 (an election year) construction or rehabilitation of over 26,000 dwellings was begun using city assistance, representing a public expenditure of $738 million. For the year starting July 1991, expenditure had dropped by a third on about 14.5 thousand units (Lambert, 1991). By 1992 commitments were further curtailed, as planned spending for the four years beginning in July 1992 was reduced from $1.34 billion to $835 million. The issue of provision for the middle class became moot as the entire program for new construction was being phased out, and activity was restricted to moderate and minor rehabilitation (Oser, 1992). The cutbacks will seriously reduce the number of units at all income levels produced by nongovernmental organizations, as their financing is usually contingent on a public contribution.

CONVERGENCE

During periods of both growth and recession the governing regimes of London and New York similarly relied on private market actors to expand their economies and provide public facilities. Although the systems of local government in the UK and the US had become less alike during the 1980s, the actions of public officials determining local initiatives became more similar. Using the tools of development agreements, development corporations, tax subsidies, advertising, public relations, and financial packaging, officials stressed the economic development function of government to the detriment of social welfare and planning.

To understand the reasons for this parallel evolution, we must look not to institutional correspondences but to economic forces as they were filtered through comparable, ideologically driven interpretations of appropriate response. Prime Minister Margaret Thatcher, in the name of freeing up the market and stimulating an enterprise culture, reduced redistributive governmental programs and forced the borough councils to make land available for private developers. Mayor Edward Koch, without precisely emulating the *laissez faire* mentality of the Republican national government, cozened developers in the name of the increasingly embattled middle class. At the national level those proposing greater state intervention in the economy and higher levels of redistribution failed to persuade the voting public that they had a formula for economic expansion. In both London and New York the national failures of the left reduced local advocates for low-income groups to relatively narrow issues and a primarily negative stance. Local officials had few alternatives but to work within the confines of the deal-based system of public-private negotiation. Although the displacement of Margaret Thatcher by John Major and the election of David Dinkins as mayor of New York augured a less assertive endorsement of private-sector initiatives, and in New York greater sensitivity to ethnic minorities, the general thrust of the programs of these new leaders remained the same as their predecessors. Only the growth of a strong ideological counter-force would be likely to cause a shift in direction in either place.

NOTES

1 The many criticisms along this line include, *inter alia*, the arguments of Altshuler (1965) that the planner's limited knowledge make special insight into the public interest and comprehensiveness impossible; of Gans (1968) that planning expressed the interests of the upper classes; and of Harvey (1978) and Foglesong (1986) that it is primarily oriented toward capital accumulation and, on the occasions when it is concerned with equity, toward legitimation.

2 The depiction here refers to those planners participating in what Beauregard (1990) calls the city-building process.

3 New York did once have a much more unified planning and development apparatus than most American cities; both the creation and the breakdown of this apparatus incorporate specifically local factors. For decades planning and development in New York City had proceeded in accordance with Robert Moses's set of priorities. When Moses's hegemony finally crumbled in the early

1960s, the reaction was to give primary responsibility for both commercial and residential planning to agencies under mayoral control. Although Moses's transportation functions were devolved to a regional agency, the city's Housing and Redevelopment Board (HRB) and Department of City Planning took charge of development planning. Later Mayor John Lindsay merged the HRB with other housing agencies to form a single "superagency," the Housing and Development Administration (HDA), with the object of creating a coherent program that would integrate preservation and redevelopment efforts. Mayoral policy insisted that priority for neighborhood and housing improvement be given to those areas that were the neediest. In its 1969 master plan, the City Planning Commission presented a general strategy of promoting incentives for office development in Manhattan and residential improvements in the boroughs. By the late 1970s, however, the Department of Housing Preservation and Development (HPD – the remodeled HDA) had few federal funds at its disposal and, because of the fiscal crisis, no city capital budget; it exercised its reduced authority mainly in the realm of housing rehabilitation and no longer played an important role in guiding development. The Department of City Planning virtually gave up any pretense of overall land-use planning and devoted itself mainly to studies of specific zoning changes and project impacts. In the meanwhile the economic development agencies became the lead players in development strategy formulation.

4 LPAC's *Strategic Planning Advice*, described in chapter 4, was intended to shape this *Strategic Planning Guidance.*

5 As will be discussed below, planning gain refers to the practice of obtaining public benefits from developers in return for planning permission.

6 Canary Wharf and Battery Park City are unusual among recent projects in the extent of the government role in supplying land, infrastructure, and facilities. The additional advantages that they give developers through tax forgiveness mean they exceed earlier renewal/regeneration programs in the amount of governmental largesse. They have also, however, required a larger private contribution for public purposes than had characterized earlier projects.

7 In a theoretical discussion of the incidence of exactions, Dick Netzer (1988, p. 49) concludes that they "are far from perfect substitutes for the ideal ways of privatizing the financing of the private goods aspects of urban public services that cannot be entirely removed from the public sector: Explicit marginal cost-based user charges would be better. But exactions, when properly structured, can be a reasonably good second-best solution."

8 This was the same planner who contended that the central government had prevailed over recalcitrant local authorities and had forced them to acquiesce to the private sector.

9 New York's Uniform Land Use Review Process (ULURP) sets forth a series of hurdles through which a project must pass before ultimately receiving city council approval.

10 As initially proposed in the mid-eighties, Trump's plans for what was then called Trump City included a regional mall, a 150-story tower, and a line of 60-story buildings blocking views of the riverfront; together these structures

would encompass 14 million square feet. The new proposal reduced the project size to 8.3 million square feet as well as providing the various contributions called for by the community groups. Although a number of community organizations agreed to the project, others remained opposed and viewed the acquiescences as sell-outs.

11 See Association of London Authorities (ALA) and Docklands Consultative Committee (DCC) (1991), and DCC (1988). The ALA is the association of borough councils under Labour leadership and the DCC is an advisory body to the Docklands boroughs; it is funded by the affected local authorities.

12 The total national grant for 1992 was £1,841.7 million; in 1991 it was £896 million; no breakdown is available to indicate the amount given to inner London housing associations (The Housing Corporation, 1992, p. 3).

13 New York used most of its CDBG for rehabilitation of city-owned, tax-foreclosed housing. In contrast, it had used urban renewal money for massive rebuilding of large areas of the city, mainly in Manhattan.

14 The change from PDC to EDC mainly involved consolidation of the city's old Department of Ports and Trade into the new agency.

15 In 1992 the City Planning Commission released a comprehensive plan for waterfront development (Dunlap, 1992a). A product of a new commission under the directorship of a Dinkins appointee drawn from academe, the document represented the first serious attempt by the agency to chart the course of development in two decades.

16 Any community group may incorporate itself simply by filing a form with the US Bureau of Internal Revenue and paying a small fee. It then becomes a "501 (C)(3)" organization, so named after the section of the Internal Revenue Code designating its tax status. For housing development corporations such a filing usually occurs at the initiative of a community group that wants to develop housing or qualify for a public program; for business development organizations it often occurs when the city government or a foundation is seeking an entity to manage services in a neighborhood and sets up a geographically based corporate structure with a local board to receive funds. There is not a precisely equivalent category within the United Kingdom. Community enterprises and cooperatives carry out similar functions, but there are far fewer of them than CDCs in the United States and they do not possess a special status under the tax code.

17 Both these organizations rely partly on philanthropic contributions for their financing, but raise most of their housing funds through a provision of the federal tax law that permits corporate tax shelters for low-income housing production. LISC was founded in 1979 by the Ford Foundation. The largest organization of its type in the United States, by 1992 it had assembled nearly $650 million from more than 875 private-sector and philanthropic investors and grantors. These funds, provided in the form of loans, grants, recoverable grants, guarantees, lines of credit, and equity investments have helped over 850 CDCs produce more than 39,000 units of housing in the United States and 7.3 million square feet of commercial space (Communication from P. Jefferson Armistead, Vice-President, LISC, May 4, 1992).

18 *In rem* housing is acquired by the city government through tax foreclosure.
19 Typically these houses contain a rental unit, which assists the owner in meeting his or her mortgage obligation.

6

Public-Private Partnerships in Action: King's Cross and Times Square

The negotiated quality of urban redevelopment schemes means that the dynamics of each one are different. The next two chapters examine four major redevelopment programs in London and New York to reveal the complex interplay of forces that operate in particular situations. My aims are: (1) to trace the source of each initiative; (2) to find out what resources the different participants had at their disposal; (3) to identify their objectives; (4) to assess their costs and benefits; and (5) to understand the values involved in reactions to them. All four of the projects discussed here are still in the process of development, and only one – downtown Brooklyn – actually has buildings completed and tenants in occupation. Consequently, evaluations of their likely outcomes are necessarily tentative.

The four cases selected for closer scrutiny constitute dual sets of similar pairs. This chapter focuses on two proposals for massive land-use changes on centrally located tracts still in active commercial use: King's Cross in London and Times Square in New York.[1] Planning for both commenced at the beginning of the 1980s real-estate boom; they each became bogged down in controversy and financial difficulties and are currently in abeyance. The proposed developments exemplify the type of massive office project that has mobilized community resistance in a number of cities.[2] The two undertakings had several common characteristics: they involved the re-use of commercial areas by different types of enterprises that would cater to new kinds of customers; they required a major restructuring of land uses and the relocation or closure of existing business premises; and they were likely to cause changes in the composition of the working and residential populations in the project areas and their surroundings. The environmental effects of these huge projects, as well as fears by residents of adjacent neighborhoods that rising property values would lead to their displacement, fueled antagonism to the schemes. After long periods of gestation and controversy, both projects have been caught in the current real-estate bust and may well come to naught, representing considerable opportunity costs foregone in planning, in preliminary investment, and in lost business for original users of the sites.

KING'S CROSS

The original effort to redevelop the railroad lands surrounding King's Cross and Saint Pancras stations began in the mid-1970s. The local authority of Camden wished to stimulate economic activity on the 134-acre site,[3] which contained derelict railroad sidings, loading depots, and storage facilities, as well as a number of "listed" (landmarked) structures, including the two railroad stations and several gas-storage tanks. Located in north-central London adjacent to a busy shopping area, the large tract lay close to the location of the new national library and was surrounded by residential areas housing people of moderate means.

During the mid-eighties the Camden council produced a strategy document calling for a comprehensive approach to the whole site rather than piecemeal improvements. It expressly limited further office development, calling instead for a mixed development including manufacturing, retail, housing, and recreational uses at relatively low densities. At the time of the first major development proposal in 1987, a number of small businesses with short-term leases were operating on the site. While some were prosperous, they all required inexpensive premises to maintain their profitability.

Two major landowners, the still publicly owned British Rail (BR) and the privatized National Freight Consortium, controlled most of the land. British Rail, which until the 1980s showed little interest in developing its landholdings, had become suddenly alert to the capital-producing potential of its property in the vicinity of London's stations. Pressures from the government on the remaining publicly owned firms in Britain to become self-financing had much to do with this heightened awareness. BR had especially great financial needs at King's Cross, because it confronted the expense of building a new concourse for the terminus of the Channel Tunnel train line and decking over its tracks.[4]

BR operated within the confines of the Thatcherite interpretation of the appropriate role of a government agency within an enterprise culture. In the words of Michael Edwards, a scholar who had assisted the King's Cross opponents:

> British Rail . . . is an instance of an essentially 80s phenomenon: a state agency increasingly deprived of state funding but still prohibited from raising money on the private markets, under increasingly strong imperatives to make profits from each and every one of its assets. Such agencies . . . tended to adopt private sector accountancy practices, basing their investment and operating decisions on short-run financial criteria. (Edwards, forthcoming)

Although BR had the capacity to act as a strategic planning body for London through its control of so much centrally located land, its public ownership did not inhibit it from behaving exactly like a speculative private landowner, gambling on an ever-increasing market for its properties.[5]

BR held a competition to select the developer for King's Cross. By requiring that the winning proposal would achieve the highest possible financial return on its land, it ensured that the developer would opt for intensive commercial use. Nevertheless, bidders had to guess what types of development would be acceptable, as the request for proposals (tender offer) and the borough's planning brief were vague. BR awarded the development contract to the London Regeneration Consortium (LRC), a partnership between National Freight and Rosehaugh Stanhope Developments, the developer of the successful Broadgate project at London's Liverpool Street Station.[6] The LRC's proposal was accepted by British Rail without any input from the community. When the development consortium later fleshed out its concept and presented its master plan to the Camden council, that body faced a *fait accompli*, since the consortium could not significantly change the plan and meet its obligations to BR (Edwards, forthcoming).

The Camden council nonetheless demanded community consultation before it would review the application for planning permission, and its planning office prepared a community planning brief stipulating its criteria for plan approval. While not specifying the scale and nature of the commercial component, the brief did lay out in general terms the council's requirements for housing, employment, shopping, recreation, design, environmental protection, transport, and traffic (Camden, 1988). The council had concluded that its only hope of obtaining much-needed housing was by tapping into private-sector funds as part of a development agreement, and it was willing to make concessions on office construction in return. The council further felt compelled to show flexibility toward the developers, since if it failed to negotiate an agreement, the Secretary of State for the Environment would probably overrule it on either a call-in or appeal. Councillors also thought that they had averted the creation of a rumored urban development corporation (UDC) for the area only by persuading the central government that they would be "reasonable." A UDC would have removed all control from the local authority.

The proposal

The initial LRC planning application called for 6.9 million square feet of office space; subsequently this was reduced first to 6.5 million, then to 5.9 million, and finally to 5.25 million square feet (Camden, 1989a, 1989b; *Camden Citizen*, 1990; *Financial Times*, August 1–2, 1992). The Camden planning director remarked that in the past "office construction on this scale was unthinkable." Now the best outcome he could envision was a modest reduction in size and the achievement of planning gain, by which the consortium would promise public benefits in return for planning permission. His aim was to get LRC to commit itself to 1,800 units of low-cost housing, a worker training scheme, a variety of community facilities, and a trust arrangement for their upkeep.

In addition to office uses the master plan, prepared by the architect Sir Norman Foster, proposed 1.3 million square feet, later increased to 1.6 million square feet, of residential space, and another 1 million square feet to be divided among retail, hotel, and public facility uses, including a park (Camden, 1989a, 1989b). Without specifying an exact target, the LRC indicated that most of the residential component would consist of social housing, developed mainly by housing associations. Although this large allocation of affordable housing reduced the project's threat to the borough's sizable low-income population, concerns remained over a potential reduction in the low-income stock as council housing tenants exercised their right to buy and resell their units.[7]

The plan assumed that King's Cross would become the main terminal for Channel Tunnel trains and included a grandiose new concourse between the two existing stations for these passengers. BR, which had pushed strongly for this routing, would have enjoyed a jump in the value of its property if the government had selected this destination. Instead, the government eventually decided that the train should enter London at Stratford, to the east, and then continue via a tunnel to King's Cross. The enormous cost of tunnel construction, however, made rather small the likelihood of this final link's ever materializing.

Responses to the plan

An umbrella organization for local community groups, the Railway Lands Community Development Group (RLCDG), formed to express opinions on the plan and received some funding from the borough council. It strongly opposed the size of the office component. A number of community groups testified in public hearings against the proposed "office city"; BR, however, refused to attend the hearing on the grounds that "it was legally inadvisable given that they were simultaneously presenting evidence on the Channel Tunnel Terminal to the House of Commons Select Committee" (Camden, 1989c). Camden officials professed bewilderment at this reasoning; the council's report on the hearing indicated that the absence of BR "was widely deplored" (Camden, 1989c).

A technical advisory group based at the Bartlett School of University College London (UCL) worked with the RLCDG on a critique of the LRC proposal and the preparation of an alternative plan.[8] Its funding came initially from the councils of Camden and Islington and the London Strategic Policy Committee, a short-lived successor body of the Greater London Council (GLC), and later from a local developer/businessman, Martin Clarke, who sought to rebuild the area according to a different strategy.[9] The advisory group disputed the amount of office space necessary to produce an acceptable rate of return to the developer. The crux of the disagreement revolved around projections of rent per square foot, with the LRC estimating £32 per square foot of office and the Bartlett group claiming that £36 was "eminently reasonable" (UCL Bartlett School, 1990, p. 44); choice of the higher figure would justify a smaller office complex.[10]

The Bartlett group also examined the employment impact of the scheme (UCL Bartlett School, 1990, chapter 3). They pointed out that the site at present housed at least 87 firms, with 1,500 employees, not all of whom were actually working on the site. Warehousing, retailing, and wholesaling accounted for the majority of businesses.[11] Although very few of these firms planned to move unless forced to do so, practically none would be able to afford premises on the redeveloped site. The majority anticipated losses in the event that they had to leave their present location, especially if they could not remain in the vicinity. Existing employment was overwhelmingly of white males, working predominantly for small firms in non-unionized, low-wage jobs. The proposed development, while increasing the work force in the area, would reduce its proportion of local residents and replace low-skilled with high-skilled jobs.

The Bartlett group's discussion of employment concluded by raising some crucial issues which apply also to the Times Square case discussed below:

> Is it correct to perceive sites like the King's Cross Railway Lands, as the developers do, as derelict and degraded property which unquestionably needs "renewal"? Or do such locations in fact play an essential part in the inner city economy by providing cheap premises for activities ranging from theatre scenery storage to cheap hostels, on which the inner city economy and society depend?
>   To what extent should a local authority be seeking to protect businesses displaced by redevelopment such as those on the Railway Lands? . . . Much of the employment provided by these firms is of a character and quality which makes only limited contributions to certain important local government policy objectives. As well as [raising] . . . issues about gender and ethnic distribution and workplace relations and conditions . . . few of the firms . . . contributed to any formal training provision. On the other hand we know that, in inner London generally, underprivileged groups have had lower chances of getting jobs in newly-generated firms than of retaining employment in established firms which survive. (*UCL Bartlett, 1990, p. 37*)

The RLCDG devised four alternative plans to the one presented by the LRC (Parkes, Mouawad, and Scott, 1991). The consultants worked out the first of these plans (the King's Cross Team [KXT] plan) in meetings with community groups; the other three resulted from an outreach effort to involve disadvantaged elements of the community that had not participated in the meetings. All four greatly reduced the scale and density of the project, as well as changing the proportions to be devoted to different uses. The KXT alternative reduced the office component to about 4 million square feet, increased the housing commitment by half, doubled the amount of space for warehousing and light industrial uses from approximately 200,000 to 400,000 square feet, and increased the area for recreational and community uses by a third. The three other alternatives differed from the KXT plan primarily in proposing yet more drastic reductions in the overall size of the project, to be achieved mainly through reducing the office portion; they varied in the number of square feet of offices proposed in a range of between one-quarter and 2 million – from one-sixteenth to one-half of the KXT amount. Calculations of the financial implications of these three alternatives presupposed large cost reductions based on either the minimization or total elimination of a railroad link to the Channel Tunnel trains. They also called for the abrogation of an up-front payment to British Rail for the land and required large governmental contributions to public facility and social housing expenditures.

The situation in 1992

The original timetable released by the borough of Camden scheduled a final council decision for March 1990. A committee report released in March 1992 indicated that the committee did not yet find the overall plan acceptable and called for more evidence that the office proposal was financially viable and appropriate for the site. It also demanded more information concerning conservation, transit, and the specifics of construction. The committee was more negative about the overall plan than the borough's planning officers, who recommended acceptance if the narrow site-planning issues were resolved. Finally in August 1992 the committee agreed to a revised proposal when the LRC agreed to further reduce the size of the office scheme to 5.25 million square feet (*Financial Times*, August 1–2, 1992).

Uncertainty, however, continued to surround the project. Although the LRC still promoted its development concept, one of the principal forces behind it, Godfrey Bradman, had been forced out of the chairmanship of Rosehaugh, and the company was in serious financial straits. Its partnership with Stanhope, which had worked well in the creation of Broadgate, had undergone strains, and talks aimed at merger between the two firms had foundered. According to the *Financial Times*, Rosehaugh no longer planned any speculative developments and had written down its King's Cross investment (Houlder, 1991). Stanhope, in the meanwhile, was entangled in the financial problems of Olympia & York (see chapter 9). Even were these firms in better condition, the state of the 1992 property market in London prevented any starts on large-scale office construction, and a spokesman for the RLC predicted that work would not begin until 1995–6 (*Financial Times*, August 1–2, 1992).

The Camden council also lacked motivation to expedite the development, since the softness of the office market undermined hopes that planning gain could provide a reliable source of funding for public amenities. Since planning gain depended on a sufficient difference between debt service and rent roll to allow the developer a profit and the locality its payoff, fulfillment of the promises to Camden would have required BR to lower its profit expectations. Despite its public-sector ownership, BR refused to do so, thereby forcing the proportions of the project to exceed a size acceptable to the community and making any start on the project impossible until the market could again absorb a large quantity of office space.[12]

TIMES SQUARE

Times Square is one of the world's most famous locales. Centrally located in midtown Manhattan, illuminated at night by kinetic megasigns, locus of the nation's most televised New Year's Eve celebration, it offers 24-hour-a-day activity. Stretching five blocks north from the intersections of 42nd Street with Broadway and Seventh Avenue, it is the center for New York's theater industry, including associated activities like restaurants, set designers, theatrical booking agents, ticket agencies, dance studios, and costume rental establishments. Alongside this socially acceptable array of entertainment activities until recently stood an extensive agglomeration of sex-related industries that gave Times Square its unsavory reputation. Pornography shops and X-rated cinemas acted as a magnet for loiterers, drug dealers, street hustlers, and prostitutes, causing the area, despite its crowds of theater-goers, tourists, and commuters, to display an intimidating aspect and register a high crime rate.

A low-rise, low-rent district, Times Square in the eighties had a number of virtues despite its blatant problems. Before the construction flurry at the end of the eighties, low building heights made it one of the few areas in Manhattan where sunlight reached both sides of the street simultaneously. Many of the theater support services, as well as other respectable but marginally profitable businesses, have relied for their continued operation on the inexpensive rents available on upper floors of nondescript structures scattered throughout the district. Obsolete construction and marginal uses, however, brought down real-estate valuations. As a result, the city received only a tiny proportion of the tax revenues potentially available from a location served by almost all major subway lines and close to the Port Authority bus terminal, the hub for commuter traffic from New Jersey.

Just to the west of Times Square lies the Clinton neighborhood, once known as Hell's Kitchen. It is the last low-income area in central Manhattan. The five-story tenements that line its streets have felt the pressure of gentrification, as landlords have forced out their tenants, often brutally, and converted their buildings into condominiums. Formerly the home of generations of longshoremen working on the nearby, now-defunct Hudson River docks, it houses people from a dazzling variety of ethnic backgrounds. Many of its residents work as laborers within the theater industry or as maids, porters, waiters, and kitchen help in the hotels and restaurants clustered around Times Square. The community contains several active Roman Catholic parishes and a parochial school; the churches, which once responded to the spiritual needs of largely Irish and Italian congregations, currently are places of worship for Filipinos, Latin Americans, Dominicans, and other Caribbean islanders.

The original impetus for the redevelopment of Times Square came from Clinton residents, theater and restaurant owners, and community leaders, especially clergy, who were dismayed by the sleaziness of the district. During the 1970s the western portion of 42nd Street had been upgraded through the construction of two large residential towers[13] and the rehabilitation of a strip of storefronts, together with a former airline terminal building, into off-Broadway theaters, performance studios, and restaurants. The replacement of prostitution and marginal business uses on these blocks by a lively, upscale entertainment scene seemed to show that physical improvements could also produce social transformation.

At the same time a group of upper-class, civic organizations, led by the Municipal Art Society, was becoming increasingly concerned with the impact of new office development on Manhattan's East Side. Home to New York's wealthiest residential community and most exclusive stores, the East Side had many leaders with easy access to decision-makers. The logical reaction was to "move development westward" (see chapter 2). The City Planning Commission responded by producing the "new midtown zoning," which limited further development on the East Side and encouraged construction to the West by raising the allowable building size there. While much publicity proclaimed the harm that further development could inflict on the East Side, neither the civic organizations nor the City Planning Commission paid great attention to the impact of higher densities on the West Side, which was simply assumed to be vastly underutilized. Moreover, the West Side was now seen as a potential magnet for firms that were threatening to flee to New Jersey or beyond. Times Square's seedy character was believed to discourage development for blocks around its central location. But if it were massively redeveloped, it could make the entire West Midtown area more desirable as an office location. Within the planners' mental maps, Times Square was shifting from being the entertainment core of Manhattan to becoming primarily an office and wholesaling district.

The proposal

Throughout the years various developers and design groups had presented proposals for redevelopment of the 42nd Street heart of the Times Square area. None attracted serious backing, however,[14] and in 1981 the city government distributed a request for development proposals that conformed to the new office-center vision and called on developers to follow a set of architectural guidelines. Devised by the firm of Cooper-Eckstut, which had created the much-praised design for Battery Park City, the specifications for Times Square emphasized a lively streetscape, to be achieved through building setbacks, glass street walls, and large neon signs. Even though the guidelines allowed for building heights up to 56 stories, at first they did not stimulate any protest.

The city government, in conjunction with the New York State Urban Development Corporation (UDC), selected a group of developers for the project, each with responsibility for a different component. Park Tower Realty, headed by George Klein, won the competition to develop the office section, which comprised the largest portion of the enterprise. The most immediately striking characteristic of the proposed development was its massive scale. The existing structures on the four corners straddling Times Square at 42nd Street would be replaced by four huge edifices, designed by Philip Johnson and John Burgee, totaling more than 4 million square feet of space. The heights of the buildings were to be 29, 37, 49, and 56 stories. Their appearance was somber compared to the existing architecture of the area, and they did not conform to the design criteria set forth in the Cooper-Eckstut guidelines. Generally the aesthetics of the buildings signified the seriousness of the business activity planned for their extensive interior spaces rather than the frenetic entertainment industry that had historically dominated the area. In addition, the UDC's plan included a 2.4 million square foot wholesale market on a corner of Eighth Avenue opposite the Port Authority Bus Terminal and a 550-room hotel facing it. It called for renovation of nine theaters on 42nd Street between Seventh and Eighth Avenues, and elaborate rehabilitation of the busy Times Square subway station. Untouched, however, would be New York's largest "adult entertainment" center, which lay directly across the street from the site.[15] Because the UDC did not do general land-use planning, its remit did not extend beyond the boundaries of the project.

The size of the office buildings and wholesale market greatly exceeded what was allowable under the city's zoning regulation. As at King's Cross, supporters justified the project's bulk on the grounds that only very large buildings would produce enough revenue to pay for land acquisition and the funding of community benefits. In both cases the public body choosing among the competing bidders used financial return rather than design as its criterion. Also similar to King's Cross, the Times Square developers believed that they could obtain financing only if they were able to promise rent levels substantially below those in more prestigious locations; therefore more space had to be provided to produce overall revenues comparable to other areas.

Responsibility for coordinating the scheme rested with a public-private partnership, the 42nd Street Redevelopment Corporation, comprising two public agencies and the private developers. On the governmental side both the UDC and the city's Public Development Corporation (PDC, later to become the Economic Development Corporation, EDC) carried out

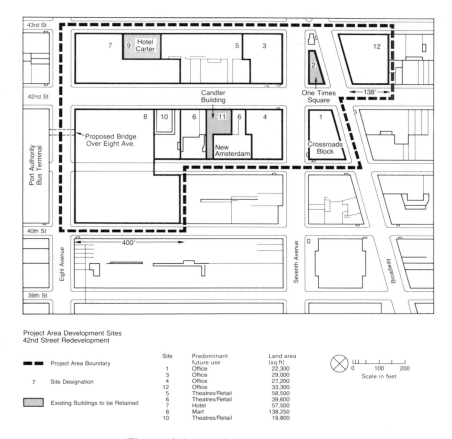

Project Area Development Sites
42nd Street Redevelopment

■ ■ Project Area Boundary

7   Site Designation

[ ] Existing Buildings to be Retained

Site	Predominant future use	Land area (sq.ft)
1	Office	22,300
3	Office	29,000
4	Office	27,200
12	Office	33,300
5	Theatres/Retail	58,500
6	Theatres/Retail	39,600
7	Hotel	57,500
8	Mart	138,250
10	Theatres/Retail	19,800

0   100   200
Scale in feet

Figure 6.1 42nd Street redevelopment

planning, staffing, and implementation functions, using the UDC's powers of eminent domain (compulsory purchase) and authority to override local zoning. On the private side, the participating developers, as well as bearing the construction costs of their buildings, would contribute to theater and subway improvements[16] and would pay for the UDC's land acquisition costs up to a specified level. The city's Board of Estimate approved the project in October 1984. In the ensuing years a series of lawsuits and other setbacks delayed its implementation, and over the course of time all the private-sector participants except the office developer and theater owners dropped out. In 1992, when the UDC began to vacate the site, the office buildings did not have any tenant commitments, while the theaters lacked adequate funding for renovations and operations.

In the meanwhile, the Department of City Planning began to respond to concerns that transformation of the area was destroying the elements that nurtured the entertainment industry. Stimulated by the permissive new midtown zoning, thirteen buildings were either under construction or planned around Times Square by 1988. All overshadowed what had been the tallest structure by at least seven stories; seven of them exceeded forty stories (Dunlap, 1988). Hoping to overcome the deadening effect of these new towers as well as of the large buildings proposed for the 42nd Street project, the city planners drafted a sign ordinance for the entire vicinity. This required all structures to provide for huge exterior signs, on the model of Piccadilly Circus in London or the Shinjuku district in Tokyo.[17]

In another, less superficial effort to maintain the character of the area as an entertainment district, the Department of City Planning also obtained city council approval for a change in the zoning, so that all buildings in the Times Square district had to devote 5 percent of their floor space to entertainment-related functions (Stasio, 1989). Office developers generally resented being forced to cater to entertainment uses at all and pressed for the most inclusive definition possible. In response to developer concerns, permissible uses, which included rehearsal halls, wigmakers' premises, and lighting designers' studios, were extended to cover record stores and movie theaters. Because the latter type of high-volume establishment generates greater rent-paying capability, it drives out the more modest kinds of activities on which the theater industry depends and will inevitably dominate the designated "entertainment-related" spaces. Many in the industry remained skeptical that the space reserved for theater support services would, in fact, keep them in Manhattan.

In 1989, responding to attacks on the appearance of the office towers,[18] the firm of John Burgee[19] redesigned them so that they reflected "the neon and honky-tonk atmosphere" of the existing district.[20] The new design incorporated setbacks, cutouts, asymmetrical grids, angled roofs, reflective surfaces in blue and green glass, and built-in multicolored neon signs (Chira, 1989). The changes, however, did little to assuage the alarm of the critics:

> The good news is that these buildings try to be entertaining; they represent a serious attempt to evolve a viable new esthetic out of Times Square's tradition of lights and signs.
>
> The bad news is that this is all cosmetics. For the problem with the original design was never just the way it looked, bad as that was; it was the fact that the towers were too big and too bulky, and threatened to put what little is left of Times Square and the theater district into shadow. (Goldberger, 1989b)

Despite the assertions of the project's planners that the only alternative to massive redevelopment was no development at all, the stretch of 42nd Street west of the project site indicated the potential for a more moderate procedure. Here the modest effort, described earlier, which produced a row of theaters and restaurants along with a low-income residential project, had greatly ameliorated the environment without a drastic reconfiguration of uses. A similar strategy addressed to the project blocks would combine rehabilitation and new construction. Under such an approach, eminent domain, by forcing out the most undesirable uses, could allow the rehabilitation of existing structures if their owners resisted upgrading. Mainly the city could have bettered the area simply through working with the property-holders from whom they seized the site.[21] It could have used tax abatement to assist the owners of the movie theaters, who claimed that they were willing to fix up their properties using their own capital without the contributions of office developers. Spot demolition would have created the opportunity for some new construction. The block closest to the existing subsidized apartment complex could have been used for a mixed residential-commercial structure, containing both market-rate and subsidized housing units. But, although such an approach could produce redevelopment without enormous disruption, it would not create the kinds of huge public and private revenues promised – although not delivered – by the city's preferred approach.

Financing

Although George Klein[22] remained the developer of the office component, the bank that was his original financial backer, Manufacturers Hanover Trust, withdrew from its commitment. The Prudential Insurance Company, which became an equity partner in the venture, then agreed to provide the financing, obtaining a $150 million letter of credit from Morgan Guaranty Trust.[23] Initially Klein's firm, Park Tower, reached a pre-leasing agreement with a large law firm; when it withdrew, Chemical Bank signed on as an anchor tenant but it subsequently also backed out. Trammell Crow, who had been selected as the developer of the wholesale market, quit the project too, as did the developer of the hotel.

While acquisition of the land and existing structures depended on the use of the UDC's power of eminent domain, purchase costs up to $150 million were to be borne by the developers. Of this amount Park Tower was originally responsible for $88 million; its commitment was increased further in subsequent negotiations (New York City PDC, n.d.; Stuckey, 1988). The remaining land purchases were covered by the city out of funds borrowed from the developer at an interest rate above the prime and returned to him through forgiveness of later payments in lieu of taxes (PILOTs) that he would owe the city once the buildings were occupied. Thus, the city was assuming land costs above a set amount and moreover would be paying the developer above-market-rate interest on his initial outlay (Hoff, 1989).

The public sector therefore incurred few of the front-end costs of the project. It did, however, commit itself to an ongoing subsidy through a tax abatement. The size of this abatement was estimated at about $650 million over fifteen years (Mollenkopf, 1985). Property tax revenues in the project area in 1982 were just $5.1 million. If the land costs did not greatly exceed the developer's contribution and if the buildings produced anything close to the predicted rate of return, the city through the PILOT would still receive considerably more revenue from the area, even under the abatement, than had previously been the case. Further financial benefits to the city included participation in rent collections from the tenants of the various structures. Title to the land and structures, which were to be leased for 99 years, would remain with UDC. After fifteen years, however, the lessees could purchase the properties; for the office buildings the buyout price was specified at only 45 percent of the average annual net rent roll.

Responses to the plan

The New York City Board of Estimate, before approving the proposals, sponsored hearings on the draft environmental impact statement and then on the final plans. Many who testified complained of the haste with which the scheme was being pressed – and certainly the subsequent eight years of delay in starting the project retrospectively raise serious questions concerning the justification for hurry. Even its supporters objected to the incomplete information on which judgments had to be based and to the size of the office towers. A group of eleven design-oriented civic groups, which had formed an association called the President's Council, expressed concerns over bulk, density, and vitality. Its membership ultimately split over whether to accept the large buildings as the price of progress. Residents of the Clinton neighborhood, located directly to the west of Times Square, mobilized against the project, contending that it would force up property values and accelerate the gentrification of their neighborhood. Community Board 4, whose constituency included Clinton, opposed the plan; Board 5, which represented the Times Square area itself and contained a number of members drawn from the business and real-estate industries, issued a catalogue of objections but did not take a firm stand. Some

Clinton groups, including the Ninth Avenue Business Association and the pastor of a major Roman Catholic Church, endorsed the proposal. Representatives of the clothing industry, located to the south of the project site, expressed fears that rents in the garment district would be forced up as office uses encroached on its territory. Although theater owners and managers supported the plan, others in the industry opposed it, fearing that entertainment uses would lose their critical mass in the area.

Politicians split on the issue, with those at higher levels, including Governor Mario Cuomo, Senator Daniel Patrick Moynihan, Mayor Edward Koch, and former Mayors Abraham Beame and Robert Wagner strongly praising the scheme. These notables even turned up to testify at the hearings, making frequent reference to the bright lights, dancing feet, and glamour that once characterized Times Square and arguing that only a tremendous redevelopment effort could restore its former glory. They did not address the problematic relationship of an office complex to this nostalgic vision. In contrast, the city council members and state assembly representatives from the area resisted the project.

The planning agencies sponsoring the venture asserted that they had consulted extensively with community groups during the years preceding Board of Estimate approval. Their communications, however, were predominately one-way, and it was only the urgency of obtaining final political approval that created any flexibility. Just before the decisive Board of Estimate vote, state and city negotiators began to engage in frenzied discussions with Clinton representatives. The key intermediaries in translating outside pressure into concessions were the elected officials rather than the planners, who until this point had remained obdurately committed to the plan. The principal concession granted was the allocation of $25 million from the regular state and city budgets to the Clinton neighborhood, to be used over the next five years for low-income housing and community development purposes. Clinton representatives failed to achieve their objective of obtaining the money from the private developers rather than public revenues. They had wanted to set a linkage precedent whereby developers would be obligated to compensate communities for project impacts. Ironically, Clinton fared much better as a result, since it began receiving its allotment at once, while eight years later the developer's obligations were not yet in force.

Unlike the King's Cross community, residents and businesses in the Times Square area did not receive public funding for support of a project area committee to advise on the plan (as was once required in the United States under federal urban renewal legislation).[24] State Senator Franz Leichter remained the project's fiercest opponent, persistently lobbying against it and publicizing what he regarded as its misguided intentions.[25] A group of developers with investments in surrounding areas bankrolled sporadic efforts at devising an alternative plan and exposing the negative financial impacts of this one.[26] The recent construction of numerous buildings in the vicinity without comparable subsidies led opponents to argue that financial assistance for the 42nd Street project was unnecessary and caused it to compete unfairly with the new structures.[27] Project sponsors responded that it was only the promise of their undertaking that created the vision of the area as an office center; without it the other structures would not have been built.

The situation in 1993

Each year after the project's approval the sponsoring agencies declared with much fanfare that work was about to begin. Lawsuits, however, kept the UDC from acquiring the site until 1990, and then negotiations with existing tenants caused further postponements. In 1992 the UDC finally evicted the occupants, but by then the enthusiasm of Prudential and Park Tower for proceeding with the project had lapsed. The empty office buildings and theaters on 42nd Street produced a ghost-town aspect to the area. Having passed into government ownership, the sites are no longer generating any real-estate taxes.[28] The relocation of 240 businesses has produced hardships for many of the companies involved, especially the smaller firms, and cost $183 million of city and investor money (Grant, 1990). Action-movie fans lament the absence of their favorite theaters: " 'They're looking to move in a new class of people here,' said Wayne Williams, a hospital worker from . . . Brooklyn. 'They want to get rid of the poor folks. Who's going to pay $22 to see Shakespeare. I want to pay $5 to see two karate movies' " (Tierney, 1991).[29] The theaters themselves, under the landlordship of the UDC, still have no operating plan, although a number of arts groups have expressed interest in using them. The costs of renovation and operation, however, remain a serious obstacle to occupancy, since they are way beyond the means of non-profit companies.[30]

Despite its considerable investment in land-taking, the Prudential Insurance Company decided in the summer of 1992 that it would not proceed with the office project. The UDC sought to hold it at its word, but finally acquiesced to a compromise in which Prudential and Park Tower agreed to reserve their right to build offices on the site (Dunlap, 1992b). Until they considered the time ripe for new construction, they would invest about $20 million in refurbishment of the existing buildings for retail, restaurant, and entertainment uses. Hence, by default, the moderate renovation of the area, in which no one was initially interested, has become the interim development plan for Times Square. Initial response to the new scheme has been very strong, with numerous prospective retail tenants seeking space (Martin, 1993).

At this point only the public agencies that originated the project appear committed to the concept of sweeping redevelopment. Their officers continue to argue that physical transformation alone can wipe out the social pathologies that bedevil the Times Square area.[31] Yet their strategy would simply relocate undesirable behavior and substitute an inhospitable physical environment for a forbidding social one. Less ambitious development and the use of regular capital budget funds for public improvements, while not as immediately lucrative for the city, would in the long run be cheaper and contribute more to the quality of life of those who live and work in the area.[32] The choice to proceed with the current strategy resulted from acceptance of the growth criterion untinctured by a commitment to equity and human scale in design and also unconstrained by caution over the likely demand for space. Because no influential political or administrative entity had seriously promoted an alternative approach, its virtues remained unexamined and the decision boiled down to either the proposed project or no project at all.

LESSONS

Initiation of both projects began within the public sector. Pressures from the public side (BR in the King's Cross case and New York City for Times Square) forced the developers to design a project that would produce the maximum return. With manufacturing regarded as a vestige of the past, public officials and developers insisted that only offices for financial and advanced-services firms could nurture economic expansion; they were extremely unwilling to entertain other possibilities. The King's Cross consortium, even when confronting a market that may not support their planned development for many years, still refuses to examine the alternative plans presented by the Railroad Lands Community Development Group. The Camden council, caught in the middle, has acquiesced in the developers' viewpoint so that it can have access to the resources offered by planning gain. In the Times Square area, the development partnership ignored the obvious strategy of an improved entertainment and retail district. Despite its reluctance, however, it eventually yielded to market pressures and endorsed the concept of its opponents, at least for the short run.

Although members of the affected communities never were able to shape the planning process to their will, they did succeed in delaying implementation sufficiently long to assure that the projects could only begin once the market had collapsed. In King's Cross, where the failure to achieve early planning permission meant that present occupants were not evicted, no drastic, disruptive change in the status quo occurred. Existing businesses, however, will have to continue operating under great uncertainty and, despite the indefinite postponement of new construction, no plans exist for intensifying uses under the current arrangements. The commitment of Camden council as well as the development consortium to comprehensive redevelopment apparently precludes short-term improvements and nurturing of existing small businesses on the site. In Times Square, even though the interim plan provides for small-scale rehabilitation, many viable businesses have already been driven out of the area, and two large office buildings, which will be extremely difficult to refill, stand empty.

Both the King's Cross and Times Square schemes point to the highly speculative element in wholesale redevelopment. By forcing the development teams to propose very large projects, the public sector increased the risk element. The opportunity costs of this strategy are quite high – its all-or-nothing approach may, with a downturn in the market, produce nothing. In both cases the obduracy of the development consortia in adhering to their aspirations for a mega-complex of offices may well have doomed their projects, not because of direct community antagonism but because their business assumptions were faulty.

Planning for the projects did not take into account the particular character of the surrounding neighborhood either in the type of jobs likely to be created by the new uses or in building on the base of commercial enterprises already there. Although large, centrally located tracts like these should be planned to serve the city as a whole, such planning need not be blind to existing strengths nor wholly ignore the particularities of locale. One cannot help but think that the slump in the office market saved King's Cross and Times Square from disaster and hope that the breathing space provided will bring greater wisdom to bear.

NOTES

1 Unless otherwise indicated, information on the cases and quotations from participants come from interviews I conducted between 1989 and 1992 for King's Cross and between 1984 and 1992 for Times Square.
2 See Squires (1989) for discussions of American cases and Brindley et al. (1989) for British examples.
3 Different documents describe the site as anywhere from 125 to 150 acres, depending on whether or not they include railroad uses.

4 Although the government eventually decided that the main terminal would be at Stratford, the train would carry passengers on to King's Cross. At the time that planning for King's Cross began, the government had not yet made its final routing decision on the connecting line to the tunnel.

5 Although not all its plans came to fruition, BR proposed developments around all the major stations. At the same time as it was working on its King's Cross enterprise, it was also participating in a large-scale proposal for the Paddington Station area in Westminster. As discussed in chapter 2, Broadgate, adjacent to Liverpool Street Station, already represented the largest redevelopment project in London outside of Docklands, and London Bridge Station formed the core of another huge, recently finished effort.

6 Rosehaugh Stanhope was itself a partnership of two firms. Rosehaugh was headed by Godfrey Bradman, characterized by the *Financial Times* (December 7–8, 1991) as "once the highest flying property developer on the stock market"; Stanhope's chair was Stuart Lipton, one of the most respected developers in Britain. Thirty-three percent of the ownership of Stanhope and 8 percent of Rosehaugh were in the portfolio of Olympia & York (*Observer*, May 7, 1992).

7 In 1989 about 44 percent of the total housing stock (about 70,000 units) in the borough was in council dwellings. Of these 31,419 council properties, 1,054 (3.4%) had been purchased under the right-to-buy program (UCL Bartlett School, 1990: 19).

8 The critique is contained in King's Cross Railway Lands Group (1989); see University College London Bartlett School (1990) for the alternative plan.

9 Communication from Michael Edwards, June 1, 1992.

10 The LRC and the Bartlett group also differed over what investing institutions would accept as the estimated capital value of the project and over the amount of professional fees that the project would incur. By 1992, when rental levels were still falling and banks were refusing to invest at all in commercial real estate, these original points of controversy appeared moot.

11 Some of the firms classified as manufacturing actually had different functions as their principal activities. Important groups of firms included construction and construction supplies; haulage and distribution; vehicle repair and hire; theater supplies; hotels and cafés; and non-profit organizations.

12 In New York the insistence by the Triborough Bridge and Tunnel Authority, which owned New York's old convention center, the Coliseum, on accepting the highest bid for its land also resulted in a building plan that aroused fierce objections to its size. Delays in accepting the plan caused by community objections got the project caught in the real-estate slump. It is currently in abeyance.

13 The two towers had received public subsidies and had been intended for middle-income owner occupancy. The location, however, deterred middle-class purchasers, and the city was desperate to fill the buildings. It ultimately received Section 8, low-income housing commitments from the federal government to subsidize rentals. Because, the structures were envisioned as a vehicle to raise the social class of the neighborhood, the city did not wish them

to be occupied by the typical impoverished recipients of public subsidies. Therefore occupancy of most of the units was restricted to households with members in the performing arts, thereby ensuring a tenant body that had a middle-class lifestyle if not a middle-class income. From the city's point of view the ploy worked extremely well, as the buildings filled up rapidly and sustain a long waiting list. Since they were originally built to high standards, the carrying costs of the structures are substantial and the subsidy per apartment extremely large; the subsidy, however, is borne by the federal government, not New York City.

14 These proposals all featured entertainment uses. Among the failed ideas were a 15-story ferris wheel to provide the centerpiece of an indoor amusement park and a "car-o-rama" featuring automobiles rotating on a moving belt behind a high glass facade.

15 Show World, as this multilevel enterprise is called, contains a large store selling pornography and sex equipment, and theaters devoted to X-rated films and live sex acts.

16 The contribution to the subway station was to be $33 million plus an inflation factor; $14 million, with an inflation adjustment, was to go toward renovation of the nine theaters.

17 Interestingly, while the playfulness of the new signs seems to arise from a postmodernist architectural orientation, the effect of fitting the signs on the buildings was to force them into a modernist mold: "It's much easier to graft exterior lighting and commercial signs onto a modern form than a classically inspired one. Can you do classical pediments and column capitals in neon?" (Goldberger, 1990).

18 The *New York Times*, whose editorial offices are located in the Times Square area, has generally supported the project, which promised to enhance the value of its real estate and the atmosphere of its surroundings. Its architectural critic, however, although normally a fan of Philip Johnson's work, joined in the vitriolic critique of the project's architectural merits: "The project's design, never any great shakes to start with, has come to seem a truly depressing prospect as the years have gone on, making this surely one of the only major works of architecture to look utterly out of date before it was even started" (Goldberger, 1989a).

19 Philip Johnson had by then retired, but he continued to act as a consultant to Burgee.

20 The stress on honky-tonk contrasts with the traditional modern architect's commitment to purity of design. If one evaluates this impulse charitably, one sees in it a reflection of the insights of Robert Venturi, Denise Scott-Brown, and Steven Izenour's *Learning from Las Vegas*, which famously declared that "BILLBOARDS ARE ALMOST ALL RIGHT" (1977, p. 6). One can also regard it as just the latest faddism on the design front. Comments by the architects could uphold both interpretations:

> Asked why the original plans . . . had not reflected the character of Times Square, Mr. Burgee and Mr. Johnson said trends in architecture as well as public opinion have changed.

"A big revolution in architecture happened in those six years," Mr. Johnson said. "We wanted to make a unified impression; we were going to make a great new Times Square, like Rockefeller Center. Now, besides the popular reaction — let's have more lights and people — inside the architecture profession we changed from classicism, like the A.T.&T. Building and copying the 1920's, to something we call the new modern." (Goldberger, 1989b)

21 The present approach to 42nd Street, adopted because the redevelopment corporation had no choice, involves just such moderate rehabilitation. Unfortunately the original owners and tenants had all been expelled from the site by the time the office project was officially postponed.

22 Also the developer of Paternoster Square in the City of London, another troubled project.

23 Prudential, which either wholly owns or participates in a number of large projects throughout the United States, differs from most insurance companies in pursuing an active role as a developer (P. Grant, 1989). Among its holdings are the Embarcadero Center in San Francisco, Century Plaza Towers in Los Angeles, Town Center outside Detroit, and the Prudential Center in Boston.

24 In Manhattan's West Side Urban Renewal Area, to the north of Clinton, the project area committee had played an important role in monitoring and changing the renewal plan throughout the 1960s and into the 1970s.

The termination of the federal urban renewal program in 1974 abrogated its citizen participation requirements, which had been built up over the years in response to protests over its neighborhood impacts. The Community Development Block Grant (CDBG) program, which replaced urban renewal in the 1974 Act, had only a vague mandate for citizen input. Under Republican administrations the federal government withdrew from oversight of local CDBG expenditures. The program, at any rate, has shrunk in size to inconsequentiality. Because CDBG funds are so limited, central business district redevelopment is rarely conducted using federal subsidies and thus need not comply with federal regulations.

25 Project supporters have accused him of fronting for rival developers who have contributed to his campaigns. He has responded that the politicians favoring the project have accepted far larger contributions from George Klein.

26 Including potential interest costs that the city might have to pay if it was forced to borrow from the developer to meet land costs, Leichter calculated that the total public subsidy could equal $1.5 billion. This amount seemingly exaggerates the savings on land and relocation costs that the developer would achieve as a consequence of UDC participation. If, however, the city incurs substantial interest payments, its overall subsidy will amount to considerably more than simply forgone taxes and infrastructure investment.

27 These buildings did receive the benefits of the more permissive zoning regulations under the special midtown zoning and a standard Industrial and Commercial Incentives Board (ICIB) tax abatement for new commercial construction.

28 Douglas Durst, a developer with interests in the area who had long opposed the project, was quoted as saying: "They've turned 42nd Street into a desolate area, decreased the value of surrounding property and eliminated about $3

million in tax revenues. They've managed to completely louse things up"
(*Crain's New York Business*, March 23, 1992).

29 The 42nd Street theaters catered to specialized tastes. A *New York Times*
reporter interviewed former viewers after the auditoriums were shuttered:

> [Fans] wish they could still watch a one-armed kung fu master. They are angry at
> the demise of the world's finest concentration of movie theaters devoted to
> zombies, nymphomaniacs, aliens, chainsaws, surfers, martial artists, cannibals
> and, of course, women in prison. . . . The government redevelopers insist they will
> put cheap entertainment – perhaps even action movies – back in some theaters,
> but the promises have not appeased serious students of The Deuce's [i.e. 42nd
> Street's] movies. These are the kind of film critics who classify works into such
> sub-genres as beasts-on-the-loose, stalk-and-slash, sword-and-sandal, and bimbos-
> behind-bars. (Tierney, 1991)

30 The landmarked New Amsterdam Theater, which the city acquired in 1982,
and which at that time was in good repair, has been allowed to deteriorate
and, due to a leaky roof, would now cost at least $50 million to restore
(Neuwirth, 1990).

31 The closing of the various entertainment attractions on the street did succeed
in dramatically reducing the crime rate.

32 The postponement of the office development plans meant that the funds
promised for subway station reconstruction vanished. The project leadership
was proposing that the Metropolitan Transit Authority (MTA) pay for
renovations out of its own capital budget, eventually to be reimbursed when
the office towers were built. The design for the renovated station, however,
was integrated into the office-tower plans and was not adaptable for the
interim use. Nor, of course, was it assured that the office buildings would ever
be constructed. The developers were in the enviable position of holding a
guarantee of enormous tax benefits if they went ahead with the project, but
were under no compulsion to do so if the market was not right.

7

Creating New Centers: Spitalfields and Downtown Brooklyn

Spitalfields and downtown Brooklyn are areas generally considered peripheral to their cities' central business districts, although more on the basis of psychological than of physical distance. Each contains under-utilized old commercial sites surrounded by very poor neighborhoods with predominantly minority populations. Their redevelopment involves an array of government subsidies; in Spitalfields the private developer has also committed a substantial contribution to the area. Although the developments proposed for these two locations involve land-use changes that threaten existing residents and businesses, they also promise employment and other economic benefits in parts of the city otherwise offering extremely little opportunity. Consequently redevelopment initiatives have found greater favor with the local community than was the case at King's Cross and Times Square. Instead many community activists see the potential for gaining commitments to their enterprises from the project's public and private sponsors.

SPITALFIELDS

Looking out of an upper-floor window of the Broadgate office complex, home to many of the world's leading financial and advanced-service firms, one can survey the sprawling structure that once held the Spitalfields Market. For over 300 years its merchants purveyed fruit and vegetables to the greengrocers and restaurants of central London.[1] The market now stands empty, awaiting transmutation into a multi-use, office-retail-residential complex, while additional sites along Brick Lane even further to the east are also being proposed as development locations.

The Spitalfields area constitutes a ward within the "neighborhood" of Bethnal Green, which itself is one of the seven components of the borough of Tower Hamlets. The boundary between the City and Bethnal Green runs through the market site. Yet, while only a block separated the financial traders in Broadgate from the produce traders of the market, they existed in separate worlds, marked by vast divergences in both land use and population. Even today clothing manufacturing ("the rag trade") and leather-working remain the principal industries of the Spitalfields area. Commercial outlets located on Brick Lane are mostly down-market "Indian" (actually Bengali) restaurants and groceries, sari shops, and workingmen's pubs. Buildings are low-rise, and many of the shops have domiciles above them. Unlike the City of London, where few people live, the area is densely populated, and the dominant form of tenancy is council housing and private-rental tenements.[2]

In the centuries since the inception of textile manufacturing by Huguenot silk-weavers, this part of East London has been the first stop for waves of immigrants entering England. After the Huguenots, Irish and Jewish groups settled in the area; now Bangladeshis comprise an estimated 80 percent of the population, with the remainder consisting of a diversity of nationalities (Community Development Group, 1989, p. 19).[3] The newcomers have lived under squalid conditions in extreme poverty:

> Despite the repeated pattern of successive migrations of peoples from rural areas to the same bad housing and the same jobs, the different groups of migrants share little else. They have found themselves in Spitalfields for many reasons, and have expected a multitude of different things from their stay. The Jews were fleeing pogroms, their previous existence was unstable, they had nowhere to return to. They came in desperation. Bangladeshis came from settled rural communities whose basic patterns were unbroken even by the British empire. They came in hope; they never expected to settle here. (Forman, 1989, p. 6)

In a recent ranking of London wards derived from four indicators of deprivation, Spitalfields ranked as the most deprived; only one ward exceeded it in unemployment, and none even approached it in levels of overcrowding (Townsend, 1987, appendix 4).[4] Those progeny who succeeded in ascending the social ladder did not stay to improve their old neighborhood but rather moved out. Although Spitalfields's "ethnic

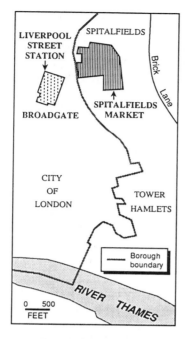

Figure 7.1 Spitalfields

color" and landmark buildings attract a certain number of visitors, it largely remains insulated from the cosmopolitan metropolis around it.

Decision-making

In 1986, in an experiment in governmental decentralization, the Tower Hamlets borough council, which had recently passed from Labour to Liberal-Democrat control,[5] divided the borough into seven districts, each with a partisan, elected council responsible for service delivery within its boundaries. Although the overall council, comprised of the aggregate of the neighborhood councils, contained a Liberal-Democrat majority, Labour continued to control some of the neighborhood bodies, including Bethnal Green's. As politicization of the East Asian community increased, its representation on the Tower Hamlets borough council grew, until there were nine Bengali councillors out of 50 in 1992, seven of whom were Labour.

Despite the rhetoric of community participation that surrounded decentralization, it won little praise from those seeking to improve conditions in the deprived areas of the borough. A Spitalfields Bengali councillor remarked that the expenditure of over £45 million had created seven layers of bureaucracy, increasing the number of civil servants while reducing service delivery. He called the 60 community advisory committees "talking shops." Another Bengali councillor commented: "The Tower Hamlets council is very strange. There is a desperate demand for money for services, but they are spending millions to build mini-town halls." An academic observer who was evaluating decentralization felt that the advisory committees were unrepresentative, dominated by the desire to exclude undesired uses, and incapable of examining the "big picture." She commented that decentralization rather than substantive programs had become the only policy of the council.

Because the central government did not recognize the authority of the neighborhood councils, the decision to grant planning permission rested with the overall borough council. Its majority saw large-scale development as providing an opportunity for planning gain and local economic improvement. According to a councillor who opposed the various development initiatives:

> In a community like this, people don't know where to go. People are out of school, they don't have any sign of employment. This is an underclass community. It is easily manipulated by the wealthy. The developers came and gave them hope, they used the leaders to manipulate the local community. The larger community will lose from development in Spitalfields. But the leaders were bought out, and the community is divided.

Community and business groups

A long history of community activism had produced a number of Bengali advocacy groups in Bethnal Green (Forman, 1989). They were rooted in two main struggles: the effort to obtain decent living accommodation for Bengali families and the need to protect the Bengali community from racialist attacks, particularly prevalent in the late 1970s. These groups had succeeded in establishing a housing cooperative, attracting several housing associations into the area, and making the neighborhood more or less secure.

Community organizations feared a repetition of the wholesale conversion and exclusion of local viewpoints that was already taking place in the Docklands (see Church, 1988a). In 1981 the London Docklands Development Corporation (LDDC) had taken over planning authority for the portion of Tower Hamlets alongside the Thames. The proposed restructuring of the western portion of Spitalfields for office uses threatened to reproduce the Docklands scenario there. The developers in the meanwhile, anticipating fierce opposition and lacking the protection of the LDDC, attempted to assuage local antagonisms through an expressed willingness to negotiate and through contributions to local betterment.

Business firms had become unusually active in sponsoring local programs within East London. Typically, British business leaders did not involve themselves in community activities: as developer interest in this area had grown, however, they began working through an association called the East London Partnership (ELP). The ELP was originally chaired by Sir Alan Shepherd, the head of Grand Metropolitan, which owned the Truman's Brewery within Spitalfields – one of the proposed development sites. An offspring of the national organization Business in the Community,[6] the ELP counted in its membership the head officers of 45 large- and medium-sized companies operating within the three East London boroughs of Hackney, Tower Hamlets, and Newham. As well as acting as a lobby on transit issues,[7] it provided small grants and technical assistance to community groups, including Bengali women's organizations, within East London.

The market site

As the City fringe began to fill up with office buildings and smart service establishments, the vegetable hawkers and the motor traffic that they attracted became more and more at odds with their surroundings. At the same time some of the historic structures surrounding the market were gaining appeal as residential locations. The psychological barrier that had separated the City of London from Tower Hamlets became breachable. The City of London Corporation, which owned the Spitalfields Market, issued a tender document for the 11-acre site in 1987; the winning bidder would commit itself to relocating the market traders in return for a long-term lease that would permit it to develop the site for office and retail uses.

A consortium consisting of three major property developers, calling itself the Spitalfields Development Group (SDG),[8] successfully proposed a multi-use, predominantly office scheme for the market buildings and their vicinity. As a first step, it expended £40 million to move the market to Hackney; before this event could happen, however, an Act of Parliament was necessary to revoke the royal charter that had established the market in the 1600s; in the more than two years that it took to achieve parliamentary assent, antagonism to the proposal built up and a "Save Spitalfields" campaign germinated. Criticism came from two sources: middle- and upper-class conservationists concerned with the project's impact on the historically significant environment; and community

Figure 7.2 Spitalfields Market, with a view of Hawksmoor's Christ Church

advocates who feared the socially and economically destabilizing effect of office and modern retail establishments on the Bengali community.

The SDG was close to receiving planning permission from the Tower Hamlets council in 1990 when the Secretary of State for the Environment called in the plan for examination of its influence on the historic setting. The Secretary of State, who has the power to remove development decisions from the jurisdiction of the local authority, was responding to pressure from the conservationists within English Heritage and the Royal Fine Arts Commission rather than from the resident community.

By the time the market relocation actually took place in 1991, the effect of the Big Bang on the office market turned out to be less than anticipated, and the SDG indicated its willingness to reduce the floor areas first proposed. After discussions with the Department of the Environment (DoE), the developers agreed to redesign their project and hired a US architect, Ben Thompson, with a British firm acting as local agent. Thompson had become famous for his design of Faneuil Market in Boston, Massachusetts – the first major festive retail mall developed on a historic market site. His modifications to the plan overcame the conservationists' objections, but Labour politicians continued to fault the scheme for its alleged insensitivity to local residents.

Planning permission was still in abeyance at the time of the market relocation in 1991. Outline consent was finally granted in 1992 by the Tower Hamlets local authority and the City of London Corporation, but as of March 1993 the DoE was still considering the proposal. The plan, as approved by Tower Hamlets, called for 1.1 million square feet of offices (including a 16-story modern glass tower, designed by Sir Norman Foster, the principal architect of the King's Cross plan, "to be a gateway into the Spitalfields site"),[9] together with 68,000 square feet of shops, and 165 flats (Houlder, 1992a).

The SDG negotiated its planning gain package with the Tower Hamlets council. The Spitalfields Community Development Group (described below) did not participate in these discussions; to the extent that local residents were represented, it was through the affected neighborhood councils. In addition to assuming the costs of market relocation, the SDG committed itself to a development agreement whereby the 127 houses on the market site would be deeded to local housing associations. It also assented to the payment of a £5 million contribution to a charitable trust (the Spitalfields Development Trust) and to a pledge of £150,000 per year for job training.

Labour politicians in Tower Hamlets continued to oppose the development on the grounds that it would result in secondary residential displacement and would drive out unskilled jobs. The developers – in a familiar refrain – contended that only a massive development could provide enough return to support the debt service, the land rent, and the planning gain package. Whereas community representatives felt that the council had succumbed to a Faustian bargain, an officer of the SDG commented to me in 1991: "If we were asked to sign up today, we wouldn't." He expressed gratitude for the delays which had held up final planning permission, given the absence of financing and the glut of office space that prevailed at that time.

Brick Lane

The prospect of a redeveloped market between the edge of the City and Brick Lane, three blocks to the east, removed the buffer that had protected the Bengali community, for which Brick Lane constituted the cultural and commercial heart. Two large parcels of land comprising 27 acres on Brick Lane – Truman's Brewery and the Bishopsgate goods yard – became identified as development sites. Truman's Brewery, like the market, was an institution centuries old; its owner, Grand Metropolitan, a large conglomerate with interests in land development as well as food and leisure activities, shut down brewing operations as it prepared a development plan for the area. British Rail saw the disused goods yard as yet another opportunity to transform its property holdings into negotiable assets.

Community groups that had unsuccessfully contested the government's plans for the Docklands and tried to block redevelopment of the Spitalfields Market turned their attention to Brick Lane. In response to the perceived threats and opportunities of large-scale commercial development there, most of these groups came together under the umbrella of the Spitalfields Community Development Group (SCDG). The SCDG, rather than simply opposing development, argued that the two Brick Lane sites should be addressed within an integrated plan for the whole area. In return for community acceptance of office uses on the two sites, they asked that part of the land should be placed in trust for the community's own uses. They envisioned a "Banglatown" shopping center which would both serve the community and draw a broader market of consumers seeking ethnic food and crafts. The SCDG also called for a training strategy and for social housing to be built before office construction.

In 1989, using funds provided by the central government's Spitalfields Task Force and by Business in the Community, it published a detailed community plan (Community Development Group, 1989). The following year, with the backing of the Bethnal Green Neighborhood Council, it achieved an agreement with Grand Metropolitan in which twelve acres would be donated to a community trust. The SCDG had three principal concerns: (1) the projects should generate retail opportunities for Bengalis; (2) garment manufacturers, especially leather goods makers, who were regarded as the only local manufacturers with market potential, would have access to capital; and (3) project sponsors would make a serious effort at implementing employment training schemes. In order to ensure that the agreement would be implemented, the SCDG demanded ongoing participation in the planning and execution of Brick Lane development, not simply a one-time Section 52 (planning gain) agreement.

City Challenge

The property slump of the early nineties caused large development schemes to stall throughout London. In Spitalfields, however, the surcease in construction activity did not quench all possibility of investment in the community as, in July 1991, Bethnal Green was awarded a City Challenge grant for a program of social and physical regeneration (see chapter 5). City Challenge was an effort spearheaded by Michael Heseltine upon his reappointment as Secretary of State for the Environment.[10] It removed money from various local aid programs in a process known as "top-slicing" and targeted it to needy places, where it would be used for coordinated programs operated by public-private partnerships. According to the Tower Hamlets general manager (i.e. chief executive officer), the winning of the grant (eleven were chosen out of 21 bidders) had largely resulted from a visit to Tower Hamlets by Michael Heseltine, who was reportedly intrigued by its experiment in devolving authority to neighborhoods and encouraged the council to submit a bid.

The City Challenge grant provided £7.5 million per year for five years. Responsibility for running the program rested with a non-profit community organization comparable to an American community development corporation.[11] Its board was to contain representatives from all the governmental and non-governmental groups with interests in the area, including the property developers, the council, the East London Partnership, the SCDG, and the housing associations. The emphasis of the program was on job training for construction, office, and child-care jobs; English language study; support for local small-business development through grants and technical assistance; and council housing renovation and new construction sponsored by housing associations. It was hoped that the relatively small government grant would act as a catalyst for private contributions. These, however, would mostly depend on implementation of schemes for the development sites.

The situation in 1992

Participants thought that the City Challenge initiative would encourage the redevelopment projects to proceed, especially on the market site, where the developer was nearing success in obtaining planning permission and had already invested a large sum in relocating the market traders. The bankruptcy of Olympia and York (O & Y) in the summer of 1992, however, called these expectations very much into question (see Chapter 9). O & Y had been the major investor within East London; it was an active force within the East London Partnership; the financial positions of other developers were entangled with its affairs; and its vast Canary Wharf complex had been envisioned as the anchor for development to the east of the City. Without resource commitments from developers, City Challenge would simply become one more underfunded inner-city program.

Governmental participation in the various Spitalfields projects did not involve the kinds of financial subventions New York City provided for developers. Public-sector incentives in Spitalfields were of two kinds: (1) The City of London offered the developers a large, central site at a low initial cost and tied future payments to returns on the property; (2) Tower

Hamlets relaxed density standards to increase the developer's profit potential. In contrast to most regeneration schemes, Spitalfields was not limited to physical redevelopment – the City Challenge grant required social planning as well. The framers of the City Challenge proposal explicitly dealt with programs to improve the language skills, job qualifications, and housing of residents. But, as in Times Square and King's Cross, neighborhood benefits were once again tied to property development that had to be sufficiently remunerative – and therefore sufficiently large – to create a financial surplus. Consequently in Spitalfields, as in the other two locations, the proposed redevelopment would result in projects strongly discordant with their surroundings and seemingly destined to transform the uses and users of the area.

DOWNTOWN BROOKLYN

Brooklyn's downtown stood as the business center of an independent municipality until New York's consolidation in 1898. From the start, however, "the city of homes and churches," as Brooklyn was labeled, lived in the shadow of Manhattan; the nearness of "the city," originally accessible by ferry and then by auto and subway, early reduced downtown Brooklyn to the status of a secondary service node (Glueck and Gardner, 1991). Once middle-class customers left the borough for the suburbs, all that remained to sustain the downtown core were government offices, one last major department store, a large but struggling group of small retailers, and the Brooklyn Academy of Music.[12] Earlier urban renewal efforts had caused the demolition of a number of buildings, but no replacements ever reached the construction stage (Willensky, 1986). In the mid-1980s several single-room-occupancy hotels housed the homeless; destitute men hung out in the refuse-strewn vacant lots; while prostitution and the drug trade flourished. The only skyscraper was the 34-story Williamsburgh Savings Bank building constructed in 1929, the year before the Great Depression signaled the end of commercial real-estate development in central Brooklyn for the next sixty years.

   While the circumstances of downtown Brooklyn throughout the forty years after World War II were shaped by depopulation and disinvestment, nearby neighborhoods had followed other paths. Brooklyn Heights, directly facing the Manhattan skyline across the East River and isolated from the rest of Brooklyn by topographic boundaries, had maintained itself as an elite white residential area throughout the period. The adjacent Cadman Plaza urban renewal scheme, which produced a shopping center and a complex of high-rise, modernist, middle-income, residential buildings, further insulated the Heights. Other districts (Park Slope,

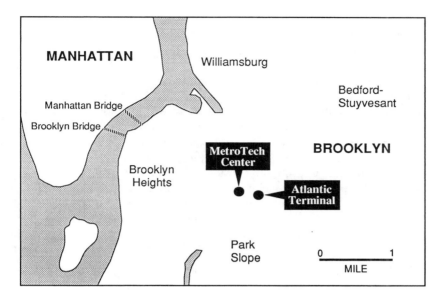

Figure 7.3 MetroTech Center

Cobble Hill, Fort Greene), in which an exodus of the original affluent inhabitants had left a large stock of handsome brownstone houses, became the targets of gentrification. The black population of Bedford-Stuyvesant and Fort Greene expanded, and large public-housing projects sheltered an increasingly impoverished population; nevertheless, parts of these neighborhoods were upgraded by middle-income, mainly black, home-owners, and the hub of African-American culture moved from Harlem to central Brooklyn. Brooklyn also became the destination for a highly diverse flow of Caribbean immigrants – estimated between 1983 and 1986 alone to include 16,000 Jamaicans, 15,000 Haitians, 12,000 Guyanese, 2,500 Granadans, 3,000 Barbadians, and 4,000 Trinidadians (Stollman, 1989, p. 12). They provided a willing low-wage labor force, and their economic ambitions stimulated the growth of small business within the borough.

A number of factors combined by the end of the 1980s to stimulate various initiatives aimed at reconstructing downtown Brooklyn. Primary was the felt need by the New York City government to compete with New Jersey in attracting the back offices of major companies. Only in the boroughs was land sufficiently cheap to allow competitively low rental prices. Shifting development interest to Brooklyn would both create a less expensive business core that could vie with out-of-state locations and deflect criticism that the mayor cared only about Manhattan. Moreover, it would respond to the urgings of the Regional Plan Association (RPA), an influential private body, which had envisioned downtown Brooklyn's elaborate transit infrastructure as creating the potential for a "third node of the Manhattan business district."

In tandem with the government's desire to see office development in the borough, private developers had begun searching more broadly for developable locations as Manhattan's construction boom absorbed the remaining parcels within its central business district. Two large Brooklyn sites presented themselves. One, adjacent to Polytechnic University, a private engineering school located on the edge of downtown, was being promoted by that institution as an ideal site, offering a potential synergy between the university's technical capacity and the needs of high-tech industry. Called MetroTech, this project opened for occupancy in 1990. The second, Atlantic Terminal, appeared the best prospect for commercial growth, as it was located above the largest confluence of subway and train lines in New York.[13] As of 1993, however, ground had not yet been broken.

MetroTech

In 1984 Polytechnic University, announced expansion plans and issued a request for proposals (RFP) to develop its surrounding area; the university's board envisioned the construction of a high-tech center, a sort of Silicon Valley East. Although the sixteen-acre site had years earlier been designated as an urban renewal area, it still housed about 100 families, 60 small businesses, and five governmental agencies. Bruce Ratner, a former New York City commissioner of consumer affairs, felt that the location had potential. He had recently entered into a joint venture arrangement with Forest City Enterprises, a Cleveland, Ohio, development firm.[14] Run by members of his family, Forest City Enterprises had interests throughout the United States. The combined New York City operation was called Forest City Ratner Companies. Ratner now persuaded the Cleveland firm to continue the alliance and respond jointly with him to Polytechnic's RFP.

Forest City Enterprises is a publicly held firm that specializes in secondary markets. Its officers describe it as an institutional rather than a speculative developer – that is, it projects future earnings on the basis of present market conditions rather than assuming increases in returns on its investments that will exceed the rate of inflation. Although its shares dropped nearly two-thirds in value between 1989 and 1992, it remained solvent by avoiding heavy leveraging; according to its founder, it had "almost no cross-collateralized mortgages or corporate guarantees. . . . no second mortgages or recourse on our mortgages" (Rudnitsky, 1992, p. 48). The firm tries to identify areas where it will not face competition, and it will not seek construction financing until the building is at least half pre-leased.[14] While superficially the places it selects appear to offer weak prospects, they present cost advantages, and public subsidies are available to further reduce risk.[15]

Polytechnic's RFP corresponded exactly with Forest City Enterprises' strategic criteria: no other developer was sufficiently interested in the area even to make a bid, and substantial governmental assistance could be obtained. According to one of the development company's officers, "Forest City Ratner realized that financial services were the high-tech firms of New York. They were big computer users. They could be advantaged by proximity to Polytechnic." The original vision of research laboratories and software outfits became transformed into yet another corporate office scheme, although somewhat disguised by the rubric of "high-tech." The development firm formulated a concept for a 4.2 million square foot office project in which it would pursue the computer processing operations of the financial industry.

Many of Forest City Ratner's staff members had worked in city government, and they knew how to use public benefits so as to bring total occupancy costs for tenants down to New Jersey levels. As a Forest City Ratner executive described the process: "Unless you worked in the public sector, understanding it is not easy. We were able to structure subsidies by setting up a 'pro forma' showing costs in Brooklyn versus New Jersey and then identifying the gap and filling it in rather than just throwing money away."

The Public Development Corporation (PDC) acted as the lead city agency on the project. At the behest of Polytechnic University and the development firm, it condemned the land, demolished the existing structures, and relocated the residents and businesses. In return, the city government was to receive a ground rent. Forest City Ratner put in about 10 percent of the private equity investment itself and obtained the rest of its financing from Japanese banks. In 1992, however, even with some of the buildings already occupied and more move-ins imminent, it had not yet been able to acquire permanent financing.

Under the city's Industrial and Commercial Incentives Program (ICIP) all firms moving into MetroTech benefited from a pass-through of property tax reductions for 22 years; a twelve-year exemption from the commercial occupancy tax; and a $500 per employee credit on the city's business profits tax for twelve years. Brooklyn Union Gas, a private utility, took advantage of the incentives and committed itself to vacating its old headquarters and moving to the nearby site; an $8 million federal Urban Development Action Grant (UDAG) supplemented the developer's

Figure 7.4 A scale model of MetroTech Center

investment in its building. The Securities Industry Automation Corporation (SIAC), a non-profit provider of computer services to the stock
exchanges, became the first tenant of the new MetroTech complex to
move from Manhattan. In addition to the standard ICIP incentives, it
received a $6 million federal UDAG, a $10 million equity investment from
the city's Municipal Assistance Corporation (MAC), and a $5.5 million
construction grant from the city's capital budget. Because New York's
extremely high utility charges penalized heavy computer users, it was
necessary to provide cheap electrical power. The company therefore
received a substantial discount from the privately owned Consolidated

Edison electrical utility, which in turn got a city tax subsidy for its largesse (Forest City Ratner, 1992; Dunlap, 1991).

The next enterprise that left Manhattan for Brooklyn did even better. The Chase Manhattan Bank in 1988 indicated that it was seriously interested in moving its data-processing operations with their 5,000-person work force to Jersey City. In exchange for reconsidering and committing itself to MetroTech, it obtained more than $100 million above the as-of-right incentives. Altogether the value of tax relief, site improvements, and electricity discounts amounted to $235 million (Lueck, 1988), and part of the tax abatement was granted to Chase's headquarters in Manhattan. In defending the arrangement against criticism of its munificence, Governor Mario Cuomo rationalized: "Nobody held us up. This is a tremendous deal." The vice-president of the RPA commended the city: "It is appropriate and a very practical approach to give away the store to get the first firms in" (Lueck, 1988). Chase bought a full-page advertisement in the *New York Times* (November 10, 1988), in which to express its gratitude for the efforts of Governor Cuomo and Mayor Koch in making Brooklyn attractive to it; according to the ad, however, "what tipped the scale in favor of New York was the simple fact that for nearly 200 years New York has been our home."

The financial concern Bear Stearns, the next company to win a special package of benefits for coming to MetroTech, did not justify its move in such sentimental terms:

> "The only way we could go to Brooklyn – because we figured that Brooklyn and Jersey City were roughly equal – was if the city would do more," Mr. Lang [its managing director] said. . . . As Mr. Lang told it, his message was: "We need relief at 245 Park [its headquarters in midtown Manhattan] or the MetroTech deal won't work. You're killing us with the real-estate taxes."
> (*Dunlap, 1991*)

The estimated value of the discretionary benefits given Bear Stearns on top of the ICIP package was $17 million, including the provision of lower-cost New York Power Authority electricity to the Manhattan building. Other reasons presented for its choice of Brooklyn were the speed with which the Dinkins administration put together the subsidy program; the fact that space in the Brooklyn Union Gas building was immediately available; and the knowledge that 57 percent of its 1,500 employees lived in Brooklyn, Queens, and Staten Island and would have difficulty commuting to New Jersey (Dunlap, 1991).

Both the Chase and Bear Stearns deals involved benefits to structures in the Manhattan CBD occupied by other sections of the target firms. Therefore, although ICIP subsidies had been deliberately removed from

Manhattan some years earlier, the outcome of directing discretionary benefits to Brooklyn was, in effect, to provide assistance in Manhattan. This breaching of the intent of the ICIP restrictions began under Mayor Koch and continued under Mayor Dinkins. Even with the resulting improvement in the Manhattan cost situation, the Bear Stearns bargain resulted in the vacating of 285,000 square feet of space there. More than three-quarters of the emptied Manhattan offices were located in two structures owned by Olympia & York, causing the *New York Times* reporter to conclude: "If there is a big loser, it may be the Reichmann family of Toronto [the owners of O & Y]" (Dunlap, 1991).

In a sense MetroTech operated as a money laundry – that is, as a device by which the government could finance investments in both economic development and community improvements off-budget. Although government's financial contribution to the project was enormous, a relatively small part of it comprised direct expenditure. In the meanwhile the developer, in addition to erecting the office towers, rebuilt a subway station and constructed or rehabilitated 59 housing units, some of them in a landmarked firehouse. The affected residents and business owners, who originally resisted being moved from the site, managed to negotiate a deal for either relocation or a buyout that they found satisfactory and dropped their lawsuit against the project (Oser, 1988). Some of the retail businesses, including Sid's hardware store, a local institution for 60 years, were assisted in returning to the project site, although in straitened and more expensive quarters.[16]

The subsidy program had suceeded in bringing enterprises to Brooklyn that otherwise would have avoided it. MetroTech, which included a three-acre outdoor commons, added a clear amenity to the decayed downtown. The complex, constructed according to a master plan created by the New York firm of Haines Lundberg Waehler, opened out onto the regular street grid, and it did not present the walled-off visage that characterizes most new development in areas perceived as dangerous. Different architects designed each building; Skidmore, Owings & Merrill, the best-known of the participating firms, was responsible for the largest amount of space. Although the architecture of the various building was undistinguished, it was not overbearing, and local people seemed to use and enjoy the greenery and special events provided in the commons. Intensive policing by both the New York Police Department and a private security force combined with a greatly increased amount of foot traffic to cause the local felony crime rate to drop by 23 percent between 1989 and 1991 (Myers, 1992).

MetroTech unquestionably revitalized the area. The development strategy produced a project over 95 percent occupied. Surrounding retail and service businesses began to feel multiplier effects (Retkwa, 1992), but they were also confronted by sharply rising rents and the arrival of competition from well-capitalized chains (Vizard, 1992). Forest City Ratner purchased the Albee Mall, a faltering nearby shopping center, with the aim of improving its appearance and merchandise. The MetroTech business improvement district (BID), funded by the businesses within the project and its vicinity, provided sanitation and security, programmed special events, and worked with community groups, merchants, and local high schools on public events and beautification projects. Receipts from the sales tax on construction purchases were set aside to fund an employment training council, and part of an office building was established as a business incubator, wherein fledgling businesses would pay low rents and receive technical and administrative services. Thus, the economic benefits of the project were spread to some degree around the surrounding area.

In the spring of 1992 black groups formed the African-American Coalition for Economic Development over the issue of jobs at MetroTech. It contended that the heavily subsidized office complex did not create employment for Brooklyn's black population. Officials at Forest City disputed this claim, arguing that the 10 percent yearly turnover in clerical jobs within the complex assured hiring of neighborhood people. Hard data is not currently available on the employment effects of the project.

Atlantic Terminal

Spurred on by their success at MetroTech, Forest City Ratner apparently decided that, with contributions from government, it could transform all of downtown Brooklyn. Except for one hotel and office complex across the street from MetroTech,[17] the firm assumed the responsibility for developing every potential commercial location in the area. Most significantly, it entered into a partnership with Rose Associates to develop the city-owned Atlantic Terminal urban renewal area, a site that had been awaiting construction activity since 1968. In 1985 Mayor Koch, with the usual publicity barrage, had announced a $255 million project to include 600,000 square feet of office space, a movie theater, 400 middle-income condominium housing units, a 45,000 square foot regional supermarket, and a shopping center.[18] The city had pledged $18.3 million of its own money toward construction, as well as the usual tax benefits. The mayor also promised that the city's Health and Hospitals Corporation (HHC) would become the anchor tenant for the office component.

The city invested $16.2 million in demolition and site improvements. However, Rose Associates, the designated developer, with long experience in the New York market as a major builder of both office and residential structures, had always followed a conservative investment strategy. After the HHC, under cost pressures and heavily criticized for extravagance, withdrew from the project, Rose apparently lost interest in moving forward. Despite Atlantic Terminal's excellent transit access Rose found the Brooklyn location too risky. Forest City Ratner's experience raised confidence in the area, and in 1991 the two firms announced their joint venture (Breznick, 1991). With little hope of finding office tenants, the partnership made the shopping center and the very large supermarket, now planned at over 50,000 square feet, its first priority.[19]

A coalition of local groups, the Atlantic Terminal Urban Renewal Association (ATURA) coalition, had formed at the time of the original 1986 project announcement to oppose the development plan. Members were particularly concerned over the possibility of secondary displacement (i.e., that development would cause surrounding areas to become unaffordable to present occupants, forcing them out) and were disturbed that on-site housing would be for middle-income owners only.[20] They recalled that years earlier, when housing on the partially vacant site had been torn down, residents had been promised replacement units. ATURA proposed a mix of affordable housing units, a greatly reduced supermarket to serve only the local community, and small-scale retail and office development; it lacked the resources, however, to formulate a full-blown alternative plan. With the assistance of pro-bono public-interest law firms, it brought three lawsuits related to the project's physical and social impacts and won one, resulting in the judge's ordering a study of its impacts on racial groups.

ATURA considered that the regional supermarket concept would bring unendurable car and truck traffic into the already heavily congested and polluted area and would negatively affect tenants of an adjacent low-income housing complex. Its stance on the supermarket and housing, however, did not attract all elements within the neighborhood. The community board saw a need for the supermarket as well as economic opportunities in the shopping center that it would anchor, and it thought that middle-income condo owners would help stabilize the neighborhood. It therefore enthusiastically supported the project. ATURA accused the board of being a rubber stamp and faulted it for not even demanding anything in return for approval.

As in Spitalfields the community split according to whether or not factions saw potential advantages to themselves if the development proceeded. The housing issue was particularly divisive since even low-income residents feared that provision of permanent housing for the homeless would worsen the social environment. Although the main criticisms of the development were based on concerns of residents for their living conditions, the African-American Coalition for Economic Development expressed its intention of monitoring Atlantic Terminal's employment outcomes. Like ATURA its interests kept it from favoring office uses, but it was not clear that it and ATURA would be in agreement on issues of scale. As at Times Square the demise of requirements for regular citizen participation by project area residents produced a situation where solicitation of community opinion depended on informal arrangements and on the willingness of elected representatives to act as advocates.

In 1992 the borough president's office set up an Atlantic Terminal advisory committee incorporating a variety of city officials and community representatives but heavily weighted toward project supporters. There were some indications that city funds would be used to change the income mix of the housing, reflecting the greater concern of the Dinkins administration than its predecessor for assisting low-income people. A proposal for a discount department store was substituted for the supermarket and greeted favorably by residents. Modifications to the parking plan lessened adverse neighborhood effects. The office component vanished from the discussion, although it was not officially withdrawn. The development team, which feared that plan modifications introduced in response to the changed real-estate market might force it to undergo the land use review process again, showed responsiveness to community concerns in the hope that its cooperativeness would prevent neighborhood groups from pressing the issue of formal reconsideration.

The situation in 1992

The real-estate slump of the nineties had a less dampening effect on the Brooklyn projects than on Manhattan development for two principal reasons. First, the city offered extremely high levels of subsidy to the area, including the commitment of some of its own agencies as tenants and assumption of site acquisition costs. Although its tax subsidies at Times Square were commensurately great, it could not justify filling that site with city offices. Rental costs would have been unacceptably high; the location was quite distant from the civic center clustered around City Hall; and the justification for building office towers on 42nd Street would have been wholly undercut.

Second, Forest City Ratner – the dominant private-sector actor in downtown Brooklyn – proved exceptionally canny in exploiting the attributes of its location. Companies like Brooklyn Union Gas had to stay in Brooklyn, and no one else was bidding for them. MetroTech's placement in Brooklyn's governmental core attracted further governmental activity to the area. Bruce Ratner's experience in city government taught him how to use the public sector to his great benefit, both through personal connections and program understanding. He took advantage of New Jersey's attraction to New York financial firms by getting the city to heap ever more subsidy on his development, and he had the backing of Brooklyn politicians who had long complained over favoritism to Manhattan.

Like Mayor Koch before him, Mayor Dinkins felt compelled to respond to every notice by a major firm that it was considering a move to New Jersey with a counter-offer. And indeed, if Manhattan was not a viable alternative for the firms that settled in Brooklyn, and if their move to New Jersey would result in heavy, long-term job loss for Queens and Brooklyn residents, encouragement of a critical mass of new construction in the latter may have been necessary for continued economic viability. If MetroTech and Atlantic Terminal do succeed in stimulating a local multiplier effect, and if pressures for employment of minority community residents prevail, the city's massive involvement in promoting Brooklyn will have important benefits for its citizens. Additionally, an environmental argument can be made for developing a business center with excellent public transit connections outside Manhattan's congested core. Unfortunately, though, Brooklyn's roadway situation and the back-ups within it caused by difficulties of automotive access to the island of Manhattan mean that growth there has serious negative environmental consequences of its own.

Whether or not New York City should incur heavy costs to entice businesses out of Manhattan to the boroughs remains controversial. A widely publicized study by New York University's urban research center argued that the city should play to its strengths and continue to emphasize its Manhattan CBD (O'Neill and Moss, 1991). By mid-1992, however, in addition to taxes forgone, the city had spent $166 million in capital improvements in downtown Brooklyn; in that year its Brooklyn expenditures amounted to nearly three-quarters of its capital budget for economic development (Myers, 1992). Forest City Ratner, for its part, had invested just $300 million, only somewhat more than twice as much as the city, yet the city had no equity participation in the project (Rudnitsky, 1992). Certainly it is hard to rationalize this extraordinary amount of public subsidy at the same time as the vacancy rate in Manhattan was soaring, and the government was sustaining a budget crisis.

Brooklyn had indeed been established as the third node of the city's business district, but not without considerable cost. At the same time as the citywide tax base was contracting as a consequence of recession, the government was giving away more tax breaks, small businesses were being forced to shoulder an increased proportion of the tax burden while larger concerns took advantage of the various tax subsidy programs, and every firm could see the logic of indicating its interest in New Jersey. MetroTech contributed to density and congestion in an area already subject to very high levels of motor vehicle traffic and consequent air pollution; Atlantic Terminal promised to add to these problems. The extent to which the economic development incorporated in MetroTech benefited the citizens of Brooklyn remained problematic. Even though the companies within MetroTech had pledged commitments to job-training and the placement of Brooklyn residents within their work forces, "the residents' biggest concern . . . is that downtown Brooklyn will become an isolated bubble, shut off from the rest of the borough" (Myers, 1992).

THE DYNAMICS OF DEVELOPMENT

Initiatives for the four redevelopment efforts described in this and the preceding chapter were fashioned by a variety of sources including private developers, community groups, and non-profit organizations, as well as government. Except in Brick Lane, however, developer interest was provoked by a government request for proposals. All four enterprises aimed at the creation of new commercial nodes in unfashionable locations, and all required considerable public investment. Despite their differing origins each bore a striking resemblance to the others in incorporating plans for very large office complexes.

The developments all threatened to overwhelm surrounding communities and provoked resistance over their physical impacts and potential displacement effects on businesses and households. The various projects involved the retention of prestigious internationally known architectural firms. Except in Brooklyn they designed complexes at odds with their surroundings, determined to make a statement and demonstrate that the redeveloped areas had a radically different character from what preceded them. Moreover, designation of the areas as renewal sites and land clearance preliminary to redevelopment had the immediate effect of dampening economic activity as the long delays and uncertainty inhibited current occupants and potential investors from improving the properties.

The relationship between the public-private partnerships sponsoring the projects and the local public affected the final outcomes. In Spitalfields and Brooklyn, where the developers showed flexibility and were somewhat responsive to the locale, the developments are more likely to proceed than in King's Cross and Times Square. In Times Square, community protest did succeed in modifying design to make it more compatible with its surroundings, and in King's Cross the developers did agree to some reduction in the size of the office complex. Nevertheless, all the projects remain much larger than the areas can readily absorb, and their local employment benefits are open to doubt.

All four cases involved conflicts of values as between local and citywide objectives, public and market criteria, and equity versus growth. Redevelopment of established areas necessarily has differential impacts on present occupants, with only a minority able to capitalize on the transformed uses. Planning agreements required compensation of residents for some of the costs to them – housing and employment programs in King's Cross, Spitalfields, and Brooklyn; a community development fund for the Clinton neighborhood next to Times Square; construction of public amenities in all four places. Some community opponents were assuaged by these side-payments, and others considered them inadequate but their only realistic option. While this type of bargaining fits well within a liberal economics paradigm of trade-offs, it fails to offer the potential advantages of planning in creating an overall environment satisfactory to the existing community.

The commercial development embodied in the projects was touted as containing growth potential for these two world cities. With manufacturing regarded as a vestige of the past, public officials and developers contended that only offices for financial and advanced services firms could nurture expanding enterprises. Even if their predictions were correct concerning the type of industry that would flourish in the future, the nature of office-centered growth seriously limited the extent to which the poor and working-class populations of inner London and New York would benefit from business expansion. While the jobs created or retained would provide few career opportunities for poorly educated citizens, the public investment involved in their creation imposed a heavier tax burden on these same citizens and on small businesses.

In both London and New York the projects had governmental sponsors, but the willingness of government to offer direct subsidy to the developer was far greater in the latter city. Neither of the two British projects was to receive any tax relief, since, except in enterprise zones, British law does not allow tax subsidies. In Spitalfields, the use of City Challenge funds to encourage private-sector activity was indirect – public capital expenditure did not directly support the private components of the developments. Thus, although all the projects tilted toward growth over equity in their value orientation, governmental expenditures in London were used for public purposes. In this respect the UK government has remained faithful to the Thatcherite image of the enterprise culture. As we shall see in chapter 9, its endorsement of the market's dispositions was less consistent on the Isle of Dogs, but even there its refusal to go all the way in assisting O & Y doomed its effort.

NOTES

1 The actual market structures were of much more recent construction, with the main building having been erected in the 1880s and the western part in the 1920s. Nevertheless, the frontage buildings of the older section are listed.

2 The area's population dropped for many years, but the effects of World War II bombing and the demolition of slum dwellings meant that there were still very high levels of crowding within the remaining housing units.

3 Population estimates for Spitalfields ward are 6,654 in 1981, of which 37 percent were born in Bangladesh, and 8,821 in 1989, with 80 percent from Bangladesh (Community Development Group, 1989, p. 18).

4 The other two indicators that composed the index were home ownership and car ownership.

5 The shift away from Labour resulted from demographic change within the borough. Under the influence of Docklands residential development, the Thameside wards filled with newcomers working as professionals, managers, or white-collar support personnel in the City. At the same time the children of the old working class increasingly moved out to more suburban locales. The council had been dominated by a traditional, male, blue-collar Labour leadership that had been unresponsive to community input both from leftists among the incoming professionals and from the immigrant community: "By the mid-1970s a group largely made up of elderly white men, with a record in organized labour, was representing a borough where one person in four was from an ethnic minority, one in five was unemployed and most of the industry had gone elsewhere or closed down" (Forman, 1989, p. 39). The Labour councillors had shown less concern over the housing problems of the Bengalis than the GLC when it was controlled by the Conservatives. Until the Liberal-Democrat takeover there had been decreasing interest in council politics, and very low voter turnout had made the task of those seeking to transform the council relatively easy.

6 Similar to the New York City Partnership, Business in the Community consists of managing directors and chief executive officers of large firms. The Prince of Wales is its president.

7 Its primary effort was to press for the routing of the Channel Tunnel train-line to Stratford in the east.

8 The SDG consisted of (1) Balfour Beatty Limited, a construction and development firm that was a wholly owned subsidiary of BICC PLC, a large holding company; (2) County and District Properties Limited, a wholly owned subsidiary of Costain Group, an international natural resources, construction, and property development company; and (3) London and Edinburgh Trust PLC, one of the UK's largest property developers, which subsequent to the original bid was taken over by a Swedish insurance company. Until the 1980s Swedish firms could not invest in property outside their country. Once able to do so, they sought control of already established firms with knowledge of local conditions.

9   The rendering of the Foster tower shows a building wholly out of character with the market and also in sharp contrast to Broadgate's more traditional masonry façade.

10 Michael Heseltine was Margaret Thatcher's original Secretary for the Environment. He returned to the position after Thatcher was deposed. His second tenure, however, proved very brief as he assumed the portfolio of the ministry of trade after John Major's victory in 1992.

11 Parliamentary legislation was required to establish this form of community corporation.

12 BAM, as this venerable institution was familiarly known, houses a major opera house and two theaters. It specializes in avant-garde works and has a devoted following. Despite some exceptional successes, however, it typically has difficulty in attracting audiences from Manhattan, who tend to regard Brooklyn as the end of the earth.

13 All the subway lines passing through Brooklyn and the Long Island Railroad have stops here.

14 The joint venture had just constructed the first high-rise office building to go up in Brooklyn in nearly 40 years, a purpose-built structure for the investment firm of Morgan Stanley, outside downtown on the edge of Brooklyn Heights. Brooklyn Heights inhabitants had vehemently opposed the building, which required a zoning change, contending that it intruded undesirable commercial uses into their quiet residential neighborhood. The city had endowed the structure with a generous package of subsidies.

15 An indicator of Forest City's unusual niche is that it was the largest single recipient of federal Urban Development Action Grants (UDAGs) within the United States.

16 One of Sid's owners, however, was not entirely happy with the move. "I had two buildings before, with 60,000 square feet. . . . Now I have about 25,000 square feet and very limited storage space" (Vizard, 1992).

17 This long-stalled project, called Renaissance Plaza, was rescued by the Dinkins administration when it signed a 20-year lease to move the Brooklyn district attorney's office out of six locations into its untenanted office tower (Mitchell, 1992). The complex would include a Hilton hotel, the first hotel to be built in Brooklyn in 50 years. The city committed itself to 360,000 square feet at a rent of $19 a square foot. The rent level was typical for class A office space in peripheral areas, but the city did not receive the rent bonuses and free fixturing that have characterized virtually all private-sector rental deals in the early nineties. The complex would also benefit from ICIP tax incentives and, of course, the public-sector occupants would be permanently exempt from sales and commercial occupancy taxes. The city's commitment put the developer, Muss Development Company, a Queens-based firm, into a better position to get financing; as of mid-1993, however, the project was not yet fully financed.

18 Two plans had preceded this one. In 1969 Mayor John Lindsay had presented a $500 million plan to build office buildings, department stores, and apartment houses there. Then in 1975 a large portion of the site had been

designated as a new campus for Baruch College, a unit of the City University. Both plans, however, were abandoned.

19 Initially the developers had proposed a publicly funded sports arena. Impassioned community opposition, as well as doubts about utilization, caused this enterprise to join the list of abandoned proposals for the spot.

20 The houses would each have rental units attached, thereby assisting the owner in covering his or her carrying costs. The rental suites would be at market rates.

8

Creating a New Address I: Battery Park City

In the spring of 1992 observers of the real-estate market were beginning to detect signs that the slump had bottomed out. Then a new tremor shook the market as the vast empire of Olympia & York (O & Y) began to founder. O & Y owned more New York commercial property than any other landlord; its Canary Wharf project was the largest development in Europe; it possessed substantial interests in other property firms; and a number of major banks held big stakes in its debt. Its inability to refinance its short-term notes and meet its interest obligations threatened the stability of the entire property market. Moreover, O & Y was not just a huge developer; it also represented the cream of the industry. Its previous enormous profitability, the scope of its projects, its responsiveness in working with government, its innovative building techniques, and the commitment of its owners, the Reichmann family, to high-quality construction and public amenities supposedly demonstrated the synergistic potential of public-private partnerships to rebuild cities.

O & Y had transformed a landfill next to New York's financial center into the most prestigious corporate address in Manhattan. Although retrospectively the World Financial Center in Battery Park City appeared to have numerous competitive advantages, the project had been on the brink of failure before the Reichmanns made their investment. Their achievement in New York made them seem invincible. When they stepped in to create an even more mammoth complex on London's Isle of Dogs, the British government, which had seen an earlier investor group withdraw, thought it had found salvation. But whereas the World Financial Center had hit the crest of the property wave, Canary Wharf was destined to plumb the trough. The overall state of the market conjoined with specific attributes of the Docklands situation to produce a failure with all the inevitability of Greek tragedy. The very qualities of the Reichmann family that had produced their previous triumphs seemed inexorably to beget their devastation.

This chapter tells the story of the rise of Olympia & York and examines the broader development scheme of Battery Park City in New York, of which O & Y's project formed the most important part. The following chapter recounts the history of development in London's Docklands, the role played there by Olympia & York, and the reasons why its Canary Wharf project on the Isle of Dogs proved a financial disaster. As in earlier chapters, my aim is to capture the dynamics of the development process, including the interplay between individual personality, economic opportunity, and governmental intervention. In the instance of the Reichmanns' developments, personality played an especially significant role. The impact of O & Y in New York and London was, for a while, so immense that it shaped general expectations concerning the future and character of the property market. Its daring and triumph in "creating a new address," as Paul Reichmann termed its achievement, made the strategy of property-led regeneration appear brilliant for a short period. Its demise raises important questions concerning governmental policies for fostering development.

THE RISE OF OLYMPIA & YORK

Paul, Albert, and Ralph Reichmann, the heads of O & Y, were among the six children of Samuel and Renée Reichmann.[1] The parents spent their youth in Hungary; they then settled in Vienna, where Samuel Reichmann established a highly successful egg-wholesaling business. As the Nazis moved into Austria, they fled with their young children first to Paris, then Madrid, and finally to Tangier. Samuel Reichmann managed to escape with some capital, and in Tangier he set up a small banking operation, specializing in currency exchange. The Reichmanns, and Renée in particular, devoted themselves to assisting Jews to escape from occupied Europe. Renée Reichmann was personally responsible for saving hundreds, perhaps thousands, of lives; she even made an extraordinarily daring rescue mission to Hungary in 1942.[2] She established relations with the major relief organizations and devised an elaborate system for sending food and clothing to concentration camp inmates; ingeniously she worked at getting them large quantities of chocolate, apparently so that they could use the candy as currency.

After the war the Reichmanns remained in Tangier, where Samuel Reichmann's business prospered. Their home was a center for displaced persons, and their reputation for piety and charity grew as they assisted camp survivors in starting new lives. Eventually the family decided to leave Tangier, and the sons, now grown, searched for an appropriate new location. As extremely orthodox Jews, the Reichmanns could reside only in a community that would support their way of life. Ultimately they picked Canada, reportedly rejecting the United States because they were repelled by McCarthyism. They moved there in 1955, with some family members living in Montreal and others in Toronto.

The brothers, whose education was within yeshivas and who were constrained by their Orthodox Judaism from pursuing a professional or technical education, started a building supply company, Olympia Tile and Wall, in the late 1950s. The company benefited from a rapidly increasing demand for lavish bathrooms. It entered the development business when it acted as its own general contractor to build a new warehouse.

The shift to property development began in earnest in 1965, when Albert and Paul Reichmann, who had formed a firm called York Developments, purchased land next to Toronto's Don Valley Parkway for $25 million from a failing New York developer, William Zeckendorf. They subdivided it and paid for the entire parcel by selling off the lots that they did not develop. In 1969 the family incorporated as Olympia & York Developments Ltd., and, while continuing to operate the tile company, proceeded rapidly to expand their development enterprises within this privately held company.

Paul Reichmann, who was the chief real-estate strategist for the family concern, foresaw the potential profits in government-sponsored central-city redevelopment. He became involved in the planning process for downtown Toronto's enormous retail and office complexes, and O & Y began work on the mammoth First Canadian Place in 1974. At the time it was built, the 3.5 million square foot size of the development was unprecedented in Canada, and skeptics doubted that it could ever be filled. The project proved immensely profitable, however, and it acted as the basis for financing later ventures. In fact, in 1988 O & Y managed to sell $400 million in bonds secured by the leases on the building without even pledging any part of the complex as collateral.

In building First Canadian Place, the brothers experimented successfully with financing and construction techniques that they later used in their other projects. Thus, they assumed the risk of borrowing short-term at variable rates, enabling them to take advantage of falling long-term rates when they became available. They also pioneered the use of new construction methods and office design. Among their innovations was a computerized system of winches, turntables, and elevators, including one that could accommodate loaded trucks, to carry materials to pre-assigned floors and thus reduce construction time. They increased their market appeal by building structures with jagged corners that allowed them to double the number of corner offices and thereby command higher rents (Lichfield, 1992).

In 1990, before the rapid devaluation of its assets that ensued shortly thereafter, the estimated value of O & Y's real estate holdings was $24 billion (Hylton, 1990b).[3] The meteoric rise in the Reichmann family's fortunes resulted from strategic low-priced acquisitions and ingenious use of financial instruments. At the depth of the New York City fiscal crisis and economic recession in 1977, it had entered the New York market, buying the properties of the Uris Brothers, another bankrupt New York firm; it paid $50 million in cash and took over mortgages worth $288 million on the eight buildings (Shachtman, 1991, p. 290).[4] A decade after their purchase, the buildings were valued at ten times the original price, and the Reichmanns had become billionaires.

The astute use of new financial instruments was another source of the family's increase in wealth. O & Y was the first to use commercial paper within the real-estate industry by issuing its own short-term notes; its reputation for success made it one of the few development firms able to raise financing on this basis. The firm also increased its operating capital through employing elaborate currency hedges and debt swaps, a practice which considerably increased its flexibility but also made its financial situation extraordinarily complex.

O & Y functioned with a lean organization and was staffed by officers widely known for their breadth and capability. A number of its high-ranking employees came out of public-sector jobs, where they had gained extensive experience in negotiating agreements with developers, learning in the process what kinds of deals could be had from government. Michael Dennis, Toronto's former housing commissioner, led the Canary Wharf enterprise from the position of executive vice-president of the firm. In 1990 the family hired John Zuccotti, formerly chair of the New York City Planning Commission and later deputy mayor, as president of its US subsidiary. An extremely well connected "fixer" within New York's governmental system, he was the first outsider to act as chief executive of one of the family's wholly owned companies. Meyer Frucher, previously the president of the Battery Park City Authority, took on the job of executive vice-president of the US company.

The Reichmann brothers represented an unusual combination of conservatism and recklessness. Despite their great wealth, they continued to live modestly in the upper-middle-class Toronto suburb of North York, within walking distance of their synagogue. Although famous for their philanthropic spending, especially but not exclusively on Jewish charities, their personal consumption habits were abstemious. They strictly observed *kashruth*, following the detailed set of rules governing Orthodox Jewish life, and totally closed down all business within the firm on Jewish holidays and the sabbath. Unlike many of the flamboyant developer heroes of the 1980s, they were extremely secretive, refusing to grant interviews or expose their family lives to public view. One journalist described them as "so colorless that they are colorful" (*Maclean's*, June 27, 1988, p. 48). Their reputation for trustworthiness in a business not known for its ethics allowed them to consummate deals with a handshake and to obtain non-collateralized loans from usually wary bankers.

At the same time they were avid speculators. Paul Reichmann's credo was that "the right time to go into any field is when the market's perception is that the time is wrong" (*US News and World Report*, March 14, 1988, p. 38). For more than two decades his contrarian tactics worked and gave O & Y the assets, the self-confidence, and the reputation to embark on ever greater gambles. The firm's mettle was shown in its willingness to risk its own funds on its ventures and in its *modus operandi* of buying out the unexpired leases of prestigious tenants to entice them to move into its properties.

The riskiest gambit of all, however, was taking on projects of prodigious size in places off the beaten track. In the words of an admiring *Business Week* (January 29, 1990, p. 33) article:

> Perhaps the most distinctive Reichmann trademark is the brothers' willingness to take huge gambles that only pay off way down the line. That's what endears them to governments. In massive public-private partnerships like the World Financial Center, they put up the financing, the government provides cheap land, and together they create whole new urban centers.

O & Y's greatest triumph, the World Financial Center in New York's Battery Park City, and its fatal failure, Canary Wharf in London's Docklands, embody the methods that brought the family first to its heights and then to its present impasse. We turn now to the story of the World Financial Center. This project seemed to demonstrate the firm's capacity to hedge its bets through using its enormous resources to assure the tenantry of its buildings. It did so by constructing a project large and luxurious enough to constitute a whole new business center and by offering sufficient incentives to attract tenants with time remaining on their existing leases.

BATTERY PARK CITY

At the southern tip of Manhattan lies a small green space now called Battery Park, created on landfill in the early nineteenth century.[5] It gained its name from a gun emplacement, the West Battery, which was situated here, overlooking New York harbor, to guard the city against naval attack. Once its military function ended, the fortification served as an entertainment arena named Castle Clinton. It next became a reception center for immigrants, later the location of the municipal aquarium, and finally a picturesque ruin. At mid-century Robert Moses, New York's highway construction czar, sought to run a ramp to his proposed Brooklyn-Battery Bridge through the park; after his plans were defeated, he still tried to destroy the historic structure. Blocked by conservationists from completely demolishing it, he left only its wall. In the postwar years Battery Park and its surroundings provided the only public waterfront access in downtown Manhattan. Directly to the north lay the towers of the downtown financial center, while to the northwest, rotting piers and unused marine facilities lined the adjacent waterfront.

During the 1960s David Rockefeller, head of the Chase Manhattan Bank, led a drive by the Downtown Lower Manhattan Association (DLMA) to retain the Wall Street area as a financial center in a period when business was increasingly moving to midtown. Part of the DLMA's strategy was to have the Port Authority construct a world trade center on a site facing the Hudson River, a few blocks north of Battery Park. Rockefeller's ambitions for the area were supported by his brother Nelson, the governor of New York State, who shepherded a bill through the state legislature allowing the Port Authority of New York and New Jersey to embark on this venture.[6] Excavation for the giant complex, harbinger of later megadevelopments, produced a great amount of debris, which could be cheaply removed if dumped in the Hudson River directly off-site. The action would create a large stretch of vacant city-owned territory close to one of the world's most densely built areas. The city's Department of Marine and Aviation, which had already proposed filling in the space around its obsolete docking facilities in the vicinity, welcomed the landfill proposal.[7]

The plan

There was considerable debate among officials of the city, the state, the Port Authority, and the DLMA as to what should be built on the new land, with many advocating the use of part of the site for subsidized housing. In

1968 state legislation set up the Battery Park City Authority (BPCA) with responsibility for financing and construction on the 92-acre site. The 1969 joint state-city "master development plan" for the tract envisioned a modernist new town, composed of superblocks constructed on platforms elevating it above its surroundings. A consortium of architects had worked on the plan, but the dominant force was Governor Nelson Rockefeller's favorite firm, Harrison and Abramovitz, progenitors of Lincoln Center for the Performing Arts and the Albany State Mall.[8] The following year the BPCA entered into a master lease with the city, which stipulated a housing mix in which each building would contain an equal number of low-, middle-, and upper-income units. The housing agreement was later discarded. Only one development was ever constructed according to the original physical plan: Gateway Plaza, a 1,712-unit middle-income rental building, was begun in 1980, its ground-breaking delayed for years by problems in obtaining Federal Housing Administration mortgage insurance. Gill (1990, p. 103) characterizes the slab-style, high-rise complex as having "a grim, gray penitentiary look."[9]

In order to finance the demolition of the old piers, complete the landfill, and build infrastructure, the BPCA issued $200 million in "moral obligation" revenue bonds in 1972. Under this now-abandoned form of financing, the state recognized an obligation to back the bonds but was not legally required to do so, thereby exempting them from the normal procedure of voter approval by referendum.[10] The landfill was not completed until 1976, by which time the city was in the throes of fiscal crisis, the office market was glutted with unused space, and federal and state housing-subsidy programs had largely vanished. New Yorkers began to use the vacant tract as an informal recreation area, and it became the location for exhibits of giant environmental sculptures. City officials started to fear the development of a "people's park," where protesters would demand that the landfill be permanently maintained as public open space.

Hugh Carey, who had become governor of New York State in 1975, sought to restart the stalled project. It was not until 1979, however, that he could gain control of its three-member board of directors. In that year the board named Richard Kahan,[11] then the head of the state's Urban Development Corporation (UDC), to the chairmanship of the BPCA. Under a memorandum of understanding with the city, the UDC condemned the site and took possession of it for a dollar. Through this act the BPCA essentially became a subsidiary of the UDC and therefore exempt from the city's planning regulations and public review procedures.[12] In exchange for giving up its ownership rights, New York City was to receive all future profits and tax equivalents.

When Kahan took over, the BPCA needed immediate approval from the state legislature to refinance its bonds, or the project would have gone into semi-permanent suspension. Kahan, who disliked the master plan he had inherited and moreover thought that its all-or-nothing approach to construction inhibited developer interest, commissioned the firm of Alexander Cooper and Stanton Eckstut to design a new plan in time to forestall legislative termination. "According to the [architects'] report, among the internal reasons for the project's failure were the master plan's 'excessively rigid large-scale development format,' which had prevented gradual development of the site; and unduly complicated controls over every detail of the project" (Gill, 1990, p. 102). The commitment to a residential income mix vanished from the prospectus.

The new plan, which provided for staged residential development spreading out from the project's nexus with the World Trade Center, attracted highly favorable comment. It freed designers from the detailed review processes of the earlier scheme, established a street-level grid, and called for architectural styles in harmony with New York's traditional commercial and residential neighborhoods:

> The physical character of the Cooper/Eckstut site plan was as much a rediscovery of New York's history of incremental private development of small land parcels as it was a romantic invocation of its most livable neighborhoods. . . . The reasons for [the] . . . enthusiastic response [to the plan] are not hard to understand. The Cooper/Eckstut plan draws on familiar New York neighborhood images and assembles them in a street and block pattern which extend (as view corridors) the Lower Manhattan streets to the waterfront. (Sclar and Schuman, 1991, p. 17)

What has been built

In July 1980 the BPCA invited development proposals for the commercial area, where financial pressures made rapid construction extremely desirable. It selected O & Y from among eleven serious bidders as the developer of a billion-dollar, 6.3 million square foot group of structures to be called the World Financial Center (WFC). As well as promising to complete the work in five years – much more quickly than any of its competitors offered – the Reichmanns undertook to put up $50 million of Olympia & York's money to guarantee the Battery Park City Authority's bond payments for 25 years (Shachtman, 1991, pp. 317-18).

O & Y held a design competition and chose the firm of Cesar Pelli & Associates, which created a cluster of four 34- to 51-story towers featuring 40,000 square foot floors. The office complex, which opened in 1985 and was completed in 1988, included Merrill Lynch, American Express, Dow Jones, and Oppenheimer & Company as its anchor tenants. In order to

Figure 8.1 The World Financial Center

bring in these prestigious firms and "create an address," O & Y took over a number of their existing tenures, thereby becoming New York City's largest landlord. Much of the space it acquired in this way needed considerable investment if it was to retain first-class office uses.

While the WFC buildings, which flanked a 3.5-acre public waterfront plaza, were in a mainly modernist style, their setbacks and masonry bases evoked Manhattan's classic skyscrapers:

> Pelli devised an artful transition from a heavy masonry base with small windows, through a series of setbacks that became progressively lighter and glassier, culminating in top stories of sheer glass crowned by illuminated spires in geometric shapes. (Ponte, 1982, p. 14).

Everything visible was built to the highest luxury standard, while the office facilities incorporated the latest technological advances.

In the midst of the office buildings, O & Y installed a "Winter Garden," a 120-foot-high vaulted atrium sheltering sixteen tall palm trees and entered by a grand marble staircase from the skyway that connects the complex to the World Trade Center.[13] The Winter Garden forms the

Figure 8.2 The Winter Garden at the World Financial Center

gateway to a shopping mall with expensive stores specializing in leather goods, stylish men's and women's clothing, designer chocolates, art books, and hand-made Italian paper. O & Y was at first reluctant to develop much retail space in the project, feeling that downtown does not draw shoppers. When it finally did agree to do so, it severely restricted the type of establishment that could rent space to only the most luxurious. The firm's first instincts appear to have been correct. Although data are not available on the success of the stores, casual observation of the number of still vacant storefronts and the quietude that lies over the occupied ones indicates that they are not doing well. The restaurants around the Winter Garden and the adjacent indoor courtyard, which operate as open-air cafés on the outdoor plaza in the summer, do however, seem to be flourishing, and the public events produced in the Winter Garden are considerable draws.

A still incomplete waterfront walkway runs along the 1.2-mile edge of Battery Park City. Its mid-section, lined with benches and decorative lampposts, reminds the stroller of the Brooklyn Heights esplanade; the park opening up on its south section, with its wild rushes and tumbling rocks, suggests the eighteenth-century shoreline; and a northern park, designed with input from residents of the new apartments and the adjoining Tribeca neighborhood, yields space for active recreation including a vast, extremely elaborate and imaginative playground. Residents and passers-by can enjoy stunning views of the harbor, Ellis Island, the Statue of Liberty, and the New Jersey shore. Battery Park City has made the waterfront accessible as never before and has given New Yorkers a uniquely spectacular open space.[14]

Figure 8.3 The Esplanade at Battery Park City

The residential section of the project is expected eventually to include up to 14,000 housing units, all at market rate. A main street forms an interior spine for the apartment groupings; service stores line its edges. In 1992 about a third of the projected housing units had been finished; the great majority were luxury condominiums, and the rest were expensive rentals.[15] Commissioned by the multiplicity of developers offered sites, different architects designed the mostly high-rise apartment buildings. In employing a variety of building materials and heights, they followed the Cooper-Eckstut design guidelines, which aimed at reproducing the feel of New York's old residential sections. None of the apartments makes a major architectural statement, but they do produce pleasant neighborhood settings. Unfortunately for the developers, the effort to imitate traditional styles with façades along the street line produced one of the typical drawbacks of standard building design – many units lacked views and consequently were difficult to sell.

Completed in 1992 at a cost of nearly $200 million, a new Stuyvesant High School occupies the north end of the site. One of the city's five competitive-entrance, elite, academic secondary schools, its students battle fiercely to gain admission. Its presence is unlikely to present any of the social problems that often afflict the environs of other New York City educational institutions.

Financial arrangements

The public role in Battery Park City consists of the $200 million landfill investment from the original bond issue; additional infrastructure investment;[16] installations, upkeep and services for the public spaces; provision of the BPCA staff; and a set of tax incentives to the developers. The World Financial Center received 150 percent of the normal tax subsidies granted under the Industrial and Commercial Incentives Program (ICIP) in determining its payment in lieu of taxes (PILOT). The residential portion was given a ten-year tax abatement under the 421a program for everything that was built before 1992, although future residential development was not to receive any abatement.

The BPCA continues to own the land and rents it to the developers on a lease that runs without a purchase option until the year 2069. It receives ground lease payments, the PILOT, and a civic facilities payment to cover upkeep expenditures on the common spaces. These revenues are aggregated ʳ⁻⁻⁻⁻⁻⁻ he debt on the various bond issues, maintenance of ⁻⁻⁻⁻⁻⁻⁻⁻⁻ BPCA's rent for its headquarters within the World ⁻⁻⁻⁻⁻⁻ staff salaries. In 1991 the authority had 62 people on ⁻⁻⁻⁻⁻ 5 during the peak building period of the mid-1980s;

according to the *New York Observer* (Golway, 1991), a number of these new hires were "well-connected political operatives." After its expenditures are netted out, the authority passes along the remainder to the city. By 1991 the BPCA had contributed close to $90 million to the general fund; in that year, however, payments dropped to roughly $18 million from about $28 million in the preceding two years. In addition, its projected revenues have supported the issuance of $400 million in bonds to pay for affordable housing elsewhere in the city (see below). Once the debt on the project is retired, all profits will go to New York City. Most of the projected $10 billion in income from the development will be generated in the twenty-first century; while the bulk of it was designated for the payment to the city, expenses, and debt service, there was still a prediction of substantial uncommitted revenues (I. Peterson, 1988).

Assessment

The physical aspects of Battery Park City have mostly won rave reviews from professional critics and the public. The *Times* architectural critic termed it "close to a miracle" when the first buildings opened (Goldberger, 1986). Later he commented: "There has been nothing like Battery Park City in New York or anywhere else in our time – a 92-acre complex of housing and office buildings in which parks, waterfront promenades, streets and public art rank as important as the buildings themselves. . . . The result is a place, not a project" (Goldberger, 1988).

Dissenters, however, dispute the mainstream consensus on the total aesthetic and social success of Battery Park City. Detractors of its physical manifestation cite its Disneyesque quality. It is too flawless, too luxurious, too unreal. Its very splendor makes it vulnerable to Michael Sorkin's (1992, pp. xii-xiii) general attack on recent planned urban developments:

> This new realm is a city of simulations, television city, the city as theme park. This is nowhere more visible than in its architecture, in buildings that rely for their authority on images drawn from history, from a spuriously appropriated past that substitutes for a more exigent and examined present. . . . Today, the profession of urban design is almost wholly preoccupied with reproduction, with the creation of urbane disguises. . . . [T]his elaborate apparatus is at pains to assert its ties to the kind of city life it is in the process of obliterating.
>
> Here is urban renewal with a sinister twist, an architecture of deception which, in its happy-face familiarity, constantly distances itself from the most fundamental realities. The architecture of this city is almost purely semiotic, playing the game of grafted signification, theme-park building. Whether it represents generic historicity or generic modernity, such design is based in

the same calculus as advertising, the idea of pure imageability, oblivious to the real needs and traditions of those who inhabit it.

Battery Park City is the antithesis of the naturally developing, heterogeneous urban district prescribed by Jane Jacobs (1961), but it incorporates many of her lessons nevertheless. It is dense, has multiple uses, short streets, buildings along the street line, and small accessible parks. Its single management permits the creation of an artificial diversity, with carefully selected tenants and idealized versions of the city of memory (see Boyer, 1983). It lacks the spontaneous contrasts of the real early twentieth-century metropolis, and social commentators fault its exclusionism, contending that even its gorgeous open spaces inhibit public access:

> How public *is* public space, when it has been embedded in a context that raises such formidable social barriers that the masses of ordinary working people (not to mention those out of work) would feel uncomfortable entering it? How many poor families may be expected to cross the raised bridge into that citadel of wealth, the World Financial Center, and wander through the privileged enclaves of South End Avenue and Rector Place before reaching their permitted perch along the waterfront? (Lopate, 1989, p. 24; italics in original)

Although Wall Street's white-collar proletariat uses the parks during weekdays, Battery Park City otherwise remains mainly a recreation zone for the relatively well-to-do.[17] The interiors of the World Financial Center are in the standard style of corporate opulence, and entry to the upper floors is totally restricted to those with reasons to be there. Despite the vaunted efforts of the planners to attach the site to the city's street grid, the bulky structures of the World Trade Center and an eight-lane highway separate Battery Park City from the rest of the financial district. Employees can easily enter their workplace from PATH train, subway, or parking garage without ever setting foot on the ground, although the attractiveness of the outdoor area may tempt them out.

Yet the ambition of the Battery Park City planners to make it part of New York does not wholly fall short. Brendan Gill[18] (1990, p. 105) did not speak only for himself when he expressed "a tentative, infinitesimal tremor of hope . . . [that] Battery Park City might have succeeded in weaving itself into the fabric of the city . . . [as] a symbol of the enduring vitality of the city." Large numbers of people do visit the area, and it is an oversimplification to dismiss the enjoyment it affords them as a sham or to decide that they are only the undeserving privileged classes.[19] The luxuriousness of Battery Park City's edifices symbolizes the reality that it shelters – the World Financial Center *is* the capital of capital, not a mere simulacrum. The parks and promenades do have genuine roots in New York's natural environment, and they are hospitable to a variety of uses and users once the psychological barrier to entering them is crossed. Leftist urban critics like to put down sanitized environments, but gritty is not necessarily preferable to pretty. There are few New Yorkers of any social stratum who do not welcome the occasional opportunity to visit a park open to the sea and unsullied by detritus; Battery Park City satisfies a genuine human need. It hints at being a cliché, at evidencing a sameness with other large developments even as it seeks distinction. Simultaneously, however, its unique natural setting and the genuine creativity of its design team cause it to rise above easy criticisms of its genesis and function. As a physical space it has power and gives pleasure.

Sponsors justify the exclusion of low-income people from the project's residences and the granting of large subsidies for luxury apartments and opulent office towers by its support of affordable housing elsewhere in the city.[20] Under 1986 state legislation, the BPCA issued $400 million of revenue bonds for low-income housing. In addition, the authority committed itself in an agreement with the city to contribute another $600 million toward the city's housing program by the year 2000 (Schmalz, 1987), but by 1992 it had placed further bond issues on hold.[21] According to a BPCA official, the postponement was a response to the turbulent state of the real-estate market and the fear that O & Y's difficulties would deter investors from buying the bonds. He indicated that the halt was only temporary. The future commitment, however, was premised on the expectation of additional office construction. Since the building of a fifth office tower is currently in abeyance, the prospects for the $600 million ever materializing are therefore questionable.

Essentially the authority acts as a device whereby the city does off-budget borrowing for housing construction. The effect would be the same if the city rather than the BPCA issued the housing bonds and the BPCA, which accordingly would not have to meet debt service on those bonds, turned over the resulting augmented revenues as part of its payment to the city. Borrowing through the authority, however, shrinks the apparent size of the city's budget, ensures that the funds are allocated to housing, isolates the revenue stream that supports it, and provides a more advantageous interest rate than the city would get using general obligation bonds.

Battery Park City then is a carefully coordinated total environment, with substantial financial benefits disseminated to the general population. Its principal private developer went beyond meeting its contractual obligations and provided the public with significant amenities. The authority has also used its funds to make the city more appealing. Nevertheless, except in some of its park planning, it has involved no public participation whatsoever. Its commercial and residential structures are reserved for the wealthiest corporations and families in the United States, although any well-behaved individual can use its public facilities on a daily basis.

In terms of the indicators of private-sector funds leveraged and jobs kept in the city, Battery Park City was an economic success. The question is always raised whether the funds and jobs would have been there regardless; given the centrifugal forces that constantly operate on New York, the answer is probably no. Moreover, thanks to its location on landfill next to the financial district, it did not displace anyone either economically or spatially. The city did receive something meaningful in exchange for its largesse. If the project is to be faulted, it must be on the grounds of opportunity costs. The public sector could hypothetically have borrowed the funds it put into capital expenditures for Battery Park City for some other, more socially beneficial purpose. The taxes forgone might have been directed toward another, more productive endeavor that would have produced more jobs for the neediest and less spatial segregation. Within the constraints of New York's political and economic situation, however, it is hard to imagine an alternative strategy for the site that would have resulted in a more desirable outcome or that, in the absence of any development there, commensurate resources would have been mobilized for a more socially beneficial cause.

NOTES

1 The history of the Reichmann family presented here is drawn from *US News & World Report* (March 14, 1988, p. 37–9); *Maclean's* (June 27 and October 24, 1988, pp. 46–7, 41–50); Lever (1988a, 1988b); *Business Week* (January 29, 1990); Hylton (1990a); and a long article by Elaine Dewar (1987) in *Toronto Life* magazine. The latter essay chronicled the family's flight from Austria to Tangier to escape the Nazis and the subsequent building of their fortune. While it specifically recounted only positive – in fact, sometimes heroic – deeds by the parents, it nevertheless nastily implied, without any supporting evidence, that still unrevealed secrets sullied the family's extraordinary reputation for probity. Thus, *inter alia*, the following comments and questions, which were never substantiated with actually damning facts, were presented:

The accepted story hardly mentioned just what it was they did in Tangier. (p. 65)
Why didn't the Reichmanns just move to New York? Was there something in their background . . . that prevented them from getting papers to enter the United States? (p. 65)
Could Renee Reichmann have been desperately sending packages and visas all over Europe while her husband and his friends helped to fuel the German war machine? Impossible. (p. 110)

Obviously, he [Samuel Reichmann] was a very clever operator, one who didn't mind
walking right on the line between legality and illegality to make a profit. (p. 166)
Had the Reichmanns done all this [worked through relief organizations to rescue
European Jews] to get rich? (p. 174)

The Reichmanns brought a libel suit against the author, the magazine, and
the *Globe and Mail*, Toronto's leading newspaper, which had published an
editorial against the suit. The article's factual narrative appears generally
correct; it was its innuendos that made it potentially libelous. Ultimately the
case was settled out of court, when the family agreed to accept a contribution
to charity and an apology by the author.

2 Dewar (1987, p. 132) quotes an interview she conducted with Edward
   Reichmann, one of the brothers: "Late in 1941 and in 1942 there were all
   kinds of rumors from Europe about a crackdown in Czechoslovakia and the
   situation of Jews there. . . .By then the war was in full swing. Mother decided
   to travel to Hungary. . . . She went to France, Italy, then Yugoslavia and into
   Hungary. Neither my father nor her friends could dissuade her. From
   Tangier, it was not clear that she could help in Europe. But it turned out she
   saved thousands. . . . She had a letter saying that she was a representative of
   the Spanish Red Cross."

3 In 1992 the company's North American property portfolio consisted of almost
   40 million square feet of mainly office space: 54 percent in New York City, 17
   percent in Toronto, 10 percent in Calgary, 5 percent in Ottawa, and the
   balance scattered among smaller cities (Hylton, 1992e).

4 When O & Y purchased the buildings, they were in the possession of National
   Kinney, a former parking-lot corporation that the late Stephen Ross renamed
   Warner Communications and used as his base ultimately to gain control of
   Time Warner Communications, one of the largest corporate buyouts in
   history. At the time the Reichmanns bought them, the properties were losing
   money. Among them was 55 Water Street, the world's largest commercial
   office building. During the mid-eighties this building became a very stylish
   address for some of New York's most active investment-banking firms,
   including Lehman Brothers, Bear Stearns, and L.F. Rothschild. In 1986 the
   building had a 99 percent occupancy rate and O & Y raised a $548 million
   Eurobond loan on it (Dizard, 1992).

5 Principal sources for the discussion of Battery Park City are Ponte (1982);
   Lopate (1989); Gill (1990); Sclar and Schuman (1991); Battery Park City
   Authority (1992); and interviews with officials of the Battery Park City
   Authority.

6 The State of New Jersey, whose agreement also had to be obtained for the
   Port Authority to proceed with the project, acceded to this investment in
   exchange for the Port Authority's assumption of the Hudson and Manhattan
   tubes, a bankrupt rail system connecting New Jersey with Manhattan.

7 The city owned all the land under water between the riverbank and the pier
   heads.

8 Harrison and Abramovitz specialized in high modernism with an overlay of
   glitz. Their post-Corbusian large structures, isolated from each other on

superblocks, embodied the style that was a particular butt of Jane Jacobs's criticism of urban renewal programs. She characterized these programs as producing:

> Luxury housing projects that mitigate their inanity, or try to, with a vapid vulgarity. Cultural centers that are unable to support a good bookstore. Civic centers that are avoided by everyone but bums, who have fewer choices of loitering place than others. . . . Promenades that go from no place to nowhere and have no promenaders. . . . This is not the rebuilding of cities. This is the sacking of cities. (*Jacobs, 1961, p. 4*)

9 The developer was the Lefrak Organization and the architect was Harrison and Abramovitz.

10 Moral obligation bonds were invented by John Mitchell, when he was a New York bond attorney. He later gained notoriety as Richard Nixon's Attorney General during the Watergate scandal.

11 Richard Kahan's career has been intertwined with most of the major public-private partnerships in New York City, on both sides of the public-private divide. Just out of Columbia Law School, he joined the UDC staff and then served as vice-president of the Lefrak Organization, one of the nation's largest development firms. Afterwards he returned to UDC, and while still in his early thirties served simultaneously as president of the UDC, the BPCA, and the Convention Center Development Corporation, which was then constructing the Javits Center. Upon leaving his public-sector posts, he joined another large development firm, Tishman Speyer, as a partner. Most recently he, along with sociologist Richard Sennett, became head of the Urban Assembly, a group aimed at improving third-world cities. He is also serving as director of Riverside South, the consortium of community groups working with Donald Trump on a plan for his West Side Yards.

In Wayne Barrett's highly critical biography of Donald Trump, he castigates Kahan for the role he played as an intermediary in Trump's remaking of the old Commodore Hotel into the Grand Hyatt. In his epilogue, however, Barrett (1992, pp. 472–3) comments: "I also have some regrets about another character in this drama who comes off badly in the text, Richard Kahan, the UDC president who helped facilitate the Hyatt deal so long ago. I have found Kahan in the years since to be a straightforward and decent man, who has made many contributions to the city. But, unfortunately, this view of him cannot alter the events of the late seventies."

12 The Battery Park City Authority, the 42nd Street Redevelopment Corporation, and the Convention Center Development Corporation all were UDC subsidiaries, partaking in the UDC's special powers.

13 While the plaza and the Winter Garden were both open to the public, they were built and held by O & Y.

14 The 1979 master plan allocated 30 percent of the land to public open space, not including streets.

15 In 1986 apartments generally sold for $350 a square foot or rented for $25 a square foot a year (*New York Times*, March 23, 1986). After the real-estate

slump, prices fell, and developers had difficulty in disposing of new units. Two builders auctioned off units in 1991, averaging $267 per square foot. Most of the original apartments were studios or one-bedrooms; later buildings contained more family-sized units.

16 By and large the authority has received nothing but praise for the lavishness of its investments in public art and landscape architecture. Recently, however, David Emil, who succeeded Meyer Frucher as president of the authority, has been criticized for ordering design changes in the third footbridge connecting Battery Park City to the rest of Manhattan. This bridge, which is attached to Stuyvesant High School, was originally to have cost $4 million. The redesigned structure will cost twice as much. In defending his decision, Emil remarked: "This will be an enchanting, beautiful bridge. . . . Bridges have inherent in them a sort of magical imagery, and for whatever reasons the bridges to the south don't capture that. This bridge will" (Golway, 1991).

17 The absence of the homeless, who inhabit Battery Park and the nearby Staten Island Ferry Terminal in large and visible numbers, from Battery Park City raises questions of how genuinely open to the public it is. BPCA officials, however, claim that the outdoor spaces are not treated differently from the rest of New York. While there is a small unarmed security patrol in addition to normal New York City Police Department coverage, it does not devote itself to keeping out unwanted sojourners. And in my own frequent visits to the site, while I have rarely seen anyone who looked particularly disreputable, neither have I seen anyone harassed. The opinion of those I have interviewed on the subject is that physical and psychological barriers keep out such people.

18 Brendan Gill was the *New Yorker* magazine's architectural critic and has been chairman of both the Landmarks Conservancy and the Municipal Art Society, civic groups concerned with protecting and improving New York's architectural heritage.

19 I know of no survey of users of Battery Park City's public areas. Casual observation reveals them as predominately white middle-class but, depending on the time of day and week, with a considerable admixture of working-class people of varying ethnicity. On summer weekends, the strollers and café patrons are New Yorkers who pursue the sun in a city park rather than retiring to their homes "in the country."

20 Gill (1990, p. 103) quotes Meyer Frucher, Richard Kahan's successor as president of the BPCA: "When Governor Cuomo asked me to become president of the Battery Park City Authority he said to me, 'Give it a soul. Without a soul the beauty will be superficial.' This was a difficult challenge, but one that I think we have met in essentially two ways: through the Housing New York Program and by making Battery Park City a destination for all New Yorkers."

21 From the initial issue, $150 million supported construction of 1,850 substantially rehabilitated apartments in Harlem and the South Bronx, to be provided to a mix of families, with the homeless constituting 30 percent, low-income 45 percent, and moderate income 25 percent (Oser, 1987).

9

Creating a New Address II: Docklands

After its great success in developing the World Financial Center (WFC) in New York, Olympia & York (O & Y) enjoyed a reputation as the world's largest and best-managed property development firm. Its owners, the Reichmann brothers, had become immensely wealthy and had begun to extend their economic power far beyond their base in property. While still in the process of constructing and tenanting the World Financial Center, they started seeking other outlets for their fortune besides high-stakes real-estate activities so as to diversify their holdings. They invested especially heavily in natural-resources firms, reportedly on the expectation that the balance sheets of such enterprises would run counter to the real-estate cycle. Thus, O & Y acquired a controlling interest in Abitibi-Price, a pulp and paper company that was the world's largest producer of newsprint, and purchased substantial holdings in Gulf Canada[1] and GW utilities. The seemingly cautious strategy of diversification, however, was undercut by the specialization in natural resources – another notoriously speculative area – which in the late 1980s proved to move in tandem with the real-estate market. And, although O & Y had previously avoided excessive indebtedness by self-financing much of its real-estate operation, it borrowed heavily for its new acquisitions.

Other investments also proved destabilizing. A takeover bid for the distiller Hiram Walker resulted in a publicly ignominious defeat. A large investment in Robert Campeau's real-estate and retailing company came to naught as well. Campeau, a Canadian entrepreneur specializing in leveraged buyouts, spent exorbitantly on the acquisition of the Allied and

Federated department-store chains in the United States. Only a few years after his lionization as the king of retailing, his entire debt edifice crashed when the revenues from the stores, diminished by weakened consumption after the 1987 stock-market collapse, fell far below the amount necessary to service his huge debt. O & Y initially rushed to his assistance with an emergency $250 million loan, then refused to bail him out further. In 1990 Campeau was forced to seek Chapter 11 bankruptcy protection in the US, devaluing the Reichmanns' equity share. A further effort at hedging likewise produced the opposite result. In order to protect its real-estate projects, O & Y bought substantial interests in competing property-development firms in Canada, the US, and England. The effect of these investments, along with accepting real estate as collateral for the loan granted to Campeau, was to increase the firm's vulnerability to the 1990s downturn in the property market.[2]

The chief cause of the Reichmanns' downfall, however, lay at the core of their principal business in property development. Overconfident from their triumph in creating a prestigious new office center on a Manhattan landfill, they tried to repeat their earlier feat in London's Docklands. In England, however, they had the misfortune to bring their property onto the market when it was plummeting into the bottom of a cycle. Moreover, they had as their partner a government that turned its back on them when they were unable to cover their obligations; a site further from the existing financial center than the one in New York; and a local market of office-users that was less willing to discard its traditional locational preferences. As a consequence, O & Y's endeavor to build an office complex more than twice as big as the WFC at Canary Wharf on the Isle of Dogs brought down its British and Canadian branches and produced, at least for the moment, the world's largest ghost town on the bank of the Thames. To understand how this result came to pass, we begin the story with a history of Docklands development

REDEVELOPMENT STRATEGIES

The name "Docklands" applies to that part of East London which borders the Thames. The East End has always been home to London's poorest inhabitants. Until the 1960s it also offered jobs to its residents – on the docks, in port-related activities, and in manufacturing. For much of this century, however, the area received almost no new private investment; its industrial structure was antiquated; and its resident population was shrinking. Principal industries in the river wards were printing, food and drink processing, engineering, and metals fabrication, mostly operating in relatively small premises. Poor motor-transport connections and obsolete facilities led industries to either move or close up rather than reinvest in the area; the trend was hastened by the closing of the docks between 1967 and 1981.[3]

In the decades following World War II, East London local authorities constructed large social-housing estates, mainly in the inner areas, with the number of units growing from 30,000 to 125,000. This redevelopment, however, did not relieve the physical congestion of those sections that remained populated, nor did it reverse decay where industry and trading activities had once flourished. Instead population became concentrated in bleak, institutional enclaves, while the extensive tracts of abandoned industrial and docking facilities appeared increasingly gloomy and forbidding (Buck et al., 1986, p. 7). Peter Marris (1987, pp. 60–1) has succinctly captured the situation at the beginning of the 1980s:

> From the outset, London's docks had been haphazardly laid out, quickly outdated, and mutually frustrating in their competition. They kept in business partly because the Port of London, however inefficient, was the capital of an empire; but even more because whenever their commercial survival was threatened, they relentlessly drove down the price of labour. The merging of the dock companies into a public authority at the beginning of this century did not fundamentally change this balance of militancy and vulnerability. When the dockers at last gained security after the Second World War, their way of life and the communities they had made, with all their pride of craft, and practical radicalism, grimness and history, were already facing drastic transformation. The old docks, trapped by the congested city which had grown up around them were not adaptable to the intensive mechanization which would keep them profitable.

The Port of London Authority (PLA), which had built a modern container port downriver at Tilbury in the 1960s, was severely criticized by Docklands community leaders and the Greater London Council (GLC) for its failure to maintain the London docks as a going concern. In a 1985 report the GLC contended that the upstream docks in the East End, while unsuitable for long-distance containerized cargo, retained usefulness for intra-European trade (GLC, 1985). Even with investment for that purpose, however, their economic value would have remained limited. The end of London's central role within world trading patterns, combined with technological change, meant that at best their employment potential was very small.

At any rate, the PLA, like the Port Authority of New York and New Jersey, began to see its inner-area facilities as more valuable for real-estate development than transport and began exploiting its property holdings as financial resources to fuel its port modernization enterprises elsewhere. During the early 1970s St Katharine's Dock, a short walk from the Tower

Figure 9.1 St. Katharine's Dock

of London, became the location of a mixed-use project of luxury flats, offices, a hotel, and a marina, indicating the possibilities for adaptive re-use. Although architecturally conventional, the complex afforded attractive views of the water, and the area around the yacht basin allowed office workers and hotel guests to take their leisure in surroundings isolated from, but close to, the bustle of the City. On the south side of the Thames in Southwark, the closing of Hays Wharf and the zoning of the area for office construction generated a rapid rise in property values, reinforcing the cost pressures that were pushing manufacturing firms out of the area (Ambrose and Colenutt, 1975, chapter 4).[4] While the mid-seventies property slump caused a hiatus in the implementation of the plans for the south side, its trajectory from industrial to office use was not reversed. At the same time mechanization and rationalization reduced the maritime labor force from 23,000 in 1969 to only 12,000 four years later and to 7,000 in 1979 (Marris, 1987, p. 61; Brindley et al., 1989, p. 98).[5]

With the closing of the docks, ancillary warehouse and transport facilities, and industrial plants, increasing amounts of land lay unused, leading the Conservative central government to establish a study team during the 1970s to assess the area's development potential. Its presentation of planning alternatives mainly stressed the commercial potential of the riverfront acres, the largest available area of inner-city land in western Europe, and was received with hostility by local community leaders (Church 1988a; Brindley et al., 1989). When a national Labour government gained power in 1974, it threw out the report and set up a strategic-planning authority for the area, the Docklands Joint Committee (DJC). The DJC included representatives from the central government, the GLC, and the local authorities, as well as the Port of London Authority and the trade unions; the associated Docklands Forum solicited citizens' opinions. The DJC produced a comprehensive plan that stressed preservation of manufacturing, council-housing production, and social programs for current residents.

The plan, however, lacked powerful backing, and the difficulty in funding it doomed it to oblivion. The election in 1977 of a Tory GLC that was antagonistic to the East London local authorities had an immediate blocking effect on implementation of the plan. Beyond that, the very large expenditures required to make the Docklands usable, the fiscal weakness of all levels of government, and the unattractiveness to private capital of the DJC plan meant that Docklands regeneration would require a major change of strategy. A substantial regeneration program required either much greater amounts of government investment than could be imagined within the political and economic context of the time or a plan that offered far greater incentives to the private sector.

The London Docklands Development Corporation

After the Conservatives returned to power nationally in 1979, they jettisoned the goals of the DJC plan. In 1981 they established the London

Docklands Development Corporation (LDDC) to promote economic development in the area (see chapter 5).[6] The administrative jurisdiction of the LDDC, which covered 8.5 square miles (5,500 acres), encompassed the riverside portions of three boroughs – Tower Hamlets, Newham, and Southwark[7] – where it became the official planning authority. It worked closely with the London office of the Department of the Environment (DoE) and involved cabinet members in decision-making on its bigger deals. It diverged from its New York counterpart, the Battery Park City Authority, by giving developers much more latitude in project selection and design. Its style was entrepreneurial, and its staff focused on implementation rather than planning (Brindley et al. 1989). As one of its executives declared to me, "There was never any grand master plan. Reg Ward [the first CEO] just wanted to make things happen."

The LDDC's principal aim was to promote growth in Greater London; improvement of the lives of those residing in the riverside localities was at best a subsidiary goal. Its consultation with local authorities was perfunctory, and it established no formal mechanisms for citizen participation. Instead of viewing the territory under its planning control as embedded within the Docklands boroughs, the LDDC pictured the riverbank as a new vibrant core for the whole metropolis. Its ambition was to attract the immense sums of private investment capable of transforming this vision into reality. Since its main asset was land rather than financial capital, it focused on turning over that asset to property developers rather than on an alternative development approach that would target operating firms. In other words, it was capable only of being a land development agency, not a development bank.

The LDDC took possession of all land within its jurisdiction owned by either the boroughs or the GLC; in addition it purchased the Port Authority's holdings within the development area and acquired additional, privately owned parcels through compulsory purchase.[8] It was responsible for preparing the land it owned for development, then disposing of it to a suitable developer. Site preparation was often a costly process, since it involved clearing structures, cleaning up environmental hazards, and filling areas under water. At first, the LDDC barely broke even on its land sales; on the Isle of Dogs its initial offerings sold for about £80,000 per acre. But by 1986 the price had shot up to £250,000 per acre, and some parcels even sold for £3 million per acre at the height of the speculative boom (Buchan, 1990). In 1988 the LDDC was receiving £165 million from central government grant and £63 million from property sales; but by 1991 income from property sales had shrunk to £27 million, while the grant had leaped to £315 million, constituting more than a third of the government's total expenditures on urban development in the country (LDDC, 1991; Fazey, 1991).

The poor transport connections of the area, where formerly workers had walked to their jobs and cargo was waterborne, meant that development for office uses required a massive transportation building program. The LDDC's initial transit investment consisted of the construction of a light railway subject to frequent breakdowns; as a result of efforts to curtail expenses, it opened with a terminus not directly accessible from the main underground system and with quite limited carrying capacity. Rebuilding it to a higher standard cost about £500 million, and, due to the problems of working on an operating system, it proved far more difficult than if the work had been done originally. Even with the improvements, the railway did not have sufficient capacity to meet anticipated demand. Consequently London Transport planned to extend the Jubilee tube line to the east. In addition, both the LDDC and the Department of Transport undertook a group of very expensive road-building projects, while the airport authority opened a facility on an island in the Thames in 1987 and intended to enlarge it. Although the LDDC identified the airport as an important catalyst for development and a generator of jobs, the GLC had opposed it on the grounds that the employment claims would not materialize, that it would contribute to air and noise pollution, and that it would displace jobs from the docks (GLC, 1985). As of 1992, the airport is little used, and the GLC's opposition to the investment appears justified; proponents, however, anticipate much greater activity once new, quieter, short-haul aircraft are introduced.

Residential development

At first, development on LDDC-controlled land advanced from the boundary with the City of London. Much of the new construction was residential. Between 1981 and 1992, over 16,000 housing units were completed within the Docklands development area, of which 78 percent were privately developed for owner occupation at market rates. By 1991 about 24,000 of the development area's 64,600 inhabitants had moved in from outside the East End, mainly into the new structures (LDDC, 1992).[9] Although some of the new units were in rehabilitated warehouses, the great majority occupied newly constructed buildings. Except for the nautical themes of their names, the residential complexes made no architectural reference to the communities which they colonized – nor, for that matter, to central London. Thus, for example, the Brunswick Quay, Surrey Quays, and Blyth's Wharf developments were indistinguishable in appearance from typical suburban blocks of low-rise flats anywhere in the southeast.

The residential strategy meant that ultimately the population would be dominated by newcomers with sharply different values, political

Figure 9.2 New residential development in Docklands

affiliations, and incomes from the original inhabitants (A. Smith, 1989). Nevertheless, the Docklands retained close to 40,000 of its original inhabitants, many displaced from their industrial and port employment, mostly living in over 13,000 council and housing association units (LDDC, 1988a, 1992). As a consequence, even with its infusion of new luxury housing, the area remained economically mixed, with stark juxtapositions of rich and poor (Brownill, 1991).[10]

After the stock market's Black Monday of October 1987, financial industry expansion triggered by the Big Bang reversed itself, and the housing market in Docklands stagnated; by 1989 the entire London private residential sector had collapsed, and a number of developers ran into severe financial trouble. Virtually all plans for additional market-rate construction were shelved the next year; several developments were halted when only partially complete; and the number of new housing units finished fell far below the LDDC's predictions.[11] Moreover, steeply rising interest rates meant that developers had to offer substantial inducements, including mortgage subsidies, in order to attract any buyers. By 1992 residential construction activity in the Docklands was limited to housing-association projects and council estate renovation, and LDDC land sales to for-profit housing developers had ended.

CANARY WHARF

As part of its effort to stimulate private investment, the Conservative government designated 482 acres of the Isle of Dogs as an enterprise zone. Originally a peninsula formed by a curve in the Thames about 2.5 miles east of the City of London, it was cut off from the adjacent land mass by a canal in the nineteenth century. In 1802 it had become the site of the West India Docks. As the docks expanded, a warehouse was built on the land between the canal and the main dock. Called Canary Wharf, it was used to store cargoes of bananas and sugar cane from the West Indies and fruits from the Canary Islands – ultimately it gave its name to the vast twentieth-century complex built on its site. By 1900 it was handling most of London's fruit and vegetable imports from South Africa and New Zealand. As late as the mid-1960s, about 20,000 men still worked at the West India Docks; by 1981, however, they were closed (Fathers, 1992).

The enterprise zone classification freed firms within the zone's boundaries from conforming to most planning regulations and from paying business rates (i.e., property taxes), as well as allowing them to deduct 100 percent of their capital expenditure on industrial and commercial construction from their corporate income taxes (Morley et al., 1989, p. 133). Benefits under the enterprise zone ended in 1992, ten years after its inception, and this deadline put considerable pressure on developers to begin construction before the tax subsidies lapsed.[12] It was estimated that, as a result of low land prices and enterprise zone incentives, net construction costs in the zone would be half as much as in central London, and occupancy costs just 59 percent (Buchan, 1990).

Initially the LDDC expected that relatively small office and industrial firms would take advantage of the enterprise zone benefits. But, as the boom of the eighties heated up, office developers began to bid on space wherever they could find it. In 1985 a consortium headed by an American developer, G. Ware Travelstead of First Boston Real Estate, proposed to build an 8.8 million square foot office development for financial and advanced services firms at Canary Wharf.[13] In return for its commitment to the development and its willingness to underwrite a proportion of the costs of upgrading the Docklands Light Railway, the consortium received a promise from the LDDC that it would continue the Docklands Light Railway westward, connecting it directly with the Bank Underground station. The Travelstead agreement also required the LDDC to provide infrastructure, primarily roads, initially estimated to cost £250 million; the

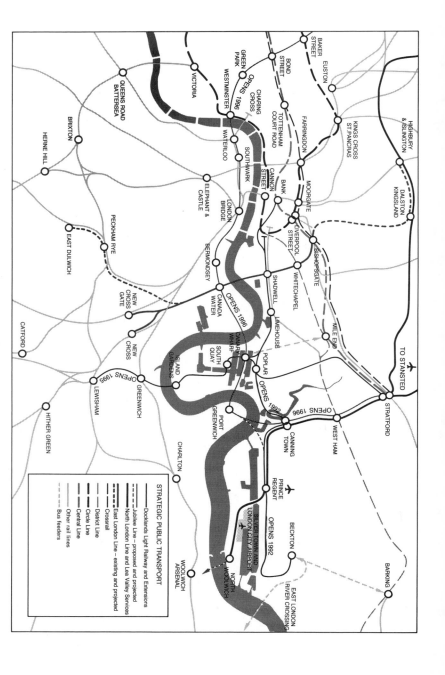

Figure 9.3 Docklands transport

STRATEGIC PUBLIC TRANSPORT

Docklands Light Railway and Extensions

Jubilee Line – proposed and projected

Crossrail

North London Line and Lea Valley Services

East London Line – existing and projected

District Line

Circle Line

Central Line

Other rail lines

Bus feeders

key to the roads plan was the Limehouse Link, which would traverse the Isle of Dogs, making the project area accessible at both its east and west ends. The road required extensive tunneling and the relocation of 558 families (LDDC, 1991, p. 12). The resulting costs made it the most expensive road per mile ever built in the United Kingdom, and eventually the LDDC's road investment vastly exceeded the originally estimated amounts.[14]

In mid-1987 the Travelstead consortium withdrew from the negotiations and, to the great relief of the government, Olympia & York stepped in. It committed itself to develop at least 4.6 million square feet of floor space by 1992, an additional 7 million square feet thereafter, pay £8.2 million for the LDDC land, and contribute £150 million toward the extension and upgrading of the Docklands Light Railway (National Audit Office, 1988, p. 19). In order to entice the Texaco Corporation into the complex, it advanced plans for construction of an additional 925 thousand square foot building, resulting in the production of more than 5 million square feet in 1991–2. Later, in its effort to persuade the government to route the proposed extension of the Jubilee tube line through Canary Wharf and to expedite its authorization, O & Y pledged £400 million to that project. Although the DoE, which participated directly in the negotiations, raised the question of receiving a share in the profits from the development, along the Battery Park City model, "both the Department and the LDDC considered that to do so might jeopardize the whole development" (National Audit Office, 1988, p. 19). As matters later turned out, perseverance could only have produced a pyrrhic victory.

The Docklands Consultative Committee (DCC), consisting of representatives of the affected boroughs, strongly attacked the LDDC for underpricing the land. It asserted that the £400,000 per acre paid by O & Y amounted to between 8 and 13 percent of its market value (DCC, 1988). Given the collapse of prices that occurred thereafter, however, and the twenty-acre size of the parcel O & Y acquired, the deal retrospectively does not seem to have unduly benefited the developer.

Design

Imitating the design precepts that guided Battery Park City, Paul Reichmann called for a plan that would give the illusion of natural growth. A number of architects, including Cesar Pelli, I.M. Pei, and Skidmore, Owings & Merrill, designed individual structures, thereby simulating the diversity of an evolving city. In order to have buildings open directly onto the street, deep excavations were dug to accommodate underground parking garages. As in the WFC, their walls feature setbacks and varieties of facing material. The edifices surrounding Westferry

Figure 9.4 Canary Wharf

Circus, the roundabout terminating the complex at the western end, mime the great squares of central London. Only the central tower, at 48 stories the tallest building in Britain, makes a deliberate break with the rest of London. Canary Wharf also resembles Battery Park City in having much of its land (more than one-third) dedicated to open space, visible fixtures of the highest quality, and buildings equipped with advanced communications technologies.

Community benefits

O & Y committed itself to hire 500 local construction workers as part of its agreement with the LDDC. It also financed the running of a construction training college, established a £2 million trust fund for local schools and colleges (Buchan, 1990),[15] and contributed £70 million to the extension of the Docklands Light Railway. When the riverbus, which offered boat service between the Docklands and Charing Cross Pier in central London, ran into financial difficulty, O & Y took it over and made up the shortfall. As in Battery Park City, the Reichmanns spared no expense in providing a high level of public amenity, manifested here in an elaborate plaza centered on a monumental fountain and full-grown trees imported from Germany.

Inducements

O & Y used a variety of extremely expensive devices to lure companies out of central London. It repeated its New York practice of attracting tenants by buying out their existing leases. Costly as this practice had been in New York, it was even more so in London, where leases are much longer, and rents much higher. In the case of American Express, O & Y agreed to take over the 240,000 square feet rented by its Lehman Brothers subsidiary in Broadgate within the City of London. The rent for the Broadgate space amounted to at least £2 million a year more than the company was to pay for the 330,000 square feet in Canary Wharf, where it was planning to consolidate its operations (Rodgers and Nissé, 1992).[16] To get the *Daily Telegraph*, already located on the Isle of Dogs, to move into Canary Wharf, the Reichmanns purchased the newspaper's South Quay building at £20 million above book value (Buchan, 1990). O & Y also offered fitting-out subsidies aggregating to £200 million and rent concessions rumored to include rent-free periods up to five years (Rodgers and Nissé, 1992; *Economist*, June 22, 1991).[17]

THE DOWNFALL OF OLYMPIA & YORK

The first real evidence that Olympia & York was in difficulty came in September 1990, when the Reichmann family attempted but failed to sell a 20 percent share in its US real-estate portfolio (Hylton, 1990b; 1992b). Although the move marked the first time that the company had sought outside investors in its real-estate portfolio, its officers denied that the offering and a subsequent refinancing of Canary Wharf obligations indicated a liquidity problem. Many observers, however, wondered whether the Reichmanns' assets were sufficient to withstand the real-estate troubles afflicting the urban centers in which the firm operated (Prokesch, 1990). Between 1990 and 1992 the family desperately strove to shore up its empire by investing $500 million of its own money, putting individual assets up for sale in order to achieve liquidity (Hylton, 1992a). It sold some of its non-property holdings at prices well below its original investment, but by 1990 the transatlantic real-estate market was dead, and it could not find purchasers willing to pay an amount exceeding the debt on any piece of property.

Even as oversupply was causing the values of its properties around the world to plummet, O & Y was continuing to invest billions in Canary Wharf, the future of which looked less and less assured. In a 1990 advertisement in the *Sunday Times*, Paul Reichmann had asserted that Canary Wharf represented less of a risk than the World Financial Center, claiming: "Doing one building there would be risky; doing nearly a dozen is not. On a scale of one to 10, if you say the risk with Battery Park was nine, here it would be one" (quoted in Sullivan et al., 1992).

Despite the optimistic predictions and all the various incentives to occupants, 53 percent of the office space nearing completion remained unlet in the summer of 1992.[18] Little of the retail space had been rented either, and without a critical mass of office workers, there was small likelihood that it would be. The *Telegraph* turned out to be the only major British tenant O & Y succeeded in attracting. The other large committed tenants, in addition to American Express and Crédit Suisse– First Boston (CSFB), were all American firms – Morgan Stanley, Bear Stearns, and Texaco.[19] The absence of a prestigious British financial or service firm meant that the Reichmanns had failed in creating an address. One developer quoted in the *Independent* argued that it was O & Y's inability to understand the mystique of the City of London for British companies that was at the root of its miscalculation: "What did Paul Reichmann do wrong? North Americans have no sense of place, or of history. He didn't realise that British people and businesses are tied by invisible threads to places: to the Bank of England or just to a set of streets, some shops, a restaurant" (Buchan, 1990, p. 5). Whether or not it was possible in the British context to overcome the appeal of central London, its failure to do so placed O & Y at a serious disadvantage in its competition with property-owners within the City of London, especially once the office glut there eroded the previous cost differential between the City and the Docklands.

The final months

A concatenation of events began in February 1992 which led irresistibly to the collapse of Olympia & York. The first of these was a downgrading of the company's commercial paper by a Canadian bond-rating service, which estimated that the value of O & Y's listed investments (i.e. investments in publicly held companies) had fallen by over 40 percent, from C$6.6 billion to C$3.9 billion, in the preceding two years (Simon, 1992b). The firm had typically borrowed on notes that matured every thirty to ninety days and would roll them over when they came due. Now it could no longer refinance its short-term debt through selling it directly to investors, nor could it find bankers willing to take up the slack. After the downgrade by the rating agency, the company began buying up about $400 million of its commercial paper itself (Hylton, 1992c).

Its situation worsened further on March 12 when Morgan Stanley won a $240 million judgment enforcing O & Y's pledge to buy its Canary Wharf building upon completion.[20] On March 22 O & Y admitted that it was sustaining a "liquidity crisis" and called a meeting of its creditors to restructure about $12 billion of its debt. Two days later Thomas S. Johnson, former president of the Manufacturers Hanover Bank of New York, was named president of O & Y, replacing Paul Reichmann. The next week the firm failed to make the first installment on its £400 million contribution toward the Jubilee Line extension.[21]

At an April 13 meeting O & Y publicly revealed its financial situation for the first time. Thomas Johnson did not appear at the meeting and, in fact, never assumed his announced position in the firm.[22] He was reportedly dissatisfied with his own financial package and with the Reichmanns' refusal to be wholly forthcoming concerning the firm's balance sheet (Farnsworth, 1992). His replacement was Gerald Greenwald. Greenwald and Robert S. Miller, who joined him in heading the O & Y negotiating team, had led Chrysler's financial rescue operation when that company was on the brink of extinction (Parker-Jervis, 1992). They asked lenders for $180 million to continue work on Canary Wharf and $84 million for the firm's Canadian operations. Three weeks later lenders were requested to forgo payments on most of O & Y's $12 billion real-estate debt for five years in exchange for a 20 percent, non-voting equity stake in the holding company and 30 percent in Canary Wharf.

In the following months O & Y missed a series of bond and mortgage payments on instruments secured by a tower in the WFC, the Aetna Center in Toronto, and First Canadian Place. In response to its increasingly frantic effort to stave off bankruptcy and to prepare Canary Wharf for tenants scheduled to arrive during the summer, it obtained two short-term bank loans adding up to $58 million. The Canadian government initially indicated that it might provide loan guarantees for the beleaguered company; it backed away from this position, however, after running into heavy political attack. On May 14 the Canadian parent company and some of its subsidiaries filed for bankruptcy protection in Canada, and some of the subsidiaries filed for Chapter 11 protection in the United States as well. The Canadian bankruptcy court restricted the firm's ability to shift money from its Canadian properties to other projects, including Canary Wharf. By the end of the year, lenders had begun to take possession of the firm's Canadian holdings.

Government response

The United Kingdom government indicated that it was considering moving the headquarters of the DoE to Canary Wharf. It stipulated, however, that it would do so only if the price were competitive with alternative locations and if O & Y made good on its contribution to the Jubilee Line. When the government continued to procrastinate on committing itself to this course of action, the banks decided they could wait no longer to take action (Peston, 1992). On May 27 the effort to save Canary Wharf from bankruptcy failed, as eleven banks with about £550 million in loans to the project refused to provide new funds to fund the Jubilee Line obligation and to keep construction going beyond the end of the month. At that time O & Y had put £1.4 billion in the project and the banks another £1.2 billion; it was estimated that an additional £600 million was required to finish construction of the first phase (Sullivan et al., 1992).

Canary Wharf was placed under the administration of three partners in the accounting firm Ernst & Young by a United Kingdom bankruptcy court. Under British law, administrators run a bankrupt company and present the court with a plan determining the company's ultimate fate. In contrast to Chapter 11 bankruptcy in the United States, where the firm's management remains in control of the organization and presents a restructuring plan that avoids liquidation of the firm, British bankruptcy procedures favor creditors (Prokesch, 1992b).

In the meanwhile, the transport and infrastructure requirements of converting the Isle of Dogs into an office center consumed more and more of the LDDC's resources. Despite the great increase in the size of its government grant, the LDDC ran into growing financial difficulties. In 1990 its chief executive, Michael Honey, abruptly resigned from his post (*Economist*, May 12, 1990, p. 71). By mid-1991 the new CEO, Eric Sorensen, a DoE civil servant, announced plans to cut its 456-member staff by 40 percent over the next two years (Houlder, 1991a). At the end of 1992 the remaining staff were anxiously awaiting final word on their fate. According to the *Economist* (May 12, 1990, p. 71), the LDDC's low salaries as compared to private firms meant that "the calibre of staff may have suffered accordingly." It also noted that "leading developers question the level of property expertise."

The US situation

As of February 1993, Olympia & York's main US subsidiary, of which the WFC formed the most lucrative part, was the only part of the firm's real-estate business not under bankruptcy protection. Despite the very high vacancy rate in downtown Manhattan, most of the O & Y properties had high occupancy rates, and the WFC remained almost fully rented. Although there was some vacant space in it, caused by shrinkage in the financial industry, responsibility for filling it rested with those tenants that had reduced their organizations. They were subletting unused parts of their leaseholds and absorbing the fairly substantial losses involved.

Two factors accounted for O & Y's more favorable position in the US (Hylton, 1992d). First, much of the financing on the New York properties was asset-based, non-recourse financing, meaning that if creditors foreclosed on the loans, they would not have access to any of the company's other assets and would have acquired properties with market values below the outstanding loans. This was the case at Tower B of the WFC and 55 Water Street, on both of which O & Y defaulted on its Eurobond payments. At 55 Water Street it warned investors that they would have to use their own resources to make necessary improvements in the building (Simon and Peston, 1992). Second, the company did not require additional cash from the banks to operate most of its properties, as was the case at Canary Wharf. Nevertheless, although the majority of its New York properties had low vacancy rates, some of them had a number of leases about to expire and required major renovations.[23] Moreover, potential tenants now feared moving into an O & Y building, not knowing whether the company would be able to maintain the premises and feeling uncertain about the quality of any future landlord, should the building change hands through liquidation (Bartlett, 1992).

O & Y was New York City's largest taxpayer, and its liquidity crisis was causing it difficulty in meeting its tax obligations, including its in-lieu payments to the Battery Park City Authority (BPCA). It managed, however, to negotiate an agreement with the city to pay its taxes and tax equivalents in installments, with interest payments to compensate for the delay (Purdum, 1992).[24] Since it would be extremely disadvantageous to both O & Y and its lenders to default on tax payments and allow the city to take the buildings under tax foreclosure, the city's revenue stream seemed reasonably secure. In the eventuality that a bank foreclosed on any of the WFC buildings, it would assume O & Y's tax-equivalent obligations to the BPCA.

Why did it happen?

The causes of the world's largest real-estate failure range from the specific to the general. They include: (1) the financial situation of O & Y; (2) personal characteristics of the Reichmanns; (3) government policy and the phasing of the development plan for Canary Wharf; and (4) the state of the international commercial property market.

Financial obstacles to salvaging O & Y

The Reichmanns' hopes that they could get agreement from their creditors on a restructuring plan that would pump necessary additional funds into their projects were unrealizable for several reasons. First, the loss in value of their properties caused by the real-estate slump meant that their liabilities exceeded their assets.[25] Consequently they no longer had unencumbered property to use as collateral against additional loans. Bankers would only be willing to acquire equity in the properties if they believed the shares were going to increase in value, but expectations for market recovery were low. Second, there were significant differences in the status of the various lender banks in their claims on O & Y's assets and revenues. Banks which had lent £500 million pounds for Canary Wharf in the 1990 refinancing had their loans secured by O & Y's assets; later lenders took shares in Canary Wharf companies as security, causing them to rank behind the former group in their claims on the parent company. Additional loans would only worsen the situation of the latter group. Third, the Reichmanns had been seeking to redeem their short-term paper, amounting to C$800 million, thus putting all the banks, which numbered about 100, behind the commercial paper holders (Peston and Simon, 1992a).[26]

Personal characteristics

The basis of the Reichmanns' wealth was a very high tolerance of risk. In staking their fortune on Canary Wharf, they apparently felt that they had a sufficient cushion to endure a market downturn. Indeed, in 1988 they were reported to have net assets of C$11 billion and borrowings of less than C$2 billion (Peston and Simon, 1992b).[27] But the internationalization of real-estate investment meant that, contrary to their expectations, markets in different cities tended to move together, so that their multiple investments did not counterbalance one another. The downturn was both longer and deeper than they predicted, and it occurred when their non-real-estate investments were going sour as well.

Many commentators have wondered why the Reichmanns took so many chances when their taste for consumption was quite limited and their fortune established. Speculations recounted by John Lichfield (1992) provide some insight into the interaction between personal characteristics and public events. He quotes a Reichmann business associate as believing that "their heads were turned" by Margaret Thatcher's personally urging them to seize the opportunity to demonstrate the vigor of capitalism in the once socialist-dominated Docklands. Lichfield repeats an explanation from a Toronto Jewish scholar that:

> After the war years, many Jewish families wanted to build a safe, secure base from which they would never have to run again. The Reichmanns appear to me driven to go beyond that, to create a base so wealthy that they could practise their own interpretation of the law without the kind of compromises – such as social contact with gentiles and non-orthodox Jews – which were forced on them in exile. And beyond that to raise the funds to begin to recreate, in scholarship at least, the shattered, enclosed world of their orthodox communities in Europe. (Quoted in Lichfield, 1992)

Finally Lichfield recapitulates the observations of Peter Forster, the author of a book on the Reichmanns:

> The key to everything is the psychology of Paul Reichmann. He is a deal junkie. Deal-making is what he lives and breathes for, the obsessive need to go on making bigger and better deals. And the need to encompass it all in his head, with no proper management structure. With most businessmen, money is not the driving force. . . . his motivation is really the game itself, to do things bigger and better, to work out ever more intricate and imaginative deals. (Quoted in Lichfield, 1992)

ECONOMIC IMPACTS OF DOCKLANDS REDEVELOPMENT

From the outset the two sides of the Docklands debate were clearly differentiated. The position of the government and its supporters was that the Docklands could be an engine of growth, propelling London into a dominant position in twenty-first-century Europe. They frequently mentioned the French success in creating a business center on the Parisian periphery at La Défense, and cited central London's restrictions on growth, congestion, and obsolescent office stock as reasons to plan a new development designed from the start to fulfill contemporary needs. The past failures of Labour governments in promoting alternative, smaller-scale strategies of growth were taken to indicate that only private capital, leveraged by strategic public-sector contributions, could succeed in converting the Docklands from wasteland to viability. Opponents of converting the Docklands into a financial and advanced services headquarters maintained that current residents would receive few housing and employment benefits; that these would only be incidental to the main goal of stimulating private property investment; and that the amount of public financing required to make the project feasible represented a perverse tax on the rest of British society, which would be deprived of adequate governmental support for other community development efforts.

Both sides of the controversy produced reams of data to demonstrate that the experience so far supported their position. The LDDC countered the stereotype of upper-class gentrifiers by showing that 58 percent of in-movers after 1980 had come from within the three Docklands boroughs (LDDC, 1992). It claimed that the number of jobs located in the urban development area had nearly doubled between 1981 and 1990 and that investments in training schemes caused many of these jobs to go to residents of the three boroughs.[28] It boasted of its great success in bringing in private capital. According to its calculations, its nearly £1.5 billion of expenditures over eleven years stimulated private investment of £9.6 billion, yielding a ratio of private to public investment of 6.7:1 (LDDC, 1992).[29]

Critics within the Association of London Authorities (ALA – the coalition of local Labour authorities) and the Docklands Consultative Committee challenged the LDDC's claims on housing, employment, and leveraging. They charged that most available housing had been priced out of the reach of ordinary people and that the LDDC's program of constructing housing for owner occupation had deprived the local authorities and housing associations of land for future social housing:

> Hundreds of these [market-rate] homes now lie vacant and unsold, a legacy of the Docklands property boom. While housing waiting lists grow, millions of pounds have been spent subsidising housing that in terms of the market nobody wants. LDDC estimate that in June 1990, 1422 units were unsold or unoccupied. One year later the figure is certainly very much higher. (ALA and DCC, 1991, p. 11)

The ALA/DCC study contests the LDDC's employment numbers, asserting that there was a net reduction rather than an increase in jobs in the 1981–90 period. Its analysis reveals that closings and relocations caused a loss of over 20,000 jobs, while new jobs amounted to fewer than 17,000. By its reasoning, the remaining jobs shown in the LDDC data should not be counted as new jobs since they were transfers from other parts of London (ALA and DCC, 1991, p. 6). The ALA/DCC group also claimed that only 3 percent of the work force of big office firms on the Isle of Dogs were Docklands residents and that development had not dented the high unemployment rate in the Docklands wards, which was 2.5 times the Greater London average. Their study accused the LDDC, once its proceeds from land sales had dried up, of cutting back sharply on social spending, which had only become a priority in 1987. In another report the

DCC questioned the LDDC leverage ratio, which calculated the relation between public and private investment. The DCC maintained that the number did not include enterprise zone tax subsidies and Department of Transport expenditures as part of the public contribution and that it excluded local-authority investment in land improvements prior to the establishment of the LDDC (DCC, 1988, chapter 7).

In 1993, with work stopped on Canary Wharf and the billions of dollars in property investment seriously devalorized,[30] the LDDC leveraging claims necessarily ring hollow. Even if the reported amount was invested, it ultimately represented a good deal more than the market value of the property involved. Under these circumstances, as a practical matter the amount of private capital used becomes a meaningless figure. Moreover, in the current situation, where the LDDC is continuing to spend money while private investment has stopped, the theoretical ratio will rapidly worsen.

Government policy and the phasing of development

The failure of O & Y to meet its financial obligations shows the deficiencies of the property-led strategy even within the terms of the Conservative objective of creating a new growth pole. The Docklands development scheme aimed at achieving the outcome of earlier British new-town investment – the instantaneous creation of a whole new urban center. The use of a development corporation as the government's instrument replicated the new-town organizational structure (Potter, 1988). But instead of using public money for the bulk of up-front capital expenditures, the Conservatives relied on the private sector to put in most of the financing and to provide major public benefits besides. It did so out of a pragmatic desire to avoid large expenditures and an ideological commitment to private enterprise. The predictable consequence was that the Docklands replicated the fate of the US new-town experience, wherein developers foundered because they could not meet their loan obligations before their projects had attained a positive revenue flow.[31] Given the size of initial investment, the length of time from project inception to conclusion, the cyclical nature of the property market, and the inability of private developers to refinance their debt when lending institutions lose confidence in the market, only under the most fortuitous circumstances could any developer carry out such a project. Olympia & York was the world's richest development firm; its failure indicates the limits on turning to the private sector for achieving public ends.

Even while the Conservative government did eventually supply considerable subsidy to the Docklands, the amounts were insufficient and too late. The government's reluctance to shoulder the full cost of the

Jubilee Line extension and build it in advance of development reflected a halfhearted commitment to Canary Wharf that foreordained its failure. The absence of adequate transportation infrastructure limited the project's appeal to both investors and tenants. Many comments have been made about Londoners' aversion to moving outside the core and the significance of the much greater distance between Canary Wharf and the City than between Wall Street and the WFC. With good road and rail connections, however, the friction of distance might well have been outweighed by the attractions of the new surroundings.

Alternative possibilities

When the Thatcher government took office, either of two alternatives to the one taken could have been chosen and, with hindsight, would have averted the present debacle. The first, laid out by Bob Colenutt, the director of the Docklands Consultative Committee, rejects the Tory conception of the Docklands as a new business and residential center for London. Colenutt (1990) has suggested instead a gradualist strategy toward regeneration that would give priority to assuaging inner-city deprivation. He has proposed, *inter alia*: (1) emphasizing job training and technical assistance to business rather than property development; (2) developing comprehensive strategic plans rather than stimulating "flagship" developments to act as magnets for growth; and (3) increasing local accountability and democracy. His approach is less flashy and, ironically, much more conservative than the Conservatives' tactics. It would be unlikely to attract large sums of capital, and, despite his call for a stronger regional planning approach, it would probably sacrifice the potential of the Docklands as a strategic resource for Greater London as a whole. Its great merit lies in its direct confrontation of the sources of social and economic inequality, its deficiency in the weakness of its stimulus to growth. Colenutt does not espouse a parochialism that would limit the benefits of Docklands development simply to its low-income residents, as did the earlier DJC plan. But neither does he indicate what would attract business to the area.

The other strategy that the government could have adopted at the onset would have emulated Paris's La Défense in its policy mechanisms as well as its physical form. This comparable project to Docklands represented a very different, far more successful approach to eliciting private-sector investment. A public corporation quickly put in the necessary infrastructure, including rail transport, at the start. As the 19 million square feet of office space within the complex went up, the government first restricted then almost halted permissions to construct commercial buildings within central Paris. When financial crisis hit during the mid-seventies, the cabinet pumped in additional public revenues as well as giving tax advantages to firms settling in La Défense (Savitch, 1988, chapter 5). Thus, while the French used private-sector resources to create a whole new section of Paris, they did not rely on the market to regulate the flow of those resources.

In contrast, the British government remained obdurate in its endorsement of market mechanisms. It refused to restrain the City of London Corporation in its competition with the Docklands, thereby insuring the oversupply of London office space that made it impossible for Docklands developers to fill their buildings. It would not release O & Y from its transport commitments, and it would move civil servants into Canary Wharf only if rentals did not exceed the lowest going rate for comparable space.[32]

Prime Minister John Major declared that the government would not bail out Canary Wharf: "The future of the development must be a matter for the administrator and for the banks, and not necessarily for the Government" (quoted in Nisse, 1992). Yet the LDDC and the whole Docklands approach was a creation of the UK central government; its latter-day puritanism about letting the market do its work contradicted the project's state-based origin. If the government initially had been content simply to await private initiatives, at most there would have been a gradual development of the Docklands, moving slowly outward from the boundary with the City.

UNRESOLVED ISSUES

Three issues are raised by O & Y's downfall: (1) its effect on the future of the commercial real-estate market in London and New York; (2) its impact on the banking system; and (3) its implications for the potential of property-led urban regeneration.

The future of the commercial real-estate market

The effect of O & Y's collapse on the London property market is much more profound than on New York's, where most of O & Y's individual properties remain viable. New York's developers will have even greater trouble obtaining financing, and downward pressure on rents will continue. But the availability of less expensive space will also help to keep firms from leaving the city, and the overall balance between supply and demand will not change. In London, however, the empty reaches of Canary Wharf represent a substantial net addition to the property market.

There are those who contend that property owners in the City of London will benefit because no one will now go to the Docklands. If so, then Canary Wharf will simply sit as an enormous white elephant, a testimonial to the overarching ambition of the Reichmann brothers. Other predictions are that it will become a satellite office center, like Croydon, where back offices and secondary firms will take advantage of low rents and luxurious accommodation. The third possibility is that despite Treasury opposition and protest by the affected civil servants, the government will move many of its operations into the buildings and pay for the entire cost of the Jubilee Line.[33] Only the third of these possibilities would make Canary Wharf a vital part of London.

Although local authorities and community groups in the Docklands boroughs ardently opposed the mode of development promoted by the LDDC and may now claim to have warned of the sorry outcome, they can take little pleasure in the consequences for themselves. The failure of office development will not cause it to be replaced in the foreseeable future by a more community-oriented scheme, and borough residents will probably lose whatever benefits they had achieved through development agreements and trickle down. Future strategies framed on the left will have to accommodate the extent of infrastructure and property development now in place in the Docklands, regardless of how misguided the original investment may have been.

The Reichmanns' failure is also likely to discredit their commitment to quality in the minds of future developers. As the *Guardian's* reporter put it:

> What made the Reichmanns stand out was not just the size of their ambitions. They gave the impression that building to last, rather than throwing up simple-minded rent slabs, gave them genuine pleasure. It was thanks to the Reichmanns that the words property developer finally shook off the worst of its [*sic*] pejorative associations from the hit-and-run 1960s . . .
>
> The Reichmanns changed all that. They discovered that office architecture didn't have to stay at the most cynical level. But now there is the worrying prospect that the humbling of Olympia & York will discredit that premise. If it is seen that for a developer to try to recreate the monumental city leads to commercial disaster, what is the point of anybody else trying to do the same. (Sudjic, 1992a)

The banks will all have to absorb very substantial losses, but, in *Business Week's* (June 1, 1992) words, "the sheer number of its [O & Y's] banks . . . has spared any single lender from a life threatening exposure." Many banks had already written off parts of their loans to the company and had put the rest in the non-performing category. Thus, their situation was not changed by the bankruptcy declarations. The real problem for the banking system, to which O & Y's failure simply added one more manifestation, was more long-term: banks lacked alternative good lending outlets; property no longer performed as reliable collateral for business loans; and the deflation in property markets could continue for a very long time, jeopardizing the health of the entire financial system. A well-known real estate analyst expressed the most pessimistic view:

> Real estate deflation is a glacial process. As long as rental rates remain depressed, owners' income will continue to fall. Construction will not contribute to the next business expansion, real-estate losses will continue to weigh on banks and insurers . . . . Wall Street has come to believe that bear markets are over in hours, days or months. Not this one. Real estate values will continue to fall and banks will continue to pay for their boomtime exuberance. (J. Grant, 1992)

In 1993 American banks were divesting themselves of the property they had taken over through default, resulting in a substantial loss in the value of their assets but much greater liquidity. For the moment, they were being saved by a dramatic fall in interest rates, which made their performing loans much more profitable. British banks had avoided the heavy property exposure of their US and Japanese counterparts; it was the latter who were suffering the most from the events in London, along with the repercussions of the puncturing of the Japanese "bubble economy."

The prospects for property-led regeneration

The whole Docklands experience exposes the fatal weakness of relying heavily on property development to stimulate regeneration – government-supplied incentives to the development industry inevitably beget over-supply if not accompanied by other measures to restrict production. Such a result of government intervention should not surprise believers in the market, as the current generation of political leaders all claim to be. They nonetheless maintain their faith in the power of real estate to produce economic growth, especially because they lack other instruments for stimulating growth that do not require an obviously enlarged governmental sector. Politicians are excited by the symbolic impact of new buildings, and they respond eagerly to lobbying from the development industry.[34] Except for the short-term boost from the expenditure of construction dollars, however, urban regeneration assuredly will not be the result of such a policy unless it is accompanied by other measures to improve the skills and housing of residents.

NOTES

1 The cost of Gulf Canada was $3 billion in 1985. By 1990 it had lost one-third of its value.

2 The *New York Times* (Hylton, 1990a) showed the company's holdings in 1990 as follows: Olympia & York Developments Ltd. wholly owned three subsidiaries – the US and London real-estate companies and Olympia & York Enterprises. The last of these was the holding company for its other equity interests. According to the *Times* (which is not entirely in agreement with other sources on percentages), O & Y Enterprises owned the following percentages in publicly owned companies: 82 percent of Abitibi-Price; 74 percent of Gulf Canada Resources; 36 percent of Trizec Corp.; 33 percent of Stanhope Properties, the British developer; 25 percent of Landmark Land Co.; 19 percent of Santa Fe Pacific; 14 percent of Trilon Financial; 10.5 percent of Campeau; and 8.2 percent of Rosehaugh PLC, another British development concern. In addition, it owned 89 percent of GW Utilities, which was another holding company that in turn owned 82 percent of Consumers' Gas Co., 41 percent of Interhome Energy, an oil and pipeline company, and 10 percent of Allied Lyons, the parent company of Hiram Walker.

3 Between 1951 and 1981 manufacturing jobs in inner southeast London dropped by 68 percent, from 148,000 to 47,000 (Buck et al., 1986, pp. 6–7).

4 The name of Hays Wharf lives on as the Hays Galleria within the London Bridge City complex, which opened in 1988 (see chapter 2).

5 There had been 52,000 registered dockers in 1920 (Marris, 1987, p. 61).

6 The original legislation did not fix the life span of the new agency, but in 1991 the government indicated its intention to terminate the country's ten urban development corporations by 1996.

7 The DJC also included parts of Greenwich and Lewisham in its planning.

8 In its first ten years of operation the corporation acquired 2,109 acres of land and water through vesting and purchase. After allowing for 401 acres of water and 483 acres for roads, railway, or environmental purposes, 1,225 acres remained for development. Land disposals to March 31, 1991 amounted to 661 acres, leaving 564 acres awaiting reclamation, being reclaimed, or awaiting development (LDDC, 1991, p. 17).

9 The number of dwelling units in the development area doubled between 1981 and 1990, with owner occupation increasing from 5 to 44 percent (LDDC, 1992).

10 The *New York Times* described the extreme contrasts involved:

> The wall, a brick sentinel that shields one world from another, stands as a symbol of sweeping change and resultant bitter divisions in London's once-derelict dock area.
>
> On one side of the wall, affluent newcomers occupy a stylish private housing development. On the other, a bleak public housing complex, with laundry hanging from balconies with peeling ceilings, is home to the working class and poor.

"The developers built that wall so those people wouldn't have to look at this," Steve Amor, chairman of the local tenants' association, said as he climbed the stairs to his cramped apartment. (Rule, 1988)

11 The LDDC expected the number of units to double between 1988 and 1990, from 12,000 to 24,000, but only slightly more than 15,000 were actually completed by then (LDDC, 1988b, 1992).

12 The enterprise zone deadline had the same effect as the scheduled termination of New York's special midtown zoning – developers rushed to construct buildings in the absence of any obvious demand for space so as to obtain the benefits before they disappeared.

13 The consortium also comprised two US-based merchant banks, Crédit Suisse–First Boston (parent company of First Boston Real Estate) and Morgan Stanley. The origin of the consortium's interest in Canary Wharf lay in the inability of the two financial firms to locate suitable office space in central London during the mid-eighties (Daniels and Bobe, 1991).

14 Road investment by the LDDC totalled £248 million in FY 1990–91 and was projected to total over £650 million for the subsequent three-year period (LDDC, 1991). Highways to be built by the UK Department of Transport, which would connect the Docklands to the national road system, were estimated in 1987 to cost another £348 million (National Audit Office, 1988, p. 14).

15 Whether or not O & Y's community commitments will be honored is at present an open question.

16 The planned consolidation of American Express's offices was to involve 1,500 employees situated in six buildings within central London.

17 After the project went into bankruptcy administration, the administrators feared that the liabilities incurred in the inducements to tenants surpassed the benefits of occupancy and calculated that the enterprise's balance sheet would improve if the committed tenants were persuaded not to come. Nevertheless, O & Y and Crédit Suisse–First Boston (CSFB), which owned one of the Canary Wharf buildings, opposed American Express's application to withdraw from its lease. As of July 1992 the question of whether American Express could withdraw was under judicial consideration. The firm had argued that O & Y had defaulted on its lease obligations when it ceased paying contractors to complete work on the structure. The judge temporarily blocked American Express from withdrawing (Simon, 1992a). Committed tenants feared that bankruptcy would free the project's sponsors from the obligation to assume their old leases, leaving them with empty, possibly unlettable space on their hands on which they would have to continue paying high rents.

18 Some companies had already moved in during the preceding year; in May 1992 the buildings were 11 percent occupied. The larger committed tenants were scheduled to arrive during the summer.

19 CSFB and Morgan Stanley were part of the original Canary Wharf consortium and remained as backers of the project, each agreeing to take an equity position in its own building. Morgan Stanley's agreement with O &

Y, however, required the developer to purchase its building upon completion if it so demanded. O & Y resisted the exercise of this option and lost in court.

20 The court battle raised some eyebrows since Morgan Stanley had a long-standing close business relationship with O & Y and continued to act as a financial adviser.

21 From March through June 1992 the tribulations of O & Y received virtually daily coverage in the business press and weeklies in both the US and the UK. For a chronology of the events recapitulated here, see the *New York Times* (May 29, 1992).

22 Speculation was that Johnson received $1.5 million for signing on and got a similar amount on his departure (Parker-Jervis, 1992).

23 Its building at 320 Park Avenue stood empty and required major investment; 60 Broad Street had a vacancy rate over 62 percent; and 2 Broadway of 40 percent. The huge structure at 55 Water Street had an asbestos problem, accounting for the very high estimate for its renovation, and 40 percent of its leases were due to expire within two years; and 245 Park Avenue likewise was threatened by the imminent loss of tenants (Bartlett, 1992).

24 More than $60 million was due on July 1, 1992. The agreement allowed O & Y to make six equal payments of about $10.5 million for a total of $63 million, plus 18 percent interest, with a little over $2 million of the interest also payable on July 1. It was hoped that monthly rent revenues would cover the installments. O & Y's total semiannual tax payment to New York was about $75 million, but not all its buildings were included in the deal (Purdum, 1992).

25 The value of O & Y's assets at the time of filing was the subject of considerable discussion. An estimate published in *Barron's* put the shortfall at between $6 billion and $10 billion (Isaac, 1992).

26 Different sources gave different figures for the number of banks involved, ranging from 91 to over 100. Major lenders, as listed in the *New York Times*, included large Japanese banks – Tokai Bank Ltd. ($250 million), Fuji ($100 million), Dai-Ichi Kangyo ($180 million), and other Japanese institutions (at least $250 million). Other bank lenders were: the Hong Kong and Shanghai Banking Corporation ($750 million); Canadian Imperial Bank of Commerce ($713 million); Royal Bank of Canada ($647 million); Commerzbank International of Frankfurt ($287.5 million); Crédit Lyonnais ($262 million); Citibank ($480 million); Barclay's ($315 million); Lloyds ($100 million) (*New York Times*, June 4, 1992; Parker-Jervis, 1992). *Barron's* (May 18, 1992) gives much larger figures for some of these banks. For example, it shows Crédit Lyonnais as being owed $1.25 billion and Citibank over $1 billion; these numbers seem much too high. The *Observer* (Sullivan, 1992) showed Citibank as holding $380 million in loans to O & Y. In addition to the bank loans, it was estimated that O & Y had about fifteen outstanding bond issues backed by mortgages on specific buildings, although some were also backed by shares in its energy and forestry companies (Hylton, 1992e).

27 This indebtedness figure seems too low in view of their earlier acquisitions of natural-resource companies.

28 Figures for 1985 produced by the LDDC indicated that 44 percent of Docklands employees lived within the three Docklands boroughs (LDDC, 1988a). Later fact sheets issued by the LDDC did not give figures for places of residence of jobholders.

29 Its breakdown of expenditures by percentage was as follows (LDDC, 1992):

Roads and transport	33
Docklands Light Rail	16
Land acquisition	11
Social housing	10
Services (e.g. utilities installation, sewage system)	10
Land reclamation	8
Environment	5
Community and industry support	5
Marketing	0.5

30 The loss in value of Canary Wharf was estimated at $2.2 billion by analysts (Hylton, 1992a). Two potential purchasers of the development concluded that the project was worth only $1.1 billion (Houlder et al., 1992); if so, the loss would be $3.6 billion from the original estimated value (the real loss to investors was less).

31 At the same time as Britain was building government-sponsored new towns, the US was offering shallow subsidies to private developers, who were supposed to install the basic infrastructure themselves and construct a critical mass of structures. Almost all the US ventures failed entirely or required financial restructuring.

32 The government's behavior in relation to the financial problems of the Channel Tunnel was similar.

33 When the World Trade Center opened in downtown Manhattan in a period of office oversupply, the Port Authority rented much of it to offices of the State of New York. (It should be remembered that David Rockefeller had led the drive for the construction of the structure, and his brother, Nelson, was governor at the time.) The gambit was extremely successful in carrying the complex through hard times. Many of the state offices moved out when other, higher-paying tenants appeared. Similarly the French government placed its civil servants in unfilled buildings at La Défense.

34 Thus, right on the heels of the O & Y disaster, the US House of Representatives, under pressure from the real-estate sector, passed legislation restoring the tax shelter for passive investors in property (Cushman, 1992). The move was aimed at bringing capital back into the industry and justified as an instrument for urban revitalization. Although the 1992 measure failed to achieve enactment, it is again being proposed.

10

Real-Estate Development: Why is it Special and What is its Impact?

Urban redevelopment has attracted the scrutiny of scholars and community activists since the inception of large government programs to rebuild cities after the Second World War. Initial interest centered on the governmental decision-making process, the role of the state, and community conflict. Although many studies identified the influence of business leaders on decisions and outcomes, there was little investigation of the factors affecting the actions of speculative developers. Their great prominence during the real-estate boom of the 1980s and their contribution to economic retreat at the beginning of the nineties have formed the central theme of this book. The conclusion of chapter 1 lists six questions that make up the framework of my inquiry. The first four – the relationship between economic restructuring and real-estate development, the contradictions within the process of development that produce oversupply, the relationship between governmental activity and property development, and the similarities and differences between London and New York – have already been considered in earlier chapters. This chapter addresses the fifth and sixth questions: the special characteristics of real estate as an economic sector and the impacts of redevelopment.

THE NATURE OF THE REAL-ESTATE SECTOR

Real-estate development shares characteristics with many other sectors of production in both its impacts and its operations; its uniqueness lies in the way it combines attributes usually belonging to quite dissimilar industries. Like manufacturers, property developers produce a tangible product. At the same time, the development industry resembles the entertainment business more than heavy manufacturing in having a profound cultural influence, in the singularity of each item produced, and in the process by which the elements of a project are combined. As in entertainment, production away from the firm's headquarters is *ad hoc*; unlike most other multinational corporations, big development companies do not set up permanent facilities around the world, but rather, like film-production companies, they use temporary field offices for specific projects. Yet, despite resemblances to film or television production, the industry is also similar to agriculture in its cyclical structure, its susceptibility to market glut, and its close relation with government. Although government does not directly control levels of production as in agriculture, the development industry depends heavily on public-sector decisions concerning investment in infrastructure, tax policy, and regulation of construction.

Organization of production

Major development firms typically differ from big industrial corporations in not producing on a mass scale. The fluctuating nature of the property market, and the fact that most purchases of space are from second-hand stock, has meant that the industry, except for large housing subdivision builders, could never count on a market sufficient to justify mass production. In the United States and the United Kingdom, development firms have also not adopted the same organizational structures as major industrial producers – they have not integrated most phases of the production process within their enterprises,[1] and they usually do not operate on a global, or even a national scale.[2]

Developers usually contract for most services with third parties rather than relying on internal provision. This strategy allows them simply to withdraw from activity during slumps, as they have little overhead to maintain (Bacow, 1990, p. 5). By providing development firms with other sources of income, like brokerage, management, and architectural fees, vertical integration could reduce their costs during peak periods and offer them protection against cash-flow problems during downturns in the development cycle. Few firms, however, have tried to adopt this model (Bacow, 1990, p. 5). Olympia & York did move toward vertical integration during the 1980s real-estate boom by issuing its own notes and retaining property for its own management operation. It also operated in a number of nations. As it turned out, both self-financing and working in unfamiliar locales contributed heavily to its undoing.

Ironically, construction used to be contrasted with integrated, mass-produced, capital-goods and consumer-durables manufacturing to demonstrate its backwardness. Now, however, the "hollow corporation" that relies on subcontractors, "just-in-time methods," and temporary staff has been touted as the leading edge of the restructured global economy. In the era of flexible organization of enterprises and short production runs, the development industry begins to look as if all along it had occupied the vanguard rather than the rear.

Property markets

The property development industry has a paradoxical situation with regard to market position[3] — it is simultaneously monopolistic and highly competitive. Although any structure monopolizes its site, and property owners can achieve monopoly pricing within districts (see Harvey, 1985), no developer or small group of developers can control overall supply in a metropolitan area.[4] Ease of entry into the market and the potential of previously undeveloped districts to compete with developed areas destabilizes market domination. Unlike farmers, whom the government compensates for accepting constraints on production, developers do not receive benefits when they are not developing; consequently they have strongly resisted governmentally imposed restrictions on supply, even though without them it becomes impossible to maintain high prices. The situation whereby a small group of owners can monopolize a niche but not a whole market contributes to the cyclical behavior of property markets. A competing node must reach a critical mass before it threatens an established area, but once it does, it upsets the entire price structure.

The 1980s witnessed a move toward dominance of the London and New York inner-city new-construction markets by a small number of big firms. Subsequent hard times, however, either drove them into default or caused them to withdraw from active production of space. In New York, commercial landlords on the midtown East Side commanded very high rents as a result of limitations on the supply of space in a uniquely prestigious area. Renovation of older buildings in adjacent areas by small-scale developers and massive new developments in other parts of Manhattan and in New Jersey, however, created "new addresses," leading office-renters to vacate large amounts of space on the East Side as they took advantage of lower prices elsewhere. The pressure on building owners burdened with so much empty space meant that they could not sustain the old rent level even after developers had stopped adding newly constructed space to the area. Thus, the value of their initial monopoly position dropped substantially. Within the City of London the loosening of restraints by the local authority along with construction elsewhere had the same effect on the price of space.

The most anomalous aspect of the pricing of real estate derives from the dual role of a building in functioning within both factor and consumption markets. In other industries, ownership of the product is distinct from ownership of the company or rights to future increases in the value of its production. A building, however, is both part of capital stock and a commodity. It is as if the cost of cars to the consumer fluctuated with the shares of General Motors or as if purchases of bread reflected the price of grain futures. (The price of these goods does, of course, to some degree reflect anticipations of future scarcity and resale possibilities.) The dual character of property as commodity and vehicle for capital accumulation explains why investors will risk funds on a property where production costs exceed capitalized revenues calculated on the basis of present value.

The general rule that a firm should produce until marginal cost equals marginal revenue is difficult to apply in the property industry since expectations about marginal revenue are extremely subjective.[5] Although calculating marginal revenue in all industries requires an estimate of a future price, in no other industry is such a prediction so uncertain, so subject to the externalities of the actions of others, and carried out over such a long time span. The price of a commercial property in ten years depends on the amount of space that others build, the desirability of the area in which it is located (which is itself very subjective and can be perturbed by unanticipated events), the changeable technical needs of the occupant (e.g. for "smart buildings," large trading floors, or private offices with windows), governmental decisions concerning infrastructure, taxation, interest rates, and regulation, and expansion and contraction of the industry for which the building is designed.

During the eighties financial institutions were willing to lend money to developers using optimistic estimates of the future value of the building rather than a simple ratio of the immediately anticipated rent roll to capital inputs. Consequently far more space was built than could be justified, based on immediate returns. As shown in chapter 3, it was this flow of capital into the property industry rather than demand that stimulated the huge amount of new construction at the end of the decade.

The contribution of property to value

Two much-discussed arguments of David Harvey bear on the issue of the consequences of property investment (see Haila, 1991); both signify that gains from property are particularly ill-gotten. First, in his theory of switched investment, Harvey (1981) argues that investment moves into the secondary circuit of capital, to which the built environment belongs, when there is overaccumulation in the primary circuit. Harvey's implication is that such switching dampens productive investment, and his use of the term "circuit" indicates that once capital moves into this realm it will stay there. Yet, as syndication and securitization make property debt increasingly negotiable, the distinction between circuits fades. There is, moreover, little evidence that the behavior of property counters movements in other parts of the economy, as would be the case if the switching argument were valid (see Beauregard, 1991). When times are generally tough, property suffers likewise. The lag in the property cycle as compared to the goods production cycle largely results from the long lead time involved in real-estate development projects.

During the 1970s in the United States there was a major shift of funds into property. This phenomenon is more convincingly regarded as the result of using property as a hedge against inflation and of tax advantages allocated to this sector than as a consequence of overaccumulation in the primary circuit. In addition, the tendency of banks, particularly those of Japan and the oil-producing countries, to overinvest in property grew partly out of the move by industrial companies toward disintermediation; the refusal of companies with large capital needs to turn to banks meant that the banks lacked outlets for their funds. The absence of investment opportunities for banks in the primary sector did not necessarily reflect overaccumulation in that sector.

Harvey (1982, pp. 266–70) develops his second argument concerning the effects of investment in property in his discussion of "fictitious capital" (defined as debt instruments). He asserts "the insanity of a society in which investment in appropriation (rents, government debts, etc.) appears just as important as investment in production" (1982, p. 269). According to both these arguments the property sector absorbs rather than generates value – value is only created through "real" production (including the actual building of a structure but not some of the other costs associated with it, such as sales taxes and interest).[6]

The classical (Ricardian) definition of land rent, which assumes a completely inelastic supply of land, likewise implies that the property sector is essentially parasitic. According to this reasoning, property attains its value from the way it is used by its occupant rather than any activity of the owner.[7] Speculative transactions appear to support this point. Thus, the spiraling price of an undeveloped piece of land that keeps changing hands on the expectation of future use illustrates the unearned quality of real-estate gains, as does a huge increase in the rent for an unchanged storefront at the expiration of a lease.

Such instances of wholly unproductive investment in real estate, however, do not prove that real-estate development does not create value beyond the cost of production. If agglomeration and access do transform territory into location; if restructured space increases business efficiency; if subdivision of land or reuse of empty warehouses creates a residential neighborhood where none previously existed; if the regulations that limit construction in a given district do actually produce a more attractive environment – then increases in land value resulting from development are genuine. The value of a tennis racket is dependent on a court, of a bedroom on a bed, of a steel mill on raw materials (and vice versa) – virtually all values exist in combinations and are increased or lowered, based on the context in which they are used. Physicality does not make a process real, nor does the intangibility of factors like agglomeration make them unreal. It is the concatenation of externalities from development that creates place, which as a whole may have a value greater than a simple summation of the costs of producing it.[8] The claim that such gains are socially created does not overturn this assertion – the question of who deserves to receive the gain is analytically separable from the issue of whether it exists. Value anticipated from development is not fictitious.

Factors causing government involvement

The inherently social nature of the production of place has underlain the historically high level of government involvement in the property sector. First, because ownership of property is a set of rights rather than physical possession, government has always regulated "private" property. How property rights are defined, bought and sold is defined by law and adjudicated through courts. Second, property development has an immediate neighborhood effect, and the aggregate of development projects has important impacts on the economic future and quality of life of an entire settlement. The use and disposal of property almost necessarily involves more parties than simply the nominal buyer and seller. Third, the obligation of government to provide public goods means that, even in the most market-driven societies, governments themselves have major landholdings and do some land-banking. Governments act as property developers when carrying out public functions ranging from assuring the water supply to constructing parks to building infrastructure. How they perform these functions significantly affects growth and the distribution of benefits within their jurisdictions.

Together public and private property development contributes significantly to the creation of place. Place has within it the elements of territory, of location, and of community (see Agnew, 1987, p. 28). Place is a critical component of human welfare for several reasons: (1) it provides a basis for human affiliation; (2) it is the setting for economic development and consumption; (3) it is the locus of political representation; and (4) it is the arena in which public policy acts on people. Given the crucial functions of place, it is not surprising that its constitution is among the most contested of policy issues.

How should we Evaluate the Places that the City Builders have made?

Practitioners of both city planning and urban sociology long held as a basic tenet that urban form shapes social life. Throughout much of this century planners, whose roots lay in the design professions, believed that well-ordered cities would make people lead better lives. During the same period urban sociologists, claiming a scientific basis for their hypotheses, were arguing that environmental factors explained human behavior – Lewis Wirth (1938), in his famous essay on urbanism that epitomized this approach, identified the size, density, and heterogeneity of a settlement as the determining elements of social relations within it.

Subsequently, however, leftist scholars disputed that place had independent effects, claiming that planners and sociologists had mistakenly confuted the results of a class-divided industrial society with the consequences of urban form and spatial clustering.[9] These later theorists argued instead that urbanism was a mediating factor based on the socio-economic relations of modern industrial capitalism. In its Marxist version this analysis regarded space as shaped by the dominant class using spatial divisions to its advantage and by subordinate classes which, on occasion, were able to mobilize from a territorial base to contest their situation.[10] More conservative thinkers did not share the Marxists' starting point in the economic structure. Nevertheless, they also increasingly saw physical form as an outcome instead of a cause of human activity, differing from the Marxists in tracing the qualities of places to popular preferences and technological imperatives rather than to the logic of capitalism (see e.g. Bish, 1971).

Most recently, urbanists, usually from a left perspective, have placed a renewed emphasis on urban design and spatial configuration, although without explicitly reviving the design or environmental reductionism of their planning and sociological forebears.[11] In line with contemporary post-structuralist thought, they have largely avoided identifying the form of the city as a direct cause of social behavior; rather they have read from the physical contours of cities the meaning of urban life. Their analyses stress the symbolic importance of design, chart the way in which it expresses relations of domination and subordination, oppression and resistance, and examine the interaction between environmental factors and human consciousness.[12] In particular, recent writings on the city have explored the inclusionary and exclusionary aspects of urban spatial formations, as part of a broad concern by their authors with the politics of diversity and a normative commitment to the acceptance of difference.[13] Whereas their Marxist predecessors had evaluated the material costs and benefits flowing from the creation and use of urban space, today's cultural critics have scrutinized the late capitalist city with "the conscience of the eye" (Sennett, 1990).

The evolving literature on the meaning of spatial configurations provides one set of concerns through which we can assess the development history of London and New York between 1978 and 1993. It also allows us to describe the culture of urban development and to understand how different social groups shape and respond to the new urban form. Nevertheless, I find serious problems in the arguments of this contemporary group of urbanists, which stem from their simultaneous embrace of the related but also contradictory values of diversity, authenticity, and democracy. In the remainder of this chapter, where I present my evaluation of redevelopment in London and New York, I distill the main elements of this recent critique of contemporary redevelopment practice drawn from a number of recent works, either generally on the making of the contemporary city or more specifically on London and New York – for simplicity's sake I label this body of analysis "post-structuralist." My presentation of the post-structuralist analysis attempts to offer a fair summary of the main arguments, but the reader should keep in mind that I am not fully in agreement with them. Afterwards, I specify what I see as the weaknesses of the approach and set forth some correctives that assist in overcoming these difficulties. Finally I discuss additional ways of understanding and evaluating urban redevelopment, based on a more materialist analysis.

The post-structuralist critique

The "public-private partnerships," which control the planning and implementation of redevelopment in American and British cities, express themselves in the lineaments of the cities that they build. Within these partnerships the private sector usually dominates the relationship through its command over investment choices; moreover, despite their hybrid status the partnerships typically adhere to a market-led, closed-to-the-public style that is a hallmark of private business. In pursuing their aims of economic expansion, public-private partnerships imprint the built environment with their attributes of privatism, competition, and commodification of relationships.[14] According to post-structuralist analysis, the resulting environment is hostile to authentic human expression and represses subordinate groups.

To ensure the safe pursuit of profit within the reconstructed city, designers intentionally set projects off from their surroundings so as to create defensible space: "Faced with the fact of social hostility in the city, the planner's impulse in the real world is to seal off conflicting or dissonant sides, to build internal walls rather than permeable borders" (Sennett, 1990, p. 201). A number of measures ensure that only certain people can gain access to the new constructions which define the urban landscape: isolation of projects behind highways, raised plazas, or actual walls; direct connections to parking garages and transit, obviating the need to use city streets; segregation of uses; extensive deployment of security measures; private ownership of outdoor parks and indoor courtyards, allowing the banning of unsavory individuals and political speech; high prices for renting attractive quarters and for buying goods sold within the new stores; stylistic markers that make lower-class people feel out of place. The unrelatedness of one project to the next further diminishes the public realm. In the words of the architect Moshe Safdie (1987, p. 153):

> The legibility of the city depends on the public domain as the connective framework between individual buildings. This is exemplified in the agora and the markets of the past, but it does not exist today. We are unable to connect buildings as part of the urban experience. The Galeria in Houston, the grand space of Philip Johnson's IDS building in Minneapolis, the great spaces created by Portman are an attempt to respond to our desire for public places worthy of the kind of urban life that we want. But, by definition, built as individual pieces, they are introverted and, hence, they are private and not connectable.

The resulting urban form is paradoxically neither coherent nor diverse. Physical incoherence, instead of fostering pluralism, produces segmentation[15] – separation rather than juxtaposition. The adjectives typically used to depict the contemporary city are "divided," "fragmented," and "fractured." Although the residences of the rich and poor were rarely in close proximity throughout the history of the industrial city, the commercial core previously retained a social heterogeneity, springing from its use by all strata of the population. The construction of fortified spaces within the city, however, allows the commuting businessperson and the resident gentry to experience urbanity without confronting "the other." In Richard Sennett's words (1990, p. 193):

> Battery Park City . . . is planned according to current enlightened wisdom about mixed uses and the virtues of diversity. Within this model community,

however, one has the sense . . . "of an illustration of life" rather than life itself.

Even projects like Covent Garden and South Street Seaport, which were modelled on the busy marketplaces of earlier times, produce only a simulacrum of urbanism – an "analogous city" (Boddy, 1992). In commenting ironically on the influence of Jane Jacobs, whose *Death and Life of Great American Cities* had espoused diversity as the prime urban value, Trevor Boddy (1992, p. 126 n.) contends:

> Sadly, the cornerstones of Jacobsian urbanism – picturesque ethnic shops piled high with imported goods, mustachioed hot-dog vendors in front of improvised streetcorner fountains, urban life considered as one enormous national-day festival – are cruelly mimicked in every Rouse market [i.e., urban shopping districts developed by the Rouse Corporation, which specializes in festive marketplaces] and historic district on the [American] continent. Contemporary developers have found it eminently easy to furnish such obvious symbols of urbanism, while at the same time eliminating the racial, ethnic, and class diversity that interested Jacobs in the first place.

To the post-structuralist critics the glory of cities lies in their capacity to bring together strangers, allowing people to move beyond the "familiar enclaves" of families and social networks "to the more open public of politics, commerce, and festival, where strangers meet and interact" (Young, 1990, p. 237). The diminution of this capacity reinforces the hegemony of the white males who designed the modern city and whose economic and political power it incorporates. In turn, the city symbolizes gendered power; popular response to its message reaffirms acquiescence to hierarchy and repressive norms of appropriate behavior. According to Elizabeth Wilson (1991, p. 25), the modern city and its postmodern successor signify the triumph of the "masculine approach" of "intervention and mastery" over feminine "appreciation and immersion." In his discussion of the City of London, Michael Pryke (1990, p. 202) comments that the value system of the English public school combined with a style of British masculinity to create there a gendered territory of "upper class patriarchy." He (1990, p. 212) argues that the introduction of information technology into these gendered confines produced "a spatial demonstration of predominantly male corporate power structures," as men staked out their positions on the trading floors of the financial firms while women assumed the jobs deskilled by computerization.

The claim that diversity is excluded while its illusion is created underlies the further accusation that, unlike the streets and markets of old, these new development projects lack authenticity:

> Places like Battery Park City, Times Square, and South Street Seaport are
> sustained . . . by the expansion of historical tourism, the desire to 'just look'
> at the replicated and revalued artifacts and architecture of another time. Yet
> to historicize is to estrange, to make different, so that a gap continually
> widens between then and now, *between an authentic and simulated experience.*
> (Boyer, 1992, p. 199; italics added)

Even the Prince of Wales has joined the attack on the failure of the modern
cityscape to conform to an authentic historical tradition, and his
intervention helped to block several of the megaprojects that would have
rent the fabric of central London.[16] As on Main Street in Disney World –
the apogee of simulated historicism – the purpose of presenting the past in
the architectural references of the postmodern office structures and festive
marketplaces is to induce consumption.[17] The granite-clad façades,
classical pediments, and restored warehouses persuade corporate officers
to pay high rents for symbols of prestige or lead tourists to buy the
unneeded commodities so fetchingly displayed. Rather than situating the
visitor in historical continuity with a real past, these imitative projects
project him or her into a fantasy world wherein an ostensibly meaningful
existence can be purchased off the rack.

In New York's Battery Park City, a residential community reminiscent
of traditional neighborhoods springs up on a site that was only recently
under water. In London's Canary Wharf streets lined with august buildings
seemingly built long ago suddenly appear on land formerly covered with
warehouses and shipping cranes. In Covent Garden and the Fulton
Fishmarket teeshirt vendors and fashionable cafés take over the same
structures occupied by the wholesale purveyors and raucous taverns of
yesteryear. Whether the projects contain new structures built to resemble
old ones or genuinely old buildings with new functions, their sameness,
their artificiality, their omnipresent security forces, all seem to validate the
post-structuralist perspective. The impulse for the critique derives from
laudable commitments to democracy and egalitarianism and a vision of the
city as a place to which all people have an equal right and which should
allow them all expression. The perspective, however, even though it is
rooted in a political and social analysis of space, suffers from weaknesses of
political and social perception. It is to these weaknesses that this discussion
now turns.

Inadequacies of post-structuralist analysis

Certain of the flaws in post-structuralist urban analysis are not
fundamental to its critique. Its crucial theses are its attack on exclusionism
and its identification of the urban core as expressing the dominance of a

ruling group or power bloc. Many of its proponents, however, base their argument on two assumptions, which they fail to justify: (1) that the city once nurtured diversity more than it does now, and (2) that a desirable city would be more authentic than the one currently being created. It is my belief that a modified version of the main contentions about exclusionism and power can be retained without accepting the two assumptions concerning a golden past and the virtue of authenticity. My discussion first explains the problems with the two assumptions, continues by examining the deficiencies of the exclusionism and domination arguments, and then attempts to salvage them.

A golden age of greater diversity?

Many of the post-structuralists quoted above assume that a golden age – or at least a better time – once existed, when cities did harbor the daily interaction of diverse people, and urban form expressed an authentic relationship with the forces of production and reproduction. Two obvious facts, however, undermine the nostalgic recollection of a past when urban space fostered greater tolerance and diversity.[18] First, in both London and New York, people deemed unacceptable by the larger society were kept out of those parts of the city where the upper classes congregated. The enforcement of vagrancy laws and the general lack of restraint on police discretion meant that the least attractive elements of society were simply contained in particular parts of town. The Bowery in New York and Limehouse in London were not necessarily the preferred location of their down-and-out denizens. They did not, however, dare to intrude into upper-class areas for fear of physical assault or incarceration at the hands of the law. In addition, the confinement of the mentally ill removed these individuals from the city streets. It is the now ubiquitous presence of the homeless, substance abusers, and the mentally ill in even the best parts of Manhattan and, to a lesser degree, central London that has stimulated the reactive construction of secure spaces.[19] Whether in sum the variety of people in central places is greater or less now than formerly is unclear. The inward-turning characteristics of the atrium hotels like New York's Marriott Marquis, the glitzy atmosphere of Covent Garden and South Street Seaport, and the isolation of megaprojects like Battery Park and London Bridge Cities do separate the users of these facilities from the rest of the population. Nonetheless, at least superficially, the range of types to be seen within the festive markets seems to exceed the spectrum of those who patronized the downtown department stores of my youth.[20] And even with the existence of "glass ceilings" for women and minorities, the corporations that populate the new office buildings are considerably more heterogeneous now than earlier in the century.

Second, in New York the exclusion of people of color from commercial spaces and housing was a fact of life and not illegal until mid-century. Even though patches of African-American habitation existed throughout Manhattan until their extirpation by urban renewal after World War II, the existence of these islands did not mean that their occupants mixed with other social groups. Moreover, until the war the great majority of the African-American population lived in the South, where it was subject to extreme legal segregation. Thus, the mechanisms that currently keep most of the now much larger populations of people of color out of certain spaces in central New York, however outrageous they may be, still are not as exclusionary as previous modes.[21]

A more authentic urban form?

The dismissal of contemporary redevelopment projects as inauthentic implies that during an earlier period authenticity reigned. While putting off momentarily a discussion of the broader meaning of the term, we can temporarily accept a limited definition of authenticity in design as either historical accuracy or lack of artifice (form following function). As part of the discussion of whether there was once a golden age of the city, we can then consider if current design is less meticulous in representing the past or a less natural outcome of the economy and daily lives of the population than the constructions of earlier generations.

With this question in mind, the censure of Battery Park City, Canary Wharf, South Street Seaport, and Covent Garden for their artificiality and historical inaccuracies seems on the face of it odd. The Western urban tradition since the Renaissance has always sustained the false front and the faulty imitation of times past. Those most urbane and praised of seventeenth-century urban squares – Madrid's Plaza Mayor and Paris's Place de Vosges – achieve their uniformity from the placement of identical façades on a hodge-podge of buildings. London's beloved Nash terraces, built in the early nineteenth century, employ columns and porticoes in imaginative imitation of Athenian architecture. New York's Metropolitan Museum of Art is basically hackneyed Roman Revival. If one can identify any characteristic style of major structures in the Western city since the Renaissance, it is bastardized historical re-creation.

Authenticity defined and evaluated

The second unsubstantiated assumption of the post-structuralist inter-pretation is the exaltation of the value of authenticity itself and the implied definition of it that underlies the attacks on new projects as inauthentic.

Although the critical literature is replete with accusations of fakery, the nature of authentic, late twentieth-century design is rarely specified. For example, Michael Sorkin (1992c, p. 216), the former architecture critic for the *Voice*, New York's leading alternative newspaper, excoriates Disneyland for its unreality: "The simulation's referent is ever elsewhere; the 'authenticity' of the substitution always depends on the knowledge, however faded, of some absent genuine." But what is the "absent genuine" in a nation whose main industries produce intangibles and whose economic stability depends on stimulating ever higher levels of consumption? Sorkin (1992c, p. 231) goes on to assert that "Disney-zone" is a meretricious fake:

> Disney invokes an urbanism without producing a city. Rather, it produces a kind of aura-stripped hypercity, a city with billions of citizens (all who would consume) but no residents. Physicalized yet conceptual, it's the utopia of transience, a place where everyone is just passing through. This is its message for the city to be, a place everywhere and nowhere, assembled only through constant motion.

Sorkin's prose interestingly echoes Manuel Castells' (1989, p. 6) description of the effect of information technology on society more generally:

> [We are seeing] the emergence of a *space of flows* which dominates the historically constructed space of places, as the logic of dominant organizations detaches itself from the social constraints of cultural identities and local societies through the powerful medium of information technologies. (italics in original)

If Castells is right, then Disney World is an *authentic* reflection of underlying economic and social processes, however little we may like them. It *is* the genuine, while the absent Main Streets and Hollywood studios have, in fact, disappeared as their economic functions have withered or are performed through other means.

Much of the post-structuralist literature rests on an unformulated premise that what is genuine comprises either the production and transportation of goods (e.g. craft workshops, steel mills, and working ports) or the housing of production workers (e.g. cottages and tenements). Spectacles and pageants are authentic if they are produced by their participants rather than fabricated to manipulate them. The subtext, based on Marxist concepts of alienation and commodity fetishism, is that virtue lies in material production and that producing for one's own consumption is better than purchasing mass-produced goods and services – that activity is always preferable to passivity (in this code of ethics, buying and using finished goods is not an active pastime).[22] Such a moral stance is increasingly at odds with the reality of an economy organized around corporate power, information flows, the manufacture of financial products, mass tourism, and the consumption of services. If we are going to criticize the new urban landscape for its significations, authenticity is not the appropriate value to apply, since deconstruction of the urban environment reveals a reasonably accurate portrayal of the social forces underlying it. Indeed, form is following function.

A deeper critique must instead show that this landscape fails to satisfy important human needs. But to do so puts the critic on the thorny ground of explicating what activities afford genuine as opposed to false satisfaction.[23] The effort to show that theme parks and shopping malls do not afford real pleasure is a reprise of old Marxist claims concerning false consciousness, and it founders on the same shoals of circular argumentation – only acceptance of identical premises concerning values and evidence can lead to the same evaluation of phenomena as genuine or false.[24] Indeed the popularity of some of the new shopping areas, mixed-use projects, and cultural centers seems to drive the cultural critics into paroxysms of annoyance as they attempt to show that people *ought* to be continually exposed to the realities of life at the lower depths.[25] Thus, a recent commentator on the Olympia & York projects in London and New York declares:

> Both Canary Wharf [in Docklands] and WFC [the World Financial Center at Battery Park City] are spectacular diversions that draw a veil over the realities of deepening social polarization, ghettoization, informalization and burgeoning homelessness which characterize London and New York. (*Crilley, 1992, p. 143*)

Such analyses place too much blame for social evil on middle-class escapism, in the limited sense of people's preference for looking at a pleasing environment.[26] A negative evaluation of Canary Wharf and Battery Park City depends on whether a feasible better option exists.[27] The alternative for Docklands development proposed by Labour in the 1970s remained unfulfilled because it rested on an obsolete vision of a manufacturing-based economy. Canary Wharf is in bankruptcy, but more as the consequence of half-hearted governmental commitment than because it was a bad concept. Battery Park City was built on a vacant tract of land adjacent to extremely expensive, very intensively used real estate, making it logical to extend the same use pattern. Unlike the predecessor plan for the site, it managed to attract investor interest, and it represents a far higher quality of development than the earlier plan. Although some of the undertakings I have described – especially the proposed schemes for King's Cross and Times Square – were located in places where better practical alternatives were possible, South Street Seaport, Covent Garden, and Battery Park City have arguably made good use of their sites and need not be condemned just because they are pretty or because they cater to the middle class. The cultural critics are frequently in the same uncomfortable position as their modernist predecessors. They justify their ideas in the name of democracy but speak for an intellectual elite, which seems to be as unanimous in its distaste for the new projects as the popular media are concerted in their praise.

The evaluation of authenticity depends heavily on the taste of the observer, and references to a previous golden age when urban life conformed more closely to the model of tolerant diversity are unconvincing. The aspects of the post-structuralist critique based on the assumptions of contemporary inauthenticity and recollection of a better past fail to persuade. Nevertheless, the core of the post-structuralist argument still remains an important starting point from which to assess the impacts of real-estate development in London and New York. The most important concern of the post-structuralists is with the relationship between spatial configuration, social diversity, and power in a context where social groups are differentiated by class and culture. This facet of their argument, however, also raises problems, which stem from the tension between majoritarian democracy and respect for difference, especially when identity is defined through membership in an ascriptive group.

Democracy, diversity, and cultural identity

The value that post-structuralists place on diversity arises from a vision of democracy in a multicultural, stratified society. Their attack on architectural repetition and spatial segregation asserts that these modes of spatial development neither respond to democratic preferences nor offer subordinate groups a place in which they can both express themselves and interact peacefully with each other. The weakness of their argument is that, if democracy is defined as majoritarianism,[28] most people do not seem to desire diversity. Thus, even though support for recognition of difference arises from a democratic impulse which maintains that people are different but equal and therefore entitled to equal privileges and respect, institutionalized democracy tends to suppress difference. Numerous theoretical and practical attempts have been made to devise a method of combining democracy with difference in the face of majorities demanding conformity, but the underlying contradiction between

234 Real-Estate Development

commitment to majority rule and recognition of the rights and dissonant interests of others remains.[29]

In a recent article, David Harvey (1992) presents the conflict over access to Tompkins Square Park in New York as paradigmatic of contests over the control of space. Parties to the dispute are: the homeless, who squat in the park; motorcycle gangs who raucously convene there; gentrifiers who live in adjacent buildings; land speculators whose property will appreciate in value if the gentrifiers succeed in routing the squatters and motorcyclists; anarchist supporters of the homeless who campaign vociferously and unpleasantly against gentrification; working-class neighborhood residents, many of them immigrants, who dislike the noise, drugs, hostility, and threats to personal safety emanating from the park but also oppose gentrification; and the city government, which eventually used the police to force the occupants out of the park.

The issues raised are classic ones in political theory bearing on the rights of minorities. Opponents of the city's eviction action contend that the government was acting on behalf of real-estate interests, not of the neighborhood (in this interpretation gentrifiers are not considered part of the neighborhood). While that may be the case, it is also true that most residents of the area, including working-class people and long-time occupants, preferred to have the park available for peaceful recreation rather than as a sanctuary for social outcasts. Harvey, to his credit, does not romanticize either the self-proclaimed revolutionaries in the drama nor the benefits of the park as a site for cultural mixing.[30] Instead he (1992, p. 591) remarks: "To hold all the divergent politics of need and desire together within some coherent frame may be a laudable aim, but in practice far too many of the interests are mutually exclusive to allow their mutual accommodation."[31] At this point in the unfolding of his argument, Harvey arrives at the same juncture that he reaches midway in his recent book (Harvey, 1989), after he has identified the set of conflicting social interests based on culture and gender that make up the condition of post-modernity. As in the book, he then escapes the implications of his thesis regarding mutually exclusive interests by reducing the production of invidious difference to capitalism. Thus, while he does not confound all social antagonism with class conflict, he (1992, p. 596) dissolves intractable divisions – differences that pit one group irreconcilably against another – by tracing them back to "the material basis for the production of difference" – that is, the capitalist mode of production.

Harvey's logic leads to the old Marxist dream of a society in which group oppression would disappear along with private ownership of the means of production.[32] Harvey's apparent adherence to this vision seems surprising, given the extent to which it has been discredited by attacks from theorists of racial and gender oppression. Since, however, he does not expect imminent socialist revolution, the point is moot. Rather than discussing system transformation, he (1991, pp. 599–600) endorses planning and public policy under the present economic system that would empower "the oppressed" and give them "the ability to engage in self-expression." The implication is that we always know who is the oppressor and who the oppressed, that the claims of the oppressed should always prevail even if they injure other groups, and that it is possible to attain these ends through democratic procedures.

Harvey's aim of restoring materialist analysis to the discussion of urban form is praiseworthy. Materialist analysis, however, should not simply mean rooting all social phenomena in the organization of production. Material interests also rest in rights to real property, not just in instruments of production (see J. Davis, 1991).[33] Privileged positions in relation to both property and consumption (status positions, in Weberian terms) are far more broadly distributed throughout the population than ownership of the means of production. Furthermore, as Sharon Zukin (1991) correctly points out, the organization of consumption is as important as production in determining relations in space. Consequently a materialist analysis must recognize that a large proportion of the population chooses to exclude others, based on rational calculation and genuine preference. The ineluctable conclusion is that many public policy choices will pit those groups that Harvey designates as oppressed against popular majorities acting on their real interests. And even if the widespread home ownership that underpins middle-class exclusionism is a product of capitalist efforts at legitimation, the interests deriving from it remain real.

There is no easy resolution of the issue of exclusion.[34] The desire of people to live with others sharing similar outlooks and modes of behavior is understandable. Indeed, the post-structuralists are generally willing to grant that right to subordinate groups if they choose to separate themselves, but not to ruling groups.[35] This is not an illogical stance, since subordinate groups are not usually denying others a material benefit (e.g. better schools, access to jobs) in making this choice. Nevertheless, the exclusionism practiced by non-elite groups complicates the problem by undercutting the principle of social integration. In addition, the wish to live in personal safety is obviously legitimate, as Harvey (1992, p. 600) acknowledges, and is most easily obtained through the creation of boundaries. Giving up exclusivity may require real sacrifice of important communal and material values by ordinary people.

In an insightful essay, the political scientist Alan Wolfe (1992) contends that the erection of boundaries may be a defensible endeavor necessary for the maintenance of community, even while it is also discriminatory and harmful to those excluded. He concludes by maintaining that there can be no universal moral principle on the subject, that judgments must be issued case by case. With Wolfe's caution in mind, along with the recognition that we must honor democratic process as well as democratic outcomes, we can examine the overall redevelopment strategy followed in London and New York, as well as the particular projects that were erected and their effects.

WHAT KIND OF PLACE HAVE THE CITY BUILDERS MADE?

London and New York, along with Tokyo, were the leading centers for financial transactions and associated services during the 1980s, a fact which was expressed symbolically and materially in their landscapes. The speculative rather than planned nature of the development process led to the inevitable crash, as too much investment went into expensive real-estate for which there was a limited market. At the same time, not all the strategies were wrong-headed, and not all the projects were ill-conceived. Expanding office employment, new technical requirements for informa-tion-based industries, and shrinking manufacturing sectors dictated revision of land uses. Competition among places for growth industries and the prior specializations of London and New York in finance and business services meant that a strategy catering to those industries made sense. Nevertheless, expansion of commercial space and a high-end service strategy did not necessitate the neglect of manufacturing industry, the almost total failure to address the housing needs of low-income people, and government's abdicating to financial institutions and developers the responsibility for decision-making concerning developmental priorities.

Redevelopment took the form of islands of glittering structures in the midst of decayed public facilities and deterioration in living conditions for the poor. The symbolic statements made by the new, completed projects are irritating – not because their internal environments are obnoxious in themselves but because of the contrast between them and the remainder of the city. The lead public institutions in implementing the development projects of the era – the London Docklands Development Corporation, the London Office of the UK Department of the Environment, the Battery Park City Authority, the New York State Urban Development Corporation, and New York City Public Development Corporation – operated in insulation from democratic inputs. By focusing on the construction of first-class office space, luxury housing, and tourist attractions and shortchanging the affordable housing, small-business, and community-based industry sectors, they encouraged developers to engrave the image of two cities – one for the rich and one for the poor – on the landscape. Private financial institutions were an equally important stimulant to the enterprises undertaken by property developers, and they encouraged the same types of developments as did the public agencies. Developers, because these sorts of projects had the greatest potential for profit, obviously wanted to build them and sold them to the government and financiers (but unfortunately not to tenants at the end).

Two types of developers operated during the boom: conservative builders, who predicted their returns based on rent rolls and did not build without tenant commitments; and speculators, who not only optimistically forecast fully rented buildings even without pre-leasing, but who based their financial projections on expectations of major appreciation in the value of the structures. The speculative developers both played the most active role in lobbying government to rely on property as the basis for economic growth and caused the overbuilding which produced the crash at the end of the decade. (Forest City Ratner, developer of MetroTech in Brooklyn, represented something of an anomaly. Although, like developers in the first category, it worked only when tenants already had signed up – and it reinforced the security of its investments by requiring substantial governmental subsidy – it ventured into untried areas where other developers would not go. Ironically it had much more difficulty obtaining financing than the highly speculative developers who operated in the most prestigious and already most expensive parts of the city.)

In the sobering aftermath of the boom, it has become clear that long-term profitability and growth were injured by the failure to rein in the speculators. Even though economic development was the justification for the pattern of investment that occurred, no one was responsible for calculating aggregate growth targets. Public officials frequently assert that such projections are outside their realm of responsibility and that it is up to private business to foresee demand and shape supply accordingly. Since public funds and deregulation underpinned redevelopment activity, however, the refusal of government to play such a role represented an irresponsible squandering of public resources. The unwillingness to plan comprehensively meant that too much space for the same kind of use was built on too large a scale, while there was insufficient production of needed housing, public services, and infrastructure (especially, in New York, efficient transit to the airports, and, in London, access to Docklands). Making financial and business services the centerpiece of each city's development strategy was not in itself a mistake; the error lay in emphasizing these sectors virtually to the exclusion of all else and relying too much on real estate as the method of encouraging them. Highly uneven outcomes were foreordained by an economic development strategy that did not stress job training and placement and did not involve aggressive efforts to identify industries with the potential to generate employment.

Developing Docklands as an office center was not wrong. The availability of a huge tract of mainly vacant land in the heart of the London metropolitan area represented an enormous asset, and one that rightfully should have been developed for the benefit of all Londoners, not just the small number of nearby residents. It was the government's refusal to bolster the enterprise with major social and educational programs, to halt competitive commercial development elsewhere, and to construct infrastructure in advance of development that created the ultimate debacle. The central government's final unwillingness to subsidize Canary Wharf through putting many of its own offices there, which offered the potential of tiding the development over until it became more accessible, reinforced the shortsightedness of the process.[36]

Some of the other projects whose histories I have chronicled have been better conceived. Plans for Spitalfields, should they ever come to fruition, combining as they do economic and social programming, represent a more sensible approach to area redevelopment than Docklands. The amount of funds committed by the government, however, is small and may well prove inadequate to support the goals of the plan. Downtown Brooklyn reflects a successful strategy to create a new business district, although the level of public subsidy – through supplying infrastructure, providing tax benefits, and renting space – justifies a greater public share of the profits. Battery Park City, despite its luxurious appearance, offers broad benefits. Ongoing governmental ownership of the land has produced significant public revenues for general purposes, for low-income housing, and for the creation of desperately needed green space on the site, which is legally as open to the public as Central Park.

The major projects, except for New York's 42nd Street Redevelopment Project (and potentially, Donald Trump's enormous Riverside South on Manhattan's West Side, which received City Council approval at the end of 1992), can be justified by the same rationale as new towns were. If development nodes are to be established in out-of-the-way locations, substantial front-end investment is necessary to create a critical mass. The periphery of the City of London (site of the Broadgate development), the Docklands, King's Cross railyards, the Battery Park landfill, and downtown Brooklyn all offer prime, vacant, or underutilized territory for large-scale development. The size of structures and types of uses to be placed on them are controversial public policy issues, but there is no *prima facie* argument against investing substantially in their comprehensive development. The great planning disasters are the excess of space put up in the City of London and scattered throughout downtown and midtown Manhattan. Many of these new buildings respond to no genuine demand, seriously overload the environment, and cannot be defended as contributing to the development of new nodes with potential to provide employment to residents living in peripheral areas.

The goal of urban diversity does not need to be met by developing each site for mixed-use, mixed-income, multicultural purposes. The provision of buffers between groups with, in Harvey's words, "interests [that] are mutually exclusive" makes some sense. Mayor David Dinkins likes to refer to the fabric of New York as a "gorgeous mosaic"; in a mosaic there is proximity but also separation. Creating spaces that many people enjoy, even if they do not faithfully reproduce the past, and even if they make some people feel like outcasts, is not in itself so terrible. If we wish to prevent the upper class from invading working-class neighborhoods or wholly isolating itself in suburban enclaves, then we ought not to forbid the creation of housing and offices for the elite in central places, if this can be accomplished without causing displacement.

London and New York have withstood the kinds of extreme exclusionism that the skyway and tunnel systems of cities like Minneapolis and Toronto have produced (Boddy, 1992). Their streets continue to teem with people of seemingly infinite variety, and their neighborhoods mainly abut one another rather than being separated by highways or tracts of wasteland. Successful popular opposition to highway construction and mobilization against some of the most egregious attempts to homogenize the environment have been important in maintaining overall diversity. Community participation, however, has not been sufficiently institutionalized to allow the public to influence the citywide allocation of investment or to formulate plans for neighborhood improvements.

The lack of "strong democracy" (Barber, 1984) and heavy reliance on market determinations has meant that political elites and property development interests have mapped the extant city. Within the realm of policy-making exclusion has indeed happened. Nevertheless, greater inclusion of the public in developmental decision-making would probably not produce the kind of urban environment the post-structuralists seek. Although more resources would find their way outside the central business districts, residents with a vested interest in upgrading the character of their area – including tenants of council housing and rent-regulated structures, as well as both resident and absentee property owners – would try to restrict nonconforming uses and screen out needy persons who threatened their security or life styles. Moreover, more democratic decision-making would unquestionably favor the interests of moderate- and middle-income people in the allocation of housing funds, rather than giving priority to the homeless.

An overall evaluation of the redevelopment process in London and New York and the role of developers within it yields similar broad generalizations to those made about other cities:[37] public-private partnerships were unequal; the process resulted in the construction of spectacular projects that changed the appearance and functioning of the cities but left other areas untouched or deteriorated; over-reliance on property development as an economic growth strategy left unpursued other strategies that would develop worker skills and directly spur job creation and placement. My final chapter proposes a more effective mode of incorporating property redevelopment into a general policy for economic improvement.

NOTES

1 Bacow (1990) indicates that the integrated firm is more common on the European continent.
2 See Logan (1992) for a discussion of the trend toward global firms in the 1980s and its breakdown in the subsequent slump.
3 Balchin et al. (1988, p. 15) list a number of factors that make the property market inefficient and always disequilibrated. These include, *inter alia*: the uniqueness of each site and building, illiquidity, the legal rights of property interests, the influence of conservationists, and the slowness of response to changes in demand.
4 At times firms have managed to obtain monopoly prices because of the scarcity resulting from governmental restrictions on construction; these restrictions, however, were ostensibly aimed at environmental protection, not price support.
5 Peter Marcuse, in a number of discussions that we have had, argues that property markets are wholly demand-driven. After considerable thought I have decided that my disagreement with him comes from differing concepts of demand. He regards demand as an objectively measurable force; I consider it to be largely a matter of perception. Consequently what I see as the supply of capital pushing developers to create the product could as well be interpreted as production being elicited by suppliers' perception of demand.
6 Harvey (1982, p. 261) comments: "Indeed, since money capitalists absorb rather than generate surplus value, we may well wonder why capitalism tolerates such seeming parasites."
7 Ball (1983, p. 146) distinguishes between rent and development profit, the latter being a consequence of development activity rather than land price. The distinction, however, is impossible to apply when urban land is in question, since land price does not exist independently of the value generated by agglomeration.
8 My argument, as should be obvious, does not rely on the labor theory of value. Rather I see value as arising more generally out of social relationships and accept the classical economist's view of the intersection of supply and demand as denoting the value of a commodity at a given time. This acceptance, however, does not imply that I regard the shape of the supply and demand curves as a legitimate outcome of a fair distribution of income or of choices

freely made. Nor does it mean that total value equals the aggregate of the individual values of commodities produced. The value of a pair of shoes versus the sum of the value of two left shoes is a mundane example of why simple aggregates fail to indicate the value of an ensemble.

Marxism has two separate concepts of value, neither one of which is satisfactory. In the first, the labor theory of value purports to explain exchange values. The observed discrepancies between the aggregated cost of average labor time in a product and the price of the product, however, force believers in the labor theory of value into endless contortions of epicyclic dimensions to retain its applicability (the distinction between productive and unproductive labor further muddles the issue). In the second, exchange values are contrasted to use values but there is no theorized relationship between use value and labor value, except that in a communist society they would be identical.

9 See Gans (1968) for analyses of the class biases of planners and their assumptions concerning the impact of physical form; see Castells (1977, chapter 5) for a critique of Wirth and the ecological approach to urban sociology.

10 See Saunders (1986) for a summary and critique of the Marxist arguments.

11 Much of this recent work traces back to Henri Lefebvre's (1991; original French edition, 1974) arguments, which, while rooting space in the mode of production, imbued it also with transcendent power: "'Change life!' 'Change society!' These precepts mean nothing without the production of an appropriate space. . . . new social relationships call for a new space, and vice versa" (Lefebvre, 1991, p. 59). Lefebvre (1991, p. 33) divides his analysis of space into three parts: (1) spatial practice, referring to the way in which space is used; (2) representations of space, alluding to the design of spatial forms; and (3) representational spaces, embodying the symbolic meaning of space.

12 An article by R.J. King (1988, p. 445) contends that "urban design is . . . concerned with *the purposive production of urban meaning* (the 'urban symbolic'), to be seen as a subset of the broader *production and reproduction (both purposive and otherwise) of urban meaning*" (italics in original).

13 See, *inter alia*, Sennett (1990); Gottdiener (1985); Sorkin (1992b); Young (1990); Harvey (1992); Soja (1989); M. Davis (1990); Zukin (1991); Judd (forthcoming).

14 Many observers have commented on the private character of the American city throughout its history (see Warner, 1968, for the best-known such analysis). Thus, the recent crescendo of opprobrium is only a matter of degree.

15 Interestingly this analysis recapitulates Dahl's depiction of pluralism in *Who Governs?*, where his picture of multiple elites depended on their each operating in their own sphere. Dahl viewed the resulting dispersion as a cause of celebration as it provided multiple spheres of power. The post-structuralists are less willing to regard those issue arenas shunned by economic dominants as domains of power.

16 Few of the post-structuralists, of course, would accept the Prince's image of a

mythologized traditional England as appropriate either.

17 R. Robertson (1990, p. 54) distinguishes between contemporary nostalgia, which he sees as intimately bound up in consumerism, and the "wilful, synthetic" nostalgia of the late nineteenth and early twentieth century, which was intended to stimulate nationalist loyalties.

18 The post-structuralist rejection of nostalgia embodied in architectural reference does not preclude the critics' own nostalgia for a time when architecture was not used for manipulative purposes.

19 Oscar Newman's (1972) pioneering work on defensible space initially appeared to be a more humane method of offering protection than the cruder devices of forcible removal or legalized violence. Present interpretations see defensible space as only a subtler form of cruelty.

20 I know of no survey research that indicates the mix of people using the new retail centers nor, if such exists, are there data that would allow us to compare it to earlier counterparts.

21 Suburban exclusion is much more extreme than what exists in the central areas. To the extent that suburbanization has meant a great increase in the absolute physical distance between different population groups and decreased the likelihood that they will ever cross paths at all, the argument that greater diversity once existed deserves credence. For people who actually enter the urban core, however, their likelihood of contact with someone very different from themselves has not clearly decreased.

22 Marx's concept of unproductive labor and David Harvey's use of the term "fictitious capital" are similar negations of activities that do not produce sweat.

23 Dennis Judd, who criticizes the exclusionary aspects of shopping malls and mixed-used megaprojects but does not go so far as to issue a blanket condemnation of all their aspects (see Judd forthcoming), commented to me that the writings on festive marketplaces and Disneyland display an unfortunate tendency to sneer at people for having fun.

24 Conventional economists avoid such arguments altogether by asserting that interpersonal comparisons of utility are impossible.

25 Gans (1988, p. x), without wholly endorsing the tastes and prejudices of middle America, reacts strongly against the cultural elite that would dismiss the middle strata as "right-wing racists, greedy materialists, or uncultured 'Joe Sixpacks.'" Many of the cultural critics seem to reject anyone who actually likes the targets of their opprobrium as manipulated or narrow-minded.

26 Within the United States, and to some extent the United Kingdom, the ability of middle-class people to escape the tax burden of supporting service-dependent populations by fleeing to the suburbs does, however, contribute substantially to the problems mentioned.

27 Paul Knox (1993, p. 258 and n.1), who edited the book in which the above quotation appears and who is otherwise generally sympathetic to post-structuralist insights, remarks in exasperation concerning David Harvey's negative assessment of Baltimore's Inner Harbor development: "Harvey does not say what alternative uses for a decaying industrial landscape he might propose." Knox notes that he was led to his observation concerning the Inner

Harbor by the enthusiasm of a black Baltimore cab driver over the business that the development had generated for him.

28 According to Tocqueville (1957, p. 264), "the very essence of democratic government consists in the absolute sovereignty of the majority."

29 The classic theoretical treatment is Rousseau's distinction between the general will and the will of all, wherein the general will represents the social good. The general will desires what everyone would want if each person understood his or her long-term interests, while the will of all embodies the self-serving, narrow interests of individuals. The practical solution incorporated in the United States Constitution and other similar founding documents invests rights in minorities that cannot be contravened by majorities.

30 Harvey's description of the situation builds on the work of Neil Smith (1992), which, more than Harvey's analysis, identifies the squatters as the good guys and the neighborhood residents who long for peace and quiet as the bad guys.

31 A socialist academic of my acquaintance, who lives near the park, admitted to me that while he strongly opposed the police action, he had found life pleasanter since its occurrence.

32 Political theorists are much more inclined than other social philosophers to regard conflicting interests as inherent in social life and to seek ways of managing conflict. Marxists and other social constructionists view conflicting interests as created by elites protecting their privileges; their aim is to dissipate hierarchy and thereby extirpate conflict.

33 J. E. Davis (1991, chapter 5) sees neighborhoods as divided into four property interest groups: property capitalists, owner-occupiers, tenants, and the homeless.

34 Contemplation of this issue caused me to list my own inclusions and exclusions and recognize their inconsistencies. I endorse women's colleges but not men's clubs. I think that public funds should fund high-brow public radio even though its listeners are a small elite group. I support racial integration in schools but not necessarily class mixing, at least in practice – I moved my family from a white lower-middle-class school district, where my children got regularly beaten up, to a racially integrated, but much more homogeneously upper-middle-class district. I attended an elite private university (as did many of the critics of Battery Park City), and while I have many ambivalences about that institution, I do not regret going there. I live in an extremely crowded, mixed-use section of Manhattan, but my favorite vacation resorts are far less diversely populated than Disney World, although mainly as a consequence of taste and inaccessibility rather than control by their owners. Although I am identifiably Jewish, I intensely dislike the particularism of American Jewish groups and strongly reject their "chosen people" stance. I favor a multicultural curriculum but feel that such an approach should criticize subordinate as well as dominant groups.

35 The analysis, however, fails to examine whether or not individuals who belong to ascriptive groups necessarily wish to identify themselves fully with their group. Thus, for example, Iris Marion Young (1990) falls into the trap of

subsuming the individual in the group and assuming that the standpoint politics of group leaders represents the genuine desire of members.

36 Critics of Docklands development oppose forced moving of civil servants to the Isle of Dogs on the grounds that they should not be made to pay for the government's mistakes. The Treasury opposes the government's paying anything but the rock-bottom rent. In New York, however, use of the strategy of relocating government offices has succeeded in stabilizing real-estate markets and is probably worth the disruption and short-term expenditures it causes.

37 See chapter 1, note 14.

11

Development Policy for the Inner City

Four intertwined aspects of inner city real-estate development define the crux of policy debate: (1) government's use of land development as an instrument for stimulating economic growth; (2) the exclusion of the public from decisions about property; (3) the impact of public and private development activity on the environment; and (4) the influence of public and private development activity on social equity. The last issue has two facets: the direct impacts of projects on different social groupings, and the extent to which the public receives the benefits of socially created gain in the value of property.

ECONOMIC GROWTH

One of the themes of this book has been the over-reliance of government on the property industry as the vehicle for growth policy. In the short run, during the peak of the real-estate market, the economic effects of property-led development were mixed. Deregulation and assistance to developers did not guarantee that benefits would be translated into increased employment. Moreover, while demand was robust, nothing forced developers to reduce prices to occupants, even when development costs had been lowered by governmental action. It appears that when prices were very high during the 1980s, government subsidy and regulatory relief had an inflationary effect, much of it being capitalized into land values rather than bringing down the cost of doing business. In its long-term effect, governmental assistance reinforced the expansion of the supply of space at the upper ends of the commercial and residential markets until supply greatly exceeded demand. At this point the market abruptly plummeted, and the large amounts of vacant space acted as a millstone on the economy.

We would like to know if firms were attracted to inner London and New York City because of the various public incentives to development. Unfortunately there is no clear-cut answer to this question. Part of the attraction of London and New York in the eighties was an amorphous quality which indicated that they were the right places to be. Governmental programs contributed to that perception. Moreover, New York, and, to a lesser extent, London faced competitive incentive programs from other cities and their own suburban peripheries which forced them into offering similar advantages. On the other hand, many firms in finance and related industries had to have offices in these global centers, regardless of comparative cost, and developers would have responded to this demand even without publicly provided incentives.

What makes the question genuinely imponderable is the agglomerative quality of urban development. Other attractions outweigh cost disadvantages in locational decision-making when a critical mass of skilled workers, market opportunities, and prestige exists in a place. Would London and New York have had such a critical mass without government prompting? At the beginning of the decade both cities were viewed as being in serious decline. They overcame this judgment, but to disentangle the role of policy in achieving this result is nearly impossible. Certainly some credit should go to governmental efforts. The policy issue is how they can be improved.

Economic planning

Public redevelopment programs and assistance to the private sector can form part of a sensible program for long-term economic growth. They need, however, to be within the context of economic planning. A good economic plan for a city would set levels of desired space for each market sector and each part of the city, with subsidies and regulatory relief geared to these objectives. The aim of policy should not simply be to create more space but rather to ensure that there is enough space to support industry without glutting the market. Such a strategy, in addition to contributing to stable economic growth, would, by maintaining price levels in the sector, make more funds available to government for social purposes, through increasing the property tax base. If government could also ensure its participation in development profit in return for its assistance, it would have a further source of revenue.

Economic planning has always been largely anathema in the United States and has no constituency among the Tories who now govern the United Kingdom.[1] But, along the Japanese model, without unduly interfering with the market, government can identify sectors it will assist and only provide that assistance if businesses within the sector conform to the government's strategy. Such planning would only represent intelligent supervision of governmental expenditure.[2] Whatever errors of forecasting might be made, they could not be worse than offering subsidies and exemptions from planning regulations indiscriminately. The assistance provided developers in London by the London Docklands Development Corporation (LDDC) and the Docklands enterprise zone and in New York by a plethora of incentive programs already constitute market intervention. What they lack are any controls to insure that the public sector will gain from its efforts.

Strategies

The governments of both London and New York not only did relatively little to encourage growth in economic sectors where large property developers were not pressing them for assistance, but they allowed important industries to be injured due to high rents. Rather than seeking ways to encourage economic diversity within the central areas, they let speculative office buildings drive out all other uses. Thus, for example, even though many studies have identified the arts as extremely significant components of the economies of New York and London,[3] arts groups were forced out of centrally located space because they could not afford it. Such was also the fate of numerous small businesses and non-profit organizations. While the New York City government was actively bringing down the occupancy costs of Chase Manhattan Bank and Morgan Stanley, it ignored the situation of drama groups, bookstores, artists' workshops, galleries, acting studios, coffeehouses, and rehearsal halls which were going bankrupt or losing their leases. In London, within the West End and the City, developers were encouraged to redevelop the "marginal" space that housed "marginal" businesses. It was somehow assumed that such businesses did not have an economic future rather than regarding them as essential components of the complex fabric of the city and the possible progenitors of future expansion.

In the speculative frenzy of the 1980s, developers projected future returns on a linear extrapolation of escalating rents and were therefore willing to pay extremely high prices for land acquisition. They thereby incurred indebtedness which could only be covered through gargantuan buildings and a wholly unrealistic rental structure that was destined to destroy their market as occupancy costs forced tenants out of business. The tragedy for the city as a whole was the destruction of industries ranging from light manufacturing to theater production, which could not easily be restored once cheap space again became available after the boom.

In the conventional theory of land markets no harm results from constant competition for space and awarding it to the highest bidder. The phenomenon of high rents chasing high profits, however, produces great instability, particularly among retailers, entertainment purveyors, and restaurateurs, as eventually they must raise their prices beyond the reach of their customers in order to pay their rent. The doctrine of "highest and best use" justifies planning that pushes low-return businesses to the periphery and reserves the center for the most remunerative. Theoretically, new nodes of experimental theater can be produced in outlying areas like Lambeth or Brooklyn; craft workshops can move to peripheral locations like Hounslow or Queens. Unfortunately, communities of specialists are not usually portable, and a critical mass may never be re-created, or at least not within the same metropolitan area. Furthermore, for those industries that require proximity to high-income consumers, the distance between Mayfair and Hounslow, the Upper East Side and Brooklyn, is insurmountable.[4]

Good economic policy would aim to stabilize those sectors which harbor innovation or give the city a unique competitive advantage. London and New York have traditionally been magnets for talented people. In addition, they afford markets for highly specialized businesses that cannot survive elsewhere. Although the gross revenues of such enterprises may not allow them to bid for expensive locations, they create a milieu that gives these cities their special attraction. Policies to encourage economic diversity would reinforce the functions of creativity and specialized activity. Inexpensive refurbishment of older buildings to serve as incubators for a variety of for-profit and non-profit businesses can assist in fostering originality and maintaining complexity. Very moderate commercial rent control, limiting rent increases to, say, 40 percent upon renewal of a lease and less thereafter, can keep the short-term greed of landlords from driving potentially long-term tenants out of business through rent rises in multiples of the original amount.

Greater emphasis on assisting the non-profit sector presents another strategy for ensuring stable growth. Within both London and New York an enormous array of non-profit organizations ranging from charitable trusts to hospitals to trade groups provide large numbers of jobs and are much more insulated from global economic competition than multinational corporations. Public-sector investment in appropriate space for such entities can contribute much more to steady overall economic growth than high public expenditure to attract front-office facilities of corporations subject to mergers. Outside the central areas much more financial and technical support for local enterprises would diminish the need to seek ways of attracting outside investors. In New York local economic development corporations (LDCs) offer a framework for such assistance, which could become much more significant if President Clinton fulfills his campaign promise to establish local development banks. Secure funding for LDCs would release their staffs from devoting the greater part of their time to raising money rather than operating programs. In London, where the LDC vehicle does not exist, cooperatives offer a similar opportunity.

I part company with many of my progressive colleagues by endorsing large-scale planned development of business centers on un- or under-utilized peripheral sites. The old central business districts of London and New York are overcrowded and distant from populations living in outer areas. Intensifying uses within them is environmentally and socially destructive. Consequently I think that Canary Wharf and MetroTech, located on largely vacant land in working-class districts sufficiently close to the old centers to be potentially attractive to business, justified government promotion. MetroTech, albeit expensive, has succeeded in stimulating the economic development of Brooklyn; its deficiencies lie in the failure of government to ensure that it be connected with job training and placement programs and that the public sector receive more financial return from its sizable input. The success of Canary Wharf would have required much greater governmental commitment to infrastructure investment, associated employment and social programs, assuring occupancy through use by its own agencies, and restrictions of development elsewhere. In return for pledging this kind of support, the government could have retained rights to the site and obtained ground rent of the sort that the Battery Park City Authority receives in New York and spends on low-income housing.

Improved public-private partnerships

There are four conceivable sources of risk capital for economic regeneration: the private, for-profit sector; the state; employee savings and benefit funds; and the non-profit sector. Each has advantages and disadvantages. To attract private capital to territories not regarded as inherently profitable by capitalist managers, state officials feel compelled to offer incentives, with all the likely negative consequences discussed in this book. Direct state participation in quasi-governmental corporations can save failing industries and permits greater public control of the outcomes than state subsidy of purely private entities. (The effect of AMTRAK, the

US passenger railroad corporation which connects a number of old US central cities and whose revival has spun off an important employment and retailing multiplier, is a good example of revitalization through the use of this kind of instrument). Such corporations, though, when they are profitable and capitalized on a large scale, tend to behave little differently from private firms (Rueschemeyer and Evans, 1985, pp. 57–9) and will also seek least-cost locations. In contrast, firms run directly by the state will be less profit-oriented and, theoretically at least, susceptible to democratic control. They tend, however, to avoid risks, invest insufficiently, and avoid cost-reduction measures.

Critics of business-dominated arrangements who recognize the necessity of tapping into private capital need to devise innovative versions of the public-private partnership. This means a reorientation away from manufacturing toward the service sector, recognition of the importance of management and entrepreneurship, and coming to terms with the multinational corporation. The reality that giant multinational, service-producing corporations dominate economic transactions means that progressive policy-makers must find ways of tapping into their economic power rather than dismissing them on moral grounds. Public-private partnerships under these conditions are inevitable; what needs to be done is ensure that the public component is more controlling and shares more in the proceeds.[5]

Public-private partnerships can involve the participation of small firms. Public assistance to consulting, computer, high-tech, restaurant franchise, nursing home, home health care, and similar enterprises, as well as small-scale manufacturing, could generate a stable, small-business sector to occupy inner-city sites. Such arrangements, however, will raise equity problems. If small businesses are to thrive, they will involve internal hierarchies with returns to managers sufficient to induce competent, experienced individuals to assume those roles. Managers will require discretion in rewarding worker performance. Under such an approach, social equalization, if it is to occur, would come through redistribution within the tax and welfare system rather than the firm. In other words, even a progressive policy toward inner-city redevelopment will generate serious inequalities in the rewards to labor if it is to stimulate growth.

Eisinger (1988) especially emphasizes the expanding public role in identifying product niches for local industry, promoting product development, training workers for firms in expanding areas, and marketing local outputs. The typical version of these endeavors, as in the public-private partnership and the venture capital funds, allows public assumption of the risk and private appropriation of the profit. A better model would be the hotel and convention bureaus of many municipalities, where a tax on receipts supports their marketing efforts.

Eisinger notes that some states participate in royalties from inventions resulting from state participation in product innovation. As a general rule, the more public bodies are assured of a revenue stream keyed to profits that derive from public investment, the better the community can protect itself from the continual undercutting of the public fisc caused by anti-tax pressures.

PRIVATE DECISION-MAKING AND PUBLIC OVERSIGHT

Developers who work within central business districts are generally inclined to think that they are dangerously over-regulated – although London's property entrepreneurs, having experienced the effect of deregulation, are having second thoughts. To the extent that regulation does exist, it is usually tied to environmental rather than economic effects. Government scrutiny of the financial viability of development enterprises is restricted to evaluating bids for particular sites in response to a government's request for proposals. The high externalities of developmental decisions, however, mean that the consequences of developers' decisions are widely felt. Therefore, as discussed above, economic planning measures are necessary.

Greater direct governmental intervention, however, would exacerbate tensions that already exist over questions of representation in planning decisions. The rise of urban development corporations in both London and New York responded to the purported inefficiencies of elected governmental bodies in determining priorities and implementing economic development strategies. These corporations exclude direct community input in their deliberations; in addition, some – like the LDDC and the New York State Urban Development Corporation – can make land-use decisions without seeking approval from the elected bodies of the territories where they work. The staff members and boards of these organizations consider that they do their best to represent the interests of the public. They view protesting community groups as narrowly favoring their own interests and unable to conceptualize or sacrifice for programs that would benefit the whole city. The community groups, on the other hand, justifiably feel that they bear the costs of improvements while others realize the gain, that wealthy citizens are rarely asked to give up their privileges for the common good, and that their intimate knowledge of their neighborhoods is disregarded.

I remember attending a meeting between the staff of New York's 42nd Street Development Corporation and the "Midtown Citizens Committee," a community group consisting predominately of major business executives and other notables in the area.[6] The event took place in the penthouse boardroom of the New York Telephone Company. The concerns of the Clinton neighborhood, which was vehemently opposing the development corporation's plans, seemed as remote to the assembled persons as the pedestrians 42 stories below. To them the working-class populace of Clinton appeared only obstructionist, and their own desire to turn Times Square into a high-rise office district seemed forward-looking and public-spirited. Many of those attending the meeting did not stand to gain personally from the project. None of them, however, was capable of the act of empathy required to put themselves in the place of the vociferous neighborhood's residents, who, unlike these suave, well-dressed "citizens," tended to be rude, scruffy, and suspicious of newcomers to the area.

It is an extremely difficult task to devise an appropriate system for land use and economic development planning that takes metropolitan area-wide considerations into account, operates efficiently and effectively, involves citizens in reviewing development proposals without succumbing to the "not-in-my-backyard" syndrome ("NIMBYism,") and responds to initiatives emanating from urban neighborhoods. Because planning must cope with genuine conflicts of interest, trade-offs between long- and short-term considerations, and considerable uncertainty over the results of any project, no process will produce a fully satisfactory result. Nevertheless, the creation of a planning framework like the old Greater London Development Plan would allow inputs at various levels.

The current jurisdictional systems of both London and New York make comprehensive planning impossible. London has no authoritative planning unit; New York has one, but only for part of the metropolitan area. London does have adequately staffed local authorities to run the process at the community level, but New York's community boards have insufficient resources and staff support to be vehicles for extensive planning. A significant planning effort in the two cities would require major institutional innovation.

The past failures of planners, as evidenced in highway programs, urban renewal, and modernist council estates, make recommendations for more planning suspect. Mine are made on the optimistic assumption that planners can learn from their mistakes, that in fact they were learning at the time the urban renewal program was terminated in the United States and council house-building virtually ended in Britain. Planners had learned to recognize the costs of destroying social communities and developing out-of-scale projects; they had increasingly incorporated citizen participation, housing rehabilitation, and coordination of housing and social services into these programs in the years before their surcease. There is, therefore, reason to hope that a revival of planning could produce a more sensitive process. Most important, without such an effort urban populations will remain hostage to "private" decisions shielded from democratic scrutiny despite their public significance.

Environmental decisions

Environmental protection and improvement have been the traditional concerns of public planning. During the 1980s restrictions on building heights, bulk, and transit impacts were jettisoned in order to encourage development. In New York planners discovered that they could use zoning bonuses to gain concessions from developers without pecuniary costs to the city. In the City of London the Corporation, threatened by competition from the Docklands, threw out environmental restrictions so that developers would continue to build there. Even though systematic extension of the central business district into derelict riverfront sites, with simultaneous restrictions on development elsewhere, represents a superior land-use strategy to intensification of development in already overbuilt areas, the London governing powers abjured such an approach. This approach would have denied autonomy to the City of London local authority – in conflict with the goal of devolving planning from the metropolitan level – and it would have contravened the avowed intention of the government to overcome obstacles to development. In the actual case, Britain got centralized decision-making for the Docklands and local jurisdiction for the City of London; this inconsistency produced the worst of all possible worlds, with massive development in both places.

Social equity

Social equity demands a balanced redevelopment policy which addresses the distributional effects of economic development and provides for consumption as well as investment needs. As most studies of redevelopment show, policy aimed at growth had little regard for social impacts. Better policy requires the coordination of economic and social programs, including the integration of employment and redevelopment programs; linking of housing and office construction; much higher and more consistent levels of subsidy for affordable housing; opportunities for small business in publicly assisted commercial developments; and measures to ensure that any corporation that receives public-sector benefits be prevented from cashing in and then decamping.

The flaw of the progressive critique of redevelopment, with which I am otherwise generally sympathetic, is that it focuses on provisions for consumption (housing, parks, daycare centers, etc.) and does not offer a formula for growth. So far the left has not discovered an effective method for stimulating substantial investment in declining areas that differs significantly from the business subsidy approach of the right, except that it would direct more assistance toward manufacturing. The task is to formulate a strategy that is as activist as and less destructive than the *modus operandi* of typical urban growth coalitions. Social democrats need to do what is necessary to foster incentives and reward entrepreneurship. Without a program for growth, progressives have little chance of achieving or retaining political power. Criticisms of the depredations caused by unregulated capital or prescriptions for cooperative industry are insufficient. Most people will accept growing inequality in preference to stagnation or absolute decline in the standard of living.

Advocates for the poor must also be mindful of the political opposition to extremely redistributional programs. In New York supporters of the homeless insist that their clients should receive absolute preference for subsidized housing. Consequently they sacrifice the political backing of the middle class and working poor. Moreover, by totally dissociating any criterion of worthiness from eligibility for public benefits, they contravene the deeply held beliefs of most people. Distinctions between the deserving and undeserving poor are indeed invidious. But refusal to recognize that low-wage workers may have as strong a claim to housing assistance as jobless substance abusers is not clearly the morally superior position. If equality is the only value one seeks to maximize, and if one sees all bad behavior as socially caused, then a purely redistributional policy is consistent. Acceptance of democratic norms that require yielding to majority views, however, as well as a desire to reward individual effort, leads to a more balanced policy that reserves a substantial portion of aid for people who are in want but are not the poorest. To say that everyone who needs it should receive assistance evades the issue of how to set priorities when resources are insufficient to fulfill that goal.

To speak of the tasks for progressive local forces without noting their national context is to dodge a central issue. Cities are limited in their autonomy not only by general economic forces but also by the national political system of which they form a part. Ideological, institutional, and fiscal factors constrain their ability to operate in political isolation from the rest of the nation. Within the United States in the Reagan-Bush years and in the United Kingdom to this date, progressive local regimes must swim against the ideological current. They have difficulty maintaining a broad base of support when the national propaganda attack pictures them as "loony' or unrealistic. In the northern European states, where planning and social welfare still retain much greater legitimacy, national regimes are less inclined to glorify the unshackled free market and therefore they give localities greater capabilities for managing development.

London and New York, despite the battering of recession, remain dominant economic powers within the world. Good redevelopment policy means nurturing the special attributes of these diverse places so that creativity is not overwhelmed by overspecialization in finance and business services. It requires recognizing the potential contribution to growth of other sectors in the economy. It further means that first priority be given to the welfare of the mass of citizens and that policy be assessed in terms of its direct effects on the comfort and employment prospects of popular majorities, with particular attention given to its impact on those most directly affected. There is no simple formula for providing growth with equity or efficient yet participatory planning. These nevertheless must be the overriding ambitions for policy-makers and the guiding propositions for their efforts at urban redevelopment.

NOTES

1 It is inconceivable that any private business would make capital expenditures without specifying output targets and calculating in advance the impacts of increasing production.
2 The Labour-sponsored Greater London Enterprise Board (GLEB) did do economic planning and provides something of a model. By refusing to accept the reality of big capital's role in shaping the city and by engaging in wishful thinking concerning the industrial future of London, however, the GLEB was not as effective as it might have been.
3 See, for example, O'Neill and Moss (1991) and Coopers & Lybrand Deloitte (1991b).
4 For a discussion of the importance of place and the effects of disaggregation, see Fainstein and Markusen (1993).
5 Robert Beauregard (1989) discusses the importance of the state playing a role in requiring preferential hiring agreements for residents when it participates in development. His analysis is restricted to construction hiring, but the principle can be extended to operating firms.
6 Its members included the president of the Shubert Organization, New York's largest theater owner; Celeste Holm, the actress; and Vincent Sardi, the owner of the famous restaurant bearing his name.

Appendix A

Social Science Analyses of Urban Redevelopment

Most analyses of urban redevelopment have been built around case studies of individual cities. The more ambitious of these works develop theories concerning the crucial determinants of urban change.[1] Understanding urban redevelopment, however, was not the central issue for the first case studies that dealt with this subject. Rather, it simply constituted an arena in which to study the question of urban power structures. Thus, Robert Dahl's *Who Governs?* (1961) and a number of subsequent reanalyses of New Haven, Connecticut,[2] examined decision-making in that city's urban renewal program but did not scrutinize the outcomes of redevelopment. Nevertheless, Dahl and his associates, Nelson Polsby and Raymond Wolfinger, generally assumed that redevelopment was a widely beneficial goal, as the title of Wolfinger's book, *The Politics of Progress* (1974) implies.[3] Critics of their work, however, attacked it for overlooking the costs of redevelopment programs to poor and minority groups (see N. Fainstein and S. Fainstein, 1986a).

For the decade of the 1960s, the power-structure debate dominated American discourse on urban politics. But as racial issues, urban social movements, and anti-poverty efforts turned the urban arena into a battlefield, the scope of discussion widened considerably beyond Dahl's initial formulation. The riots and urban social movements of the later part of the decade made racial divisions a central issue for urban research, whereas Dahl had omitted discussions of race almost entirely from his investigation of New Haven. Bachrach and Baratz (1962), in their critique of the pluralists, argued that in order to understand power, one must ask who benefits as well as who governs. As their thesis began to prevail, analyses of decision-making shifted to examinations of the effects of public policy, and the benign assumptions concerning the progressive qualities of urban renewal were dropped.[4] Thus, doubtless to the surprise of Robert Dahl, *Who Governs?* stimulated a body of research that ultimately connected redevelopment policy with the social and economic roots of decision-making and formed the basis for much of the later writing on urban political economy, as will be discussed below. Although these studies conflicted on whether redevelopment coalitions could actually claim credit for economic growth, they generally agreed on the regressive distributional consequences of almost all central-city redevelopment programs.[5]

In the United Kingdom urban politics emerged more slowly as a field of study than it did in the US. The much weaker position of British local government, as well as the lesser prominence of urban social movements there, had much to do with this relative obscurity. Studies of redevelopment were carried out for a variety of purposes rather than, as in the US, to contribute to the evolving debate on community power. A number of works stressed planning, housing, and redevelopment for their own sake, reflecting the much stronger UK planning tradition. Unlike the Americans, British investigators spent little time debating whether seeming consensus on redevelopment programs had been manipulated, since the conflicting programs of the Labour and Conservative Parties made dissension obvious. Rather they concerned themselves more with the functions of planning for capital accumulation and legitimation. British authors were less inclined from the start to examine public decision-making in isolation from its broader economic and social context, and they therefore scrutinized the relationship between economic transformation, class structure, and urban form earlier than did their American counterparts.[6]

EXPLANATIONS OF REDEVELOPMENT POLICY

Explanations for the redevelopment story described in chapter 1 fit into liberal and structuralist frameworks, with an overlapping third category designated regime theory. At the risk of injustice to the range of works within the types described, the next sections provide a brief overview of the principal arguments.

Liberal theories

Liberal analyses stress the importance of choice in producing redevelopment scenarios. They can be divided according to their stress on economic or political factors in shaping redevelopment activities. Conventional economically oriented studies identify regularities in the urban growth process and generally trace the changing fortunes of cities to the effects of economic competition, suburbanization, and technological change on the attractiveness of places (see, for example, Sternlieb and Hughes, 1975; P. Peterson, 1981). The response of city officials to urban decline, according to this depiction, results from the need to compensate for competitive disadvantage by offering incentives to industry. This viewpoint is not incompatible with structuralist analysis but rather, within that framework, represents a superficial explanation, since it does not account for the forces underlying the ceaseless competition among places, the contradictions that such competition creates, the necessary relationship between uneven development and profit, the dependence of the democratic state on capital, and the power exerted by business to bias the outcomes of the process.

Another, more political strand of liberal thought separates economic and political power and stresses the role of political decisions. Dahl (1961) and Polsby (1963), writing before the resurgence of Marxist thought in the 1970s, were more concerned with contesting the single-elite model than with confronting structuralism. Implicit in their focus on local decision-making, however, was a rejection of economic determinism. They regarded the local decision-making stratum as comprising multiple elites that specialized in different issue areas. Redevelopment was only one of these areas and was not of great salience to most people. The key decision-making role belonged to public officials, who were checked by popular sentiment as expressed through elections. Savitch (1988) provides an updated version of pluralist thought. While incorporating state theory into his model and thus somewhat parting company with his predecessors, he explicitly repudiates neo-Marxist arguments, contending that the most power is held by elected officials, who "can pursue an autonomous path and exercise great discretion" (Savitch, 1988, p. 7). The numerous critiques of pluralism in the power structure debate focused on its failure to comprehend the systemic privileging of business and to examine the distribution of benefits.

The more radical writers within the liberal tradition consider redevelopment a more central issue than do the pluralists and regard politics as the confrontation between elite and community rather than the jockeying of constrained elites acting within the confines of popular consensus. This group differs from the structuralists, however, in identifying progrowth coalitions rather than ineluctable economic pressures as the reason why business elites are favored within the redevelopment process (Mollenkopf, 1978; Molotch, 1980; M. Smith, 1988). This argument allows for greater local variation and the overcoming of dominant coalitions by counter-mobilization through both protest movements and voting. It stresses voluntarism in the formation of political groupings rather than the economic logic that structuralists see as causing people to join urban social movements.

The left liberals, however, fail to demonstrate that redevelopment programs ever favor non-elite groups over the long term. Such a finding would be necessary in order fully to contradict structuralist analyses. Their argument that business groups do not get their way automatically but must organize themselves and follow conscious political strategies indicates indeterminacy in the urban system. But it does not show that outcomes can routinely favor majorities of the population or that lower-income groups typically participate in dominant coalitions or that the democratic capitalist system offers the potential for such a situation. They create a straw person by caricaturing the Marxist argument as depicting absolute domination by business and the logic of capital rather than only claiming the privileged position of capital and the dependence of government and the working population on the investment decisions of capitalists.

Structuralist theory

I use the term "structuralist" to refer to theories giving primacy to economic relations in determining social actions. Although such theories are rooted in Marxist thought, their more recent manifestations break with Marxist determinism and economic reductionism to such an extent as to make the label "Marxist" misleading.

Contemporary structuralist explanations refer to the logic of capital operating in an era of global restructuring and the class antagonism arising from the economic system. Within this tradition, however, analyses vary as to whether they stress production or collective consumption in their analysis of the built environment.

Functions of redevelopment

Many observers, liberal and structuralist alike, have noted the correlation between urbanization and economic growth. Employers need proximity to labor pools, and producers require access to suppliers and to markets. Economic actors therefore cluster around each other or near to transportation nodes and telecommunications facilities so as to overcome the friction of distance. The structuralist twist on this recognition of the advantages of agglomeration displays two aspects: first, that the form of agglomeration is in tune with the interests of capitalists rather than the preferences of workers or consumers; and second, that any particular agglomeration is unstable because it embodies underlying contradictions. In the words of David Harvey (1985a, p. 190):

> Capital flow presupposes tight temporal and spatial coordinations in the midst of increasing separation and fragmentation. It is impossible to imagine such a material process without the production of some kind of urbanization as a "rational landscape" within which the accumulation of capital can proceed. Capital accumulation and the production of urbanization go hand in hand.
>
> This perspective deserves modification on two counts. Profit depends upon realizing the surplus value created in production within a certain time. The turnover time of capital . . . is a very important magnitude. . . . Competition produces strong pressures to accelerate turnover time. The same pressure has a spatial manifestation. Since movement across space takes time and money, competition forces capitalism toward the elimination of spatial barriers and "the annihilation of space by time." Building a capacity for increased efficiency of coordination in space and time is one of the hallmarks of capitalist urbanization. Considerations derived from a study of the circulation of capital dictate, then, that the urban matrix and the "rational landscape" for accumulation be subject to continuous transformations. In this sense also, capital accumulation, technological innovation and capitalist urbanization have to go together.

In this view economic expansion requires the constant demolition of the fixed investment in buildings and infrastructure that supported the previous round of economic transactions. Government-sponsored redevelopment, according to the model set by Haussmann in nineteenth-century Paris and emulated by Robert Moses in twentieth-century New York, provides a vehicle for "continuous transformations." Since, however, the city remains the realm of collective consumption, capitalist efforts to reconstitute it are perennially contested by communities of residents and by those businesses that still benefit from the older spatial arrangements. Urban politics arises from this contested terrain.[7]

Castells (1977), in his early work, traced urban social movements to the inequalities arising in the workplace and contended that urban political conflict represented a displacement of conflict from the realm of production into consumption. His approach, and that of others who examined the heightened importance of local state services (see Preteceille, 1981), rooted the activities of the local state in various of the contradictions arising from the capitalist mode of production. Urban redevelopment efforts, as well as being required to improve production, were needed in order to reproduce the labor force through the provision of housing and other services. The functionalism underlying this argument contrasts sharply with the voluntarism embodied in liberal pluralist thought.

For the purposes of my discussion there are four important points deriving from the structuralist position presented thus far:

1   The local state necessarily becomes involved in the capitalist demand for a more efficient urban landscape, since capitalists cannot carry out the task of redevelopment on their own.
2   Redevelopment policy is an arena for class- and community-based conflict in which resident groups confront capital indirectly through the local state.
3   State actors, in pursuing their own aims of maintaining revenues and power, depend on private capital investment to reproduce and expand the urban environment, resulting in a bias toward capital.
4   The redevelopment process itself requires specialists in property development. They, however, have a collective interest in the profitability of the buildings they finance and construct rather than the operations that go on within them and this interest can put them at odds with other capitalists. Moreover, the particular structure of their industry, as detailed in chapters 2 and 3, leads them to take speculative risks that differentiate them from other producers and generate an added element of instability in the urban system.

Rent theory

A subset of structuralist studies concentrates on the Marxian theory of value and the theory of rent derived from it, in an effort to connect land use and development to production more generally.[8] While a theory of rent has also been developed within conventional economics, it does not play a central role in analyses of urban redevelopment.

Neo-Marxist arguments concerning rent bear directly on the character of the investment market in real estate and thereby on the strategies of the actors within it. The return which investors in property receive is divided between the earnings from: (1) greater output or lower costs of production enabled by physical improvements on land; and (2) rent. Rent, in orthodox Marxist analysis, refers to the amount extracted from surplus value that is transferred to the owner of a property simply as a consequence of his or her holding a legal right of possession. As such, it involves a mere transfer rather than an addition to value or a lowering of production costs. The concept has a moralizing flavor since it refers to an income which neither contributes to production, as does the investment of capital in machinery, nor flows from labor.

The significance of rent to the question of urban redevelopment relates to the impact of public subsidies on economic growth and the benefits from it. If the subsidies simply become capitalized as returns to landowners – that is, as rent – rather than lowering the costs of production and offering an incentive to economic expansion, they constitute a transfer to a fraction of capital.[9] Furthermore, if rents increase as a consequence of the behavior of the collectivity – that is, if they result from factors external to the property – but are privately appropriated, then the landlord realizes an unearned increment, having contributed nothing him/herself.

Regime theory

Regime theory straddles the boundary between the liberal and structuralist formulations. The original liberal concern with decision-making gave rise to this broader approach to the study of redevelopment, which takes into account dominant ideology, agenda setting, access networks, and latent power.[10] Clarence Stone (1989, p. 234) delineates its applicability to Atlanta:

> [The business] . . . elite controls resources of the kind and in the amount able to enhance the regime's capacity to govern. Minus these business-supplied resources, governing in Atlanta . . . would consist of little more than the provision of routine services. In Atlanta, then, the very capacity for strong governance is dependent on active business collaboration.
>
> The position of Atlanta's business elite in the affairs of the community is *not* that of a passive partner in a courtship conducted by public officials. The elite has collective aims that it is mobilized to pursue. (italics in original)

While Stone describes the "collective aims" of the business elite, he does not probe how these aims are constructed. Rather he (1989, p. 241) focuses on how they are enforced:

> The business elite is small and homogeneous enough to use the norms of class unity and corporate responsibility to maintain its cohesion internally. In interacting with allies [including middle-class blacks], the prevailing mode of operation is reciprocity, reinforced in many case by years of trust built from past exchanges.

Regime theory, in its discussion of the social bases of conflict and cooperation in redevelopment, more easily accommodates racial differentiation and ideological forces than do most structuralist critiques. It detects structural biases within the political economic system of capitalism that channel the redevelopment process but, more than the clearly Marxian analyses, it accepts the importance of political and ideological factors.

INTERESTS AND THEIR INTERPRETATION

My own approach largely embraces the tenets of regime theory, but it also attempts to unravel the economic factors that lead to a particular political-ideological construction of material interest by social groups. Balbus (1971, p. 167) defines the Marxian concept of interest as follows: "Individuals whose life-chances are similarly *affected* by similar objective social conditions are said to have a *common interest* whether they perceive any such interest or not."[11] But even if, in the case of property developers, individuals perceive a common interest, ideology and uncertainty affect their view of how that interest can best be served. In turn different interpretations of their interest by powerful groups make possible different social outcomes.

My formulation differs from arguments like that of Kevin Cox,[12] who takes a more fixed view of interest formation. In asserting that the class interest of locally dependent capitalists drives urban redevelopment, he assumes that local dependence is a wholly obvious characteristic. Yet, as the following illustration shows, its definition is malleable and varies according to the particular strategies that individual actors adopt. For example, the managers of a downtown department store may invest heavily in branches and disinvest or close the main store; they may participate in a downtown growth coalition, renovate their original store, move upmarket, and endow a foundation that supports affordable housing; or they may, as employees of a multi-locational retail conglomerate, transfer to another subsidiary in a completely different part of the country and take no interest in the redevelopment program of their original location. In this instance, even though the alternatives are all premised on economic interest alone, they reflect different readings of a situation and indicate how the circumstance of local dependency results from perception and activity. Moreover, each choice can alter the "objective situation" in which the actors find themselves, as well as the fate of downtown redevelopment.

In other words, perceived interest is neither an automatic response to economic position nor a wholly voluntaristic option among possible stances. It rather comprises a structured position derived from the interaction between economic, communal, and ideological forces at a particular historical moment. While the tools that are used in this book for detecting the economic factors driving interest formation come primarily from structuralist thought, it is not expected that economic factors produce only one possible interpretation of interest or that economic situation (as opposed to community, race, and gender) is the only "objective social interest" to be maximized. Instead the formation of interest is the subject of exploration, particularly as it is construed by non-governmental (business and community) redevelopment actors.

Because the definition of interest contains such an important interpretative element, factors that shape consciousness are of particular importance in affecting human action. Value traditions, ideology, and personality are therefore underlying causes of urban development. They cannot simply be reduced to the social relations of production, because their origins, even if economically based, may be traced back to earlier historical periods or be the products of social fragments rather than the totality of relations in a society. Moreover, group identifications may be at odds with economic interests – and not simply as a result of manipulation by privileged elites.

WHAT MATTERS?

The chief difference between the liberal and structuralist explanations of the urban redevelopment process is the insistence in the former on the importance of power and decision-making and in the latter on economic logic and class domination in explaining the course of events.[13] For pluralist liberals, power is not a simple manifestation of economic ascendancy but requires choosing to expend resources. These resources extend beyond money to organization, political support, and conviction. Marxists trace all forms of power to the relations of production and regard the strategic choices of actors as the consequence of their economic position; more flexible structuralists identify large areas of relative autonomy in social institutions and identify race and gender as separable determinants. For the regime theorists, who represent something of a synthesis of the two outlooks, control of capital outweighs other sources of power, but the development process cannot be understood simply through examining a "logic" of capitalism, since that logic is itself fabricated through human activity, including the resistance by other groups to capitalist aims.[14]

NOTES

1 See Cox (1991) who doubts the theoretical coherence of the empirical literature.
2 See Wolfinger (1974); Domhoff (1978); Polsby (1963); Bachrach and Baratz (1962); Yates (1973, 1977) for discussions of New Haven in relation to the power-structure debate.
3 Paul Peterson's (1981) controversial argument that economic development programs enjoy consensual support goes over Dahl's and Wolfinger's New Haven findings once again, ignoring all the subsequent studies that undermine that conclusion.
4 See, for example, Stone (1976).
5 The literature on American urban redevelopment is enormous. See especially Altshuler (1965); Beauregard (1989); Caro (1974); Cummings (1988); S. Fainstein et al. (1986); Judd and Parkinson (1990); Logan and Swanstrom (1990b); Friedland (1983); Mollenkopf (1983); Parkinson et al. (1988); Rosenthal (1980); M. Smith and Feagin (1987); Squires (1989); Stone (1976, 1989); Stone and Sanders (1987); Swanstrom (1985); Wilson (1966).
6 Early important works on British planning, housing, and development activities include Foley (1972); Pahl (1970); Young and Willmott (1957); Marriott (1967).
   Peter Hall's (1963, 1973, 1989) immensely influential works on urban growth and change were more directed to influencing policy-makers and thus less critical of observed trends than those within the structuralist tradition. But even he criticizes "conservationist planning" for protecting the upper-class way of life while crowding the working class into "a more sanitary version of the labourer's cottage of a century ago." (Hall et al., 1973, p. 628). These, however, are not, according to Hall, the "true victims" of the planning system; the biggest losers are the poor, occupying private rental housing in the central city, who cannot gain entry into either the suburban owner-occupier market or the public housing sector.
   Additional British studies of redevelopment include Simmie (1974, 1981); Saunders (1979); Marris (1987); Brindley et al. (1989); Goss (1988).
7 The attacks on Harvey's formulation that pepper the literature (see, e.g., Saunders, 1986, chapter 7; M. Smith, 1988) accuse him of regarding the results of urban political controversies as predetermined to favor capital rather than subject to contingency and the intervention of human agency. In fact, while Harvey lapses into mechanistic language in his more abstract theorizing, he more than anyone has looked historically at the agency through which redevelopment has occurred (see the long chapter on Paris in Harvey, 1985b).
8 See Haila (1991) for a summary of the various theories and for a discussion of the economic functions of land markets and the return to investment in land and property.
9 Harvey (1985c) is more generally concerned with the functions of rent in allocating land uses and coordinating the flow of capital into the built

environment. These functions and the impacts of different types of rent need not concern us here.

10 Elkin (1987, p. 68), discussing the meaning of a business-dominated regime, comments: "The heart of the entrepreneurial political economy was the business elite's ability to create and maintain a political system in which those who held elected and appointed office did not have to be told what to do." Norman Fainstein and I (1986b) use the term "directive" to describe those urban regimes that planned large-scale redevelopment with little opposition and consequently made few concessions to non-elite interests.

11 Italics in original

12 See Cox (1991) and my response, S. Fainstein (1991b).

13 There is, of course, a marked difference in vocabulary: "economic development" versus "capital accumulation"; "businesspeople" versus "capital"; "rate of return," "profit," or "earnings" versus "surplus value"; "recession" versus "crisis of accumulation."

14 In a more recent formulation, Stone (1993) states: "[Regime theory] . . . recognizes the enormous political importance of privately controlled investment, but does so without going so far as to embrace a position of economic determinism. . . . Regime analysts explore the middle ground between, on the one side, pluralists, with their assumption that the economy is just one of several discrete spheres of activity, and, on the other side, structuralists, who see the mode of production as pervading and dominating all other spheres of activity, including politics."

Appendix B

Population and Economy of London and New York

Table B.1 Greater London population, 1940–91 (thousands)

		Percent born in New Commonwealth[a] & Pakistan	Non-white
1931	8,110		
1951	8,197		
1961	7,992		
1971	7,452	13	
1981	6,696	18	
1991	6,680		20

[a]Includes Caribbean, India, Pakistan, Bangladesh, Cyprus, Gibraltar, Malta, Gozo, and the Far East

Sources: Great Britain, *Annual Abstract of Statistics* (London: HMSO, 1987), table 2.8; UK, *1991 Census of Population*.

Table B.2   New York City population, 1940–90 (thousands)

	1940	1950	1960	1970	1980	1990
New York City	7,455	7,892	7,782	7,895	7,072	7,323
Percent White[a]	94	90	85	n.a.	61	52
Manhattan	1,890	1,960	1,698	1,539	1,428	1,456
Percent White	83	79	74	n.a.	59	59
Brooklyn	2,698	2,738	2,627	2,602	2,231	2,301
Percent White	95	92	85	n.a.	56	47
Bronx	1,395	1,451	1,425	1,472	1,169	1,173
Percent White	98	93	88	n.a.	47	36
Queens	1,298	1,551	1,810	1,986	1,891	1,911
Percent White	97	96	91	n.a.	71	58
Staten Island	174	192	222	295	352	371
Percent White	98	96	95	n.a.	89	85

[a]Individuals of Hispanic origin are included in both white and non-white categories depending on how they identified themselves. The city contained 21 percent of Hispanic origin in 1980 and 24 percent in 1990. Percentage white is not supplied for the year 1970 because the treatment of those of Hispanic origin in that year differed from the rest of the series. Groups not included in the "white population" are blacks, native Americans, Asian/Pacific Islanders, and "others."

Sources: L.C. Rosenwaike, *Population History of New York City* (Syracuse: Syracuse University Press, 1972), pp. 121, 133, 136, 141, 197; US Bureau of the Census, *State and Metropolitan Area Data Book 1986*, p. 202, table A; Port Authority of New York and New Jersey, *Demographic Trends in the NY-NJ Metropolitan Region*.

Table B.3 London employment by industry, 1960–91 (thousands)

	1961	*1981*	*1991*	
Manufacturing, mining, energy, and agriculture	1,468	690	399	(12%)
Construction	281	165	118	(4%)
Transportation, utilities, wholesale distribution	740	663	954	(29%)
Retail trade	506	300	n.a.	
Finance and business services	462	593		
FIRE			283	(9%)
Business services			451	(14%)
Other services	384	265	1,049[a]	(32%)
Government (health, education, welfare, public administration)	606	890	n.a.	
TOTAL EMPLOYMENT	4,447	3,566	3,354[b]	

[a] Includes figures for retail trade and government for 1991.
[b] It is estimated that employment in London fell by 251,000 between its December 1988 peak and June 1991 (LPAC, Errata for LPAC 1991 annual review).

Sources: Derived from Nick Buck, Ian Gordon, and Ken Young, *The London Employment Problem* (Oxford: Clarendon Press, 1986), tables 4.1, 4.2; LPAC, *Strategic Trends & Policy, 1991 Annual Review* (London: LPAC, 1991); Amer K. Hirmis, "Labour market and industry structure: Greater London," draft (London: LPAC, 1992).

Table B.4   New York employment by industry, 1950–90 (thousands)

	1960	1970	1980	1990
Manufacturing	949	768	497	346
Construction	125	110	77	110
Transportation and utilities	318	323	257	222
Wholesale and retail trade	745	736	613	614
Finance, insurance, and real estate	386	460	448	512
Services	607	785	894	1,184
Government	408	563	516	607
TOTAL EMPLOYMENT	3,538	3,745	3,302	3,575

Sources: Temporary Commission on City Finances, *The Effect of Taxation on Manufacturing in New York City*, December 1976, table 1; Real Estate Board of New York, *Fact Book 1983*, October 1982, table 56; US Bureau of Labor Statistics, *Employment and Earnings*, 37 (December 1990).

Bibliography

Advisory Commission on Intergovernmental Relations (ACIR) 1987: *Significant Features of Fiscal Federalism*. Washington, DC: ACIR.

Agnew, John. 1987: *Place and Politics*. Winchester, MA: Allen & Unwin.

Alcaly, R.E., and Mermelstein, David (eds) 1976: *The Fiscal Crisis of American Cities*. New York: Vintage.

Alterman, Rachelle, and Kayden, Jerold S. 1988. "Developer provisions of public benefits: toward a consensus vocabulary," in Rachelle Alterman (ed.), *Private Supply of Public Services*. New York: New York University Press, pp. 22–32.

Altshuler, Alan A. 1965: *The City Planning Process*. Ithaca, NY: Cornell University Press.

Ambrose, Peter. 1986: *Whatever Happened to Planning?* London: Methuen.

—— and Colenutt, Bob. 1975: *The Property Machine*. Harmondsworth, Middlesex: Penguin.

Amin, Ash, and Thrift, Nigel. 1992: "Neo-Marshallian nodes in global networks." *International Journal of Urban and Regional Research*, 16 (December), 571–87.

Association of London Authorities (ALA) and Docklands Consultative Committee (DCC). 1991: *10 Years of Docklands: How the Cake Was Cut*. London: ALA and DCC.

Bachrach, Peter, and Baratz, Morton S. 1962. "Two faces of power." *American Political Science Review*, 56 (December), 947–52.

Bacow, Lawrence S. 1990: "Foreign investment, vertical integration and the structure of the U.S. real estate industry." *Real Estate Issues*, 15 (Fall/Winter 1990), 1–8.

Badcock, Blair. 1984: *Unfairly Structured Cities*. Oxford: Blackwell.

Bagli, Charles V. 1991: "Old foes make strange bedfellows on Trump's long-fought project." *New York Observer*, April 22.

Balbus, Isaac. 1971: "The concept of interest in pluralist and marxian analysis." *Politics and Society*, 1 (February), 151–78.

Balchin, Paul N., Kieve, Jeffrey L., and Bull, Gregory H. 1988: *Urban Land Economics and Public Policy*. 4th edn. London: Macmillan.

Ball, Michael. 1983: *Housing Policy and Economic Power*. London: Methuen.

—— Bentivegna, V., Edwards, M., and Folin, M. 1985: *Land Rent, Housing and Urban Planning*. London: Croom Helm.

Barber, Benjamin R. 1984: *Strong Democracy*. Berkeley: University of California Press.

Barnekov, Timothy, Boyle, Robin, and Rich, Daniel, 1989: *Privatism and Urban Policy in Britain and the United States*. Oxford: Oxford University Press.

Barrett, Wayne. 1992: *Trump*. New York: HarperCollins.

Bartlett, Sarah. 1992: "Holding vast space and vast debt." *New York Times*, April 24.

Battery Park City Authority (BPCA). 1992: *Battery Park City Fact Sheet*. New York: BPCA.

Beauregard, Robert A. 1991: "Capital restructuring and the new built environment of global cities: New York and Los Angeles." *International Journal of Urban and Regional Research*, 15 (1), 90–105.

—— 1990: "Bringing the city back in." *Journal of the American Planning Association*, 56 (Spring), 210–15.

—— (ed.) 1989: *Atop the Urban Hierarchy*. Totowa, NJ: Rowman & Littlefield.

Berry, Mike, and Huxley, Margo, 1992: "Big build: property capital, the state and urban change in Australia," *International Journal of Urban and Regional Research*, 16 (March), 35–59.

Bish, Robert L. 1971: *The Public Economy of Metropolitan Areas*. Chicago: Markham.

Boddy, Trevor. 1992: "Underground and overhead: building the analogous city," in Michael Sorkin (ed.), *Variations on a Theme Park*. New York: Hill and Wang, pp. 123–53.

Boyer, M. Christine. 1992: "Cities for sale: merchandising history at South Street Seaport," in Michael Sorkin (ed.), *Variations on a Theme Park*. New York: Hill and Wang, pp. 181–204.

—— 1983: *Dreaming the Rational City*. Cambridge: MIT Press.

Branson, Noreen. 1979. *Poplarism, 1919–1925*. London: Lawrence and Wishart.

Breznick, Alan. 1991: "Forest City will join big Brooklyn project." *New York Times*, February 18.

Brilliant, Eleanor, 1975: *The Urban Development Corporation*. Lexington, MA: D.C. Heath.

Brindley, Tim, Rydin, Yvonne, and Stoker, Gerry. 1989: *Remaking Planning*. London: Unwin Hyman.

Brownill, Sue. 1991: "London Docklands: social or physical regeneration? The need for a reassessment of regeneration dichotomies." Paper presented at the joint meeting of the Association of Collegiate Schools of Planning and the Association of European Schools of Planning, Oxford, UK, July.

Bruck, Connie. 1989: *The Predators' Ball*. New York: Penguin.

Buchan, James. 1990: "A high-risk business." *Independent on Sunday, Sunday Review*, December 16, 2–5.

Buck, Nick, Drennan, Matthew, and Newton, Kenneth. 1992: "Dynamics of the metropolitan economy," in Susan S. Fainstein, Ian Gordon, and Michael Harloe (eds.), *Divided Cities*. Oxford: Basil Blackwell, pp. 68–103.

Buck, Nick, and Fainstein, Norman. 1992: "A Comparative History, 1880–1973," in Susan S. Fainstein, Ian Gordon, and Michael Harloe (eds.), *Divided Cities*. Oxford: Basil Blackwell, pp. 29–67.

Buck, Nick, Gordon, Ian R., and Young, Ken. 1986: *The London Employment Problem*. Oxford: Oxford University Press.

Burrough, Bryan, and Helyar, John. 1990: *Barbarians at the Gate: The Fall of RJR Nabisco*. New York: Harper & Row.

Byrne, Therese E., and Shulman, David. 1991: *Manhattan Office Market II: Beyond the Bear Market*. New York: Salomon Brothers Bond Market Research–Real Estate, June.

—— and Kostin, David J. 1990: *London Office Market II: Breaking the Code*. New York: Salomon Brothers Bond Market Research–Real Estate, August.

Camden, London Borough of. 1989a: *King's Cross Development Proposals: Progress Report on the Planning Application: Main Report*. September 19.

—— 1989b: "King's Cross development proposals. The new scheme: Have they got it right?" Photocopied flyer.

—— 1989c: "King's Cross development proposals. A development benefitting the community or an 'office city'? Report back." September.

—— 1988: *The King's Cross Railway Lands: A Community Planning Brief*. June.

Camden Citizen. 1990: King's Cross development: the new proposals. Supplement 1.

Caro, Robert. 1974: *The Power Broker: Robert Moses and the Fall of New York*. New York: Knopf.

Castells, Manuel. 1989: *The Informational City*. Oxford: Blackwell.

—— 1985: "High technology, economic restructuring, and the urban-regional process in the United States," in Manuel Castells (ed.), *High Technology, Space, and Society*. Beverly Hills: Sage, pp. 11–40.

——1977: *The Urban Question*. Cambridge, MA: MIT Press.

Chira, Susan. 1989: "New designs for Times Square try to reflect neon atmosphere." *New York Times*, August 31.

Church, Andrew. 1988a: "Demand-led planning, the inner-city crisis and the labour market: London Docklands evaluated," in B.S. Hoyle, D.A. Pinder, and M.S. Husain (eds.), *Revitalising the Waterfront*. London: Belhaven Press, pp. 199–221.

—— 1988b: "Urban regeneration in London Docklands: A five-year policy review." *Environment and Planning C: Government and Policy*, 6, 187–208.

Clavel, Pierre. 1986: *The Progressive City*. New Brunswick, NJ: Rutgers University Press.

Clawson, Marion, and Hall, Peter, 1973: *Planning and Urban Growth: An Anglo-American Comparison*. Baltimore: Johns Hopkins University Press.

Colenutt, Bob. 1990: "Urban development corporations – the Docklands experiment." Summary of a paper presented at Conference on Economic Regeneration, Chicago, September.

Colliers International Property Consultants. 1991: *Colliers International Worldwide 1991 Office Survey.* July 29.

Commission on the Year 2000. 1987: *New York Ascendant.* New York: Commission on the Year 2000.

Community Development Group (Spitalfields). 1989: *Planning Our Future.* London: Community Development Group.

Cooke, Philip (ed.). 1989: *Localities.* London: Unwin Hyman.

Coopers & Lybrand Deloitte. 1991a: "Wealth creation in world cities." Annex to London Planning Advisory Committee (LPAC), *London: A World City Moving into the 21st Century.* London: LPAC.

——— 1991b: *London, World City.* Consultants Stage II Report. London: LPAC.

Cox, Kevin. 1991: "Questions of abstraction in studies in the new urban politics." *Journal of Urban Affairs*, 13 (3), 267–80.

Crain, Rance. 1992. "By keeping city's lid on, Dinkins revives '93 hopes." *Crain's New York Business.* May 11.

Crilley, Darrel. 1993. "Megastructures and urban change: aesthetics, ideology and design," in Paul L. Knox, ed., *The Restless Urban Landscape.* Englewood Cliffs, NJ: Prentice-Hall, pp. 127–64.

Cross, Malcolm, and Waldinger, Roger. 1992: "Migrants, minorities, and the ethnic division of labor," in Susan S. Fainstein, Ian Gordon, and Michael Harloe (eds.), *Divided Cities.* Oxford: Blackwell, pp. 151–74.

Cummings, Scott (ed.). 1988: *Business Elites and Urban Development.* Albany, NY: SUNY Press.

Cushman, John H. 1992: "House approves tax bill with $14.4 billion in breaks." *New York Times,* July 3.

Dahl, Robert. 1961. *Who Governs?* New Haven: Yale University Press.

Daniels, P.W., and Bobe, J.M. 1991. "High rise and high risks: office development on Canary Wharf." SIRC Working Paper no. 7. Portsmouth Polytechnic. May.

——— 1990: "Information technology and the renaissance of the City of London office building." SIRC Working Paper no. 3. Portsmouth Polytechnic. December.

Danielson, Michael N. and Doig, Jameson W. 1982: *New York: The Politics of Urban Regional Development.* Berkeley: University of California Press.

Davis, John Emmeus. 1991: *Contested Ground.* Ithaca, NY: Cornell University Press.

Davis, Mike. 1990: *City of Quartz.* London: Verso.

Dear, Michael, and Scott, Allen J. (eds), 1981: *Urbanization and Urban Planning in Capitalist Society.* London: Methuen.

Dewar, Elaine. 1987: "The mysterious Reichmanns: the untold story." *Toronto Life,* November, 61–186.

Dijkstra, Fer. 1991: Address given at the annual meeting of the Institute of British Geographers. Sheffield, UK, January.

Dizard, John. 1992: "Boom to tomb at 55 Water St. as prestigious leases expire." *New York Observer,* April 13.

Docklands Consultative Committee (DCC). 1988. *Urban Development Corporations: Six Years in London's Docklands*. London: Docklands Consultative Committee.

Domhoff, William. 1978: *Who Really Rules?* Santa Monica, CA: Goodyear.

Downs, Anthony. 1985: *The Revolution in Real Estate Finance*. Washington, DC: Brookings Institution.

Drennan, Matthew. 1988: "Local economy and local revenues," in Charles Brecher and Raymond D. Horton (eds), *Setting Municipal Priorities, 1988*. New York: New York University Press, pp. 15–44.

Dror, Yehezkel. 1968: *Public Policy Reexamined*. San Francisco: Chandler.

Dunlap, David W. 1993: "Council's land-use procedures emerging." *New York Times*, Section 10, January 3.

—— 1992a: "Charting the future of the waterfront." *New York Times*, Section 10, November 15.

—— 1992b: "New Times Sq. Plan: Lights! Signs! Dancing! Hold the offices." *New York Times*, August 20.

—— 1991: "How developers and city hall retain big tenants." *New York Times*, June 16.

—— 1988: "From dust of demolition, a new Times Square rises." *New York Times*, July 6.

Edwards, Michael. (Forthcoming.) "A microcosm: redevelopment proposals at King's Cross" in Andy Thornley (ed.), *The Crisis of London*. London: Routledge.

Eisinger, Peter K. 1988: *The Rise of the Entrepreneurial State*. Madison: University of Wisconsin Press.

Elkin, Stephen L. 1987: *City and Regime in the American Republic*. Chicago: University of Chicago Press.

Epstein, Jason. 1992: "The tragical history of New York." *New York Review of Books*, April 9, 45–52.

Fainstein, Norman I., and Fainstein, Susan S. 1988: "Governing regimes and the political economy of development in New York City, 1946–1984," in John Hull Mollenkopf (ed.), *Power, Culture, and Place*. New York: Russell Sage Foundation, pp. 161–99.

—— 1987: "Economic restructuring and the politics of land use planning in New York City." *Journal of the American Planning Association*, 53 (Spring), 237–48.

—— 1986a: "New Haven: the limits of the local state," in Susan S. Fainstein et al., *Restructuring the City*. Rev. edn. New York: Longman, pp. 27–79.

—— 1986b: "Regime strategies, communal resistance, and economic forces," in *Restructuring the City*. Rev. edn. New York: Longman, pp. 245–82.

—— 1985: "Is state planning necessary for capital?" *International Journal of Urban and Regional Research*, 9 (4), 485–507.

—— 1979: "National policy and urban development." *Social Problems*, 26 (December), 125–46.

—— and Schwartz, Alex. 1989: "Economic shifts and land-use in the global city: New York, 1940–87," in Robert Beuregard (ed.), *Atop the Urban Hierarchy*, Totowa, NJ: Rowman and Littlefield, pp. 45–86.

Fainstein, Susan S. 1992: "The second New York fiscal crisis." *International Journal of Urban and Regional Research*, 16 (March), 129–38.

——— 1991a: Rejoinder to: "Questions of abstraction in studies in the new urban politics." *Journal of Urban Affairs*, 13 (3), pp. 281–7.

——— 1991b: "Promoting economic development: urban planning in the United States and Great Britain." *Journal of the American Planning Association*, 57 (Winter): 22–33.

——— 1990a: "The changing world economy and urban restructuring," in Dennis Judd and Michael Parkinson (eds.), *Leadership and Urban Regeneration*. Newbury Park: Sage, pp. 31–47.

——— 1990b: "Economics, politics and development policy: the convergence of New York and London." *International Journal of Urban and Regional Research* 14(4), 553–75.

Fainstein, Susan S., Fainstein, Norman I., Hill, Richard Child, Judd, Dennis, and Smith, Michael Peter. 1986: *Restructuring the City*. Rev. edn. New York: Longman.

Fainstein, Susan S., Gordon, Ian, and Harloe, Michael (eds), 1992: *Divided Cities*. Oxford: Blackwell.

Fainstein, Susan S., and Harloe, Michael. 1992: "Introduction," in Susan S. Fainstein, Ian Gordon, and Michael Harloe (eds), *Divided Cities*. Oxford: Blackwell, pp. 1–28.

Fainstein, Susan S., and Markusen, Ann R. 1993: "Urban policy: bridging the social and economic development gap." *University of North Carolina Law Review*, 71 (June), 1701–24.

Fainstein, Susan S., and Young, Ken. 1992: "Politics and state policy in economic restructuring," in Susan S. Fainstein, Ian Gordon, and Michael Harloe (eds), *Divided Cities*. Oxford: Blackwell, pp. 203–35.

Faludi, Andreas. 1987: *A Decision-Centered View of Environmental Planning*. New York: Pergamon.

——— 1986: *Critical Rationalism and Planning Methodology*. London: Pion.

Farnsworth, Clyde H. 1992: "Reichmanns and official in dispute." *New York Times*, April 11.

Fathers, Michael. 1992: "What went wrong with what went up." *The Independent on Sunday*. May 17.

Fazey, Ian Hamilton. 1991: "Urban development bodies plan their own extinction." *Financial Times*, February 21.

Feagin, Joe R., and Parker, Robert. 1990: *Rebuilding American Cities: The Urban Real Estate Game*. 2nd edn. Englewood Cliffs, NJ: Prentice-Hall.

Foglesong, Richard E. 1986: *Planning the Capitalist City*. Princeton: Princeton University Press.

Foley, Donald L. 1972: *Governing the London Region*. Berkeley: University of California Press.

Forest City Ratner Companies. 1992: MetroTech Center Fact Sheet. February.

Forman, Charlie. 1989: *Spitalfields: A Battle for Land*. London: Hilary Shipman.

Frantz, Douglas. 1991: *From the Ground Up*. New York: Henry Holt.

Frieden, Bernard J. and Sagalyn, Lynne B. 1990: *Downtown, Inc.* Cambridge, MA: MIT Press.

Friedland, Roger. 1983: *Power and Crisis in the City*. New York: Schocken.

Friedmann, John. 1986: "The world city hypothesis." *Development and Change*, 17, 69–83.

Friedmann, John, and Wolff, Gortz 1982: "World city formation: an agenda for research and action." *International Journal of Urban and Regional Research*, 6(3), 69–83.

Fujita, Kuniko. 1991: "A world city and flexible specialization: restructuring of the Tokyo metropolis." *International Journal of Urban and Regional Research*, 15(2), 269–84.

Gans, Herbert J. 1988: *Middle American Individualism*. New York: Oxford University Press.

—— 1968: *People and Plans*. New York: Basic Books.

Gill, Brendan. 1990: "The sky line: Battery Park City." *New Yorker*, August 20, 99–106.

Glassberg, A. 1981: *Representation and Urban Community*. London: Macmillan.

Glueck, Grace, and Gardner, Paul. 1991: *Brooklyn: People and Places, Past and Present*. New York: Harry N. Abrams.

Goldberger, Paul. 1990: "A huge architecture show in Times Square." *New York Times*, September 9.

—— 1989a: "Times Square: lurching toward a terrible mistake?" *New York Times*, February 19.

—— 1989b: "New Times Square design: merely token changes." *New York Times*, September 1.

—— 1988. "Public space gets a new cachet in New York." *New York Times*, May 22.

—— 1986: "Battery Park City is a triumph of urban design." *New York Times*, August 31.

Golway, Terry. 1991: "Battery Park City's Emil is assailed as a meddler." *New York Observer*, August 5–12.

Goss, Sue. 1988: *Local Labour and Local Government*. Edinburgh: Edinburgh University Press.

Gottdiener, M. 1985: *The Social Production of Urban Space*. Austin: University of Texas Press.

Gourevitch, Peter. 1986: *The Politics of Hard Times*. Ithaca, NY: Cornell University Press.

Grant, James. 1992: "The Olympia ordeal: it won't end soon." *New York Times*, Section 3, May 24.

Grant, Peter. 1990: "Tenants see tricks, no treats, with shift." *Crain's New York Business*, October 22.

—— 1989: "Why Prudential needs Times Square." *Crain's New York Business*. September 4.

Greater London Council (GLC). 1985: *London Industrial Strategy: The Docks*. London: GLC.

Green, Roy E., ed. 1991: *Enterprise Zones*. Newbury Park: Sage.

Haila, Anne. 1991: Four types of investment in land and property. *International Journal of Urban and Regional Research*, 15(3), 343–65.

—— 1988: Land as a financial asset: the theory of urban rent as a mirror of economic transformation. *Antipode*, 20(2), 79–100.

Hall, Peter. 1989: *London 2001*. London: Unwin Hyman.

—— 1980: *Great Planning Disasters*. Berkeley: University of California Press.

—— 1963: *London 2000*. London: Faber and Faber.

Hall, Peter, Gracey, Harry, Drewett, Roy, and Thomas, Ray. 1973: *The Containment of Urban England*. London: Allen & Unwin.

Hambleton, Robin. 1989: Urban government under Thatcher and Reagan. *Urban Affairs Quarterly*, 24(3), 359–88.

Hamnett, Chris, and Randolph, Bill. 1988: *Cities, Housing & Profits*. London: Hutchinson.

Harding, Alan. 1990: "Property interests and urban growth coalitions in the U.K.: a brief encounter?" Centre for Urban Studies, University of Liverpool, Working Paper no. 12.

Harloe, Michael, and Fainstein, Susan S. 1992: "Conclusion: The divided cities." in Susan S. Fainstein, Ian Gordon, and Michael Harloe (eds), *Divided Cities*. Oxford: Blackwell, pp. 236–67.

—— Marcuse, Peter, and Smith, Neil. 1992: "Housing for people, housing for profits," in Susan S. Fainstein, Ian Gordon, and Michael Harloe (eds), *Divided Cities*. Oxford: Blackwell, pp. 175–201

—— Pickvance, Chris, and Urry, John (eds) 1990: *Place, Policy and Politics: Do Localities Matter?* London: Unwin Hyman.

Harvey, David. 1992: "Social justice, postmodernism and the city." *International Journal of Urban and Regional Research*, 16 (December), 588–601.

—— 1989: *The Condition of Post-Modernity*. Oxford: Blackwell.

—— 1985a: *The Urbanization of Capital*. Baltimore: Johns Hopkins University Press.

—— 1985b: *Consciousness and the Urban Experience*. Baltimore: Johns Hopkins University Press.

—— 1985c: "Class-monopoly rent, finance capital, and the urban revolution," in David Harvey, *The Urbanization of Capital*. Baltimore: Johns Hopkins University Press, pp. 62–89.

—— 1982: *The Limits to Capital*. Chicago: University of Chicago Press.

—— 1981: "The urban process under capitalism: a framework for analysis," in Michael Dear and Allen J. Scott (eds), *Urbanization and Urban Planning in Capitalist Society*. London: Methuen, pp. 91–121.

—— 1978: "Planning the ideology of planning," in Robert Burchell and George Sternlieb (eds), *Planning Theory in the 1980s*. New Brunswick, NJ: Rutgers University Center for Urban Policy Research, pp. 213–34.

—— 1973: *Social Justice and the City*. Baltimore: Johns Hopkins University Press.

Healey, Patsy. 1990: "Understanding land and property development processes: some key issues," in Patsy Healey and Rupert Nabarro (eds), *Land and Property Development in a Changing Context*. Aldershot, Hampshire: Gower, pp. 3–14.

Healey, Patsy, and Barrett, Susan M. 1990: "Structure and agency in land and property development processes: some ideas for research." *Urban Studies*, 27(1), 89–104.

Healey, Patsy, and Nabarro, Rupert (eds). 1990: *Land and Property Development in a Changing Context*. Aldershot, Hampshire: Gower.

Healey, Patsy, Davoudi, Simin, Tavsanoglu, Solmaz, O'Toole, Mo, and Usher, David. 1992. *Rebuilding the City: Property-Led Urban Regeneration*. London: E. & F.N. Spon.

Hoff, Jeffrey. 1989: "Who should pay to transform Times Square?" *Barron's*, September 25.

Houlder, Vanessa. 1992: "Two projects in the City come nearer to fruition." *Financial Times*. March 28/29.

—— 1991a: "Docklands body to cut 40% of staff." *Financial Times*. April 30.

—— 1991b: "Rosehaugh losses grow to £226.6 m after provisions." *Financial Times*. December 7/8.

—— Smith, Michael, Rudd, Roland, and Dawnay, Ivo. 1992: "Hanson believes Canary Wharf project is worth £600m at most." *Financial Times*, June 2.

Housing Corporation. 1992: *Annual Accounts, 1991/1992*. London: The Housing Corporation.

Hudson, James R. 1987: *The Unanticipated City*. Amherst, MA: University of Massachusetts Press.

Hylton, Richard D. 1992a: "Olympia to disclose lost value." *New York Times*, July 1.

—— 1992b: "$240 million demand on developer." *New York Times*, January 16.

—— 1992c: "Slumping real estate leaves giant reeling." *New York Times*, March 24.

—— 1992d: "Focus is shifting to debt talks on US assets." *New York Times*, May 29.

—— 1992e: "Banks fear losses as builder reels." *New York Times*, March 30.

—— 1990a: "Olympia & York selling stake in U.S. holdings." *New York Times*, September 20.

—— 1990b: "Reshaping a real estate dynasty." *New York Times*, November 28.

Isaac, Paul J. 1992: "Just the beginning." *Barron's*, May 18.

Jacobs, Jane. 1961: *The Death and Life of Great American Cities*. New York: Vintage.

Jenkins, Peter. 1988: *Mrs Thatcher's Revolution*. Cambridge, MA: Harvard University Press.

Jones Lang Wootton Consulting and Research. 1987: *The Central London Office Market*. London: Jones Lang Wootton.

Judd, Dennis R. (Forthcoming). "The rise of the new walled cities," in Helen Liggett and David C. Perry (eds), *Representing the City*. Newbury Park: Sage.

Judd, Dennis, and Parkinson, Michael (eds). 1990: *Leadership and Urban Regeneration*. Newbury Park, CA: Sage.

Key, Tony, Espinet, Marc, and Wright, Carol. 1990: "Prospects for the property industry: an overview," in Patsy Healey and Rupert Nabbaro (eds), *Land and Property Development in a Changing Context*. Aldershot, Hampshire: Gower, pp. 17–41.

King, Anthony D. 1990: *Global Cities*. London: Routledge.

King, Desmond S. 1989: "Political centralization and state interests in Britain: the 1986 abolition of the GLC and MCCs." *Comparative Political Studies*, 21 (January), 467–94.

King, R.J. 1988: "Urban design in capitalist society." *Environment and Planning D: Society and Space*, 6, 445–474.

King's Cross Railway Lands Group (KCRLCDG). 1989: *The King's Cross Development–People or Profit?* London: KCRLCDG.

Klosterman, Richard. 1985: "Arguments for and against planning." *Town Planning Review*, 56(1), 5–20.

Knox, Paul L. 1993: "The postmodern urban matrix," in Paul L. Knox (ed.), *The Restless Urban Landscape*. Englewood Cliffs, NJ: Prentice-Hall, pp. 207–36.

Koch, Edward I. 1984: *Mayor*. New York: Simon and Schuster.

Krauskopf, James A. 1989: "Federal aid," in Charles Brecher and Robert D. Horton (eds), *Setting Municipal Priorities 1990*. New York: New York University Press, pp. 117–37.

Krieger, Joel. 1986: *Reagan, Thatcher, and the Politics of Decline*. New York: Oxford University Press.

Krumholz, Norman, and Forester, John. 1990: *Making Equity Planning Work*. Philadelphia: Temple University Press.

Lamarche, Francois. 1976: "Property development and the economic foundations of the urban question," in Chris Pickvance (ed.), *Urban Sociology*. New York: St. Martin's, pp. 85–118.

Lambert, Bruce. 1991: "The way cleared for long-delayed housing." *New York Times*, Section 10, April 14.

Lassar, Terry Jill (ed.). 1990. *City Deal Making*. Washington, DC: Urban Land Institute.

Lawless, Paul. 1990: "Regeneration in Sheffield: from radical intervention to partnership," in Dennis Judd and Michael Parkinson (eds), *Leadership and Urban Regeneration*. Newbury Park, CA: Sage, pp. 133–51.

—— 1989: *Britain's Inner Cities*. 2nd edn. London: Paul Chapman.

—— 1987: "Urban development," in Michael Parkinson (ed.), *Reshaping Local Government*. New Brunswick, NJ: Transaction Books, pp. 122–37.

Lefebvre, Henri. 1991: *The Production of Space*, trans. Donald Nicholson-Smith. Cambridge, MA: Blackwell.

Lever, Lawrence. 1988a: "Canary Wharf saviour sings Britain's praise: born again Anglophile of Docklands." *Financial Times*, May 9.

—— 1988b: "Reichmanns aim for Stanhope." *Financial Times*, May 11.

Levy, John M. 1990: "What local economic developers actually do: location quotients versus press releases." *Journal of the American Planning Association*, 56 (Spring), 153–60.

Lewis, Michael. 1989: *Liar's Poker*. New York: Penguin.

Leyshon, Andrew, Thrift, Nigel, and Daniels, Peter. 1990. "The operational development and spatial expansion of large commercial property firms," in Patsy Healey and Rupert Nabarro (eds), *Land and Property Development in a Changing Context*. Aldershot, Hampshire: Gower, pp. 60–97.

—— 1987: "The urban and regional consequences of the restructuring of world financial markets: the case of the City of London." University of Bristol and Service Industries Research Centre, Portsmouth Polytechnic. Working Papers on Producer Services no. 4. July.

Lichfield, John. 1992: "Downfall of a towering ambition." *Independent on Sunday*, May 17.

Lichtenberger, Elisabeth. 1991: "Product cycle theory and city development." *Acta Geographica Lovaniensia*, 31, 88–94.

Lin, Paul. 1991: "The super-agency." *City Limits*, 16 (November), 8–10.

Logan, John. R. 1992: "Cycles and trends in the globalization of real estate," in Paul L. Knox (ed.), *The Restless Urban Landscape*. Englewood Cliffs, NJ: Prentice-Hall, pp. 36–54.

Logan, John R. and Molotch, Harvey. 1987: *Urban Fortunes*. Berkeley: University of California Press.

Logan, John R., and Swanstrom, Todd, 1990a: "Urban restructuring: a critical view," in John R. Logan and Todd Swanstrom (eds), *Beyond the City Limits*. Philadelphia: Temple University Press, pp. 3–24.

—— (eds) 1990b: *Beyond the City Limits*. Philadelphia: Temple University Press.

London Docklands Development Corporation (LDDC). 1992: *LDDC key facts and figures to the 31st March 1992*. London: LDDC.

—— 1991: *Annual Report & Financial Statements for the Year ended 31 March 1991*. London: LDDC.

—— 1988a: *London Docklands Development Corporation*. London: LDDC. Ref: 134A.1, March.

—— 1988b: *London Docklands* (promotional brochure). London: LDDC.

London Planning Advisory Committee (LPAC). 1991: *London: World City*. London: LPAC.

—— 1988: *Strategic Planning Advice for London. Policies for the 1990s*. London: LPAC.

Lopate, Phillip. 1989: "The planner's dilemma." *7 Days*, February 15.

Loughlin, M., Gelfand, M.D. and Young, K. (eds). 1986: *Half a Century of Municipal Decline, 1935–1985*. London: Allen and Unwin.

Low, N.P., and Moser, S.T. 1990: "Markets as political structures, the case of Melbourne's central city property boom." Paper presented at the World Congress of Sociology, Madrid, July.

Lueck, Thomas J. 1988: "New York gives a bank a break; the return is uncertain." *New York Times*, November 13.

McCormick, M., O'Cleireacain, C., and Dickson, E. 1980: "Compensation of municipal workers in large cities: a New York City perspective." *City Almanac*, 15, 1–9, 16–20.

Mackintosh, Maureen, and Wainwright, Hilary. 1987: *A Taste of Power: The Politics of Local Economies*. London: Verso.

McNamara, Paul. 1990: "The changing role of research in investment decision making," in Patsy Healey and Rupert Nabarro (eds), *Land and Property Development in a Changing Context*. Aldershot, Hampshire: Gower, pp. 98–109.

Marcuse, Peter. 1987: "Neighbourhood policy and the distribution of power: New York City's community boards." *Policy Studies Journal*, 16, 277–89.

—— 1981: "The targeted crisis: on the ideology of the urban fiscal crisis and it uses." *International Journal of Urban and Regional Research*, 5(3), 330–55.

Markusen, J.R., and Scheffman, D.T. 1978: "The timing of residential land development: a general equilibrium approach." *Journal of Urban Economics*, 5 (October), 411–24.

Marriott, Oliver. 1967: *The Property Boom*. London: Hamish Hamilton.

Marris, Peter. 1987: *Meaning and Action*. London: Routledge & Kegan Paul.

Martin, Douglas. 1993: "42d Street project remains on track." *New York Times*, January 25.

Massey, Doreen. 1984: *Spatial Divisions of Labour*. London: Macmillan.

—— and Catalano, A. 1978: *Capital and Land*. London: Edward Arnold.

Meuwissen, J., Daniels, P.W., and Bobe, J.M. 1991: "The demand for office space in the City of London and the Isle of Dogs: Complement or Competition?" SIRC Working Paper no. 9. Service Industries Research Centre, Portsmouth Polytechnic, October.

Mills, David E. 1980: "Market power and land development timing." *Land Economics*, 56 (February), 10–20.

Mitchell, Alison. 1992: "Brooklyn office project gets long-term tenant." *New York Times*, February 26.

Mittlebach, Margaret. 1991: "Suburbs in the City." *City Limits*, 16 (May), 12–16.

Mollenkopf, John Hull. 1992: *A Phoenix in the Ashes: The Rise and Fall of the Koch Coalition in New York City Politics*. Princeton: Princeton University Press.

—— 1988: "The place of politics and the politics of place," in John Hull Mollenkopf (ed.), *Power, Culture, and Place*. New York: Russell Sage Foundation, pp. 273–84.

—— 1985: "The 42nd Street Development Project and the public interest." *City Almanac*, 18 (Summer), 12–15.

—— 1983: *The Contested City*. Princeton: Princeton University Press.

—— 1978: "The postwar politics of urban development," in William K. Tabb and Larry Sawers (eds), *Marxism and the Metropolis*. New York: Oxford University Press, pp. 117–52.

—— and Castells, Manuel (eds). 1991: *Dual City*. New York: Russell Sage.

Molotch, Harvey. 1980: "The city as a growth machine: toward a political economy of place." *American Journal of Sociology*, 82 (September), 309–32.

Morley, Stuart, Marsh, Chris, McIntosh, Angus, and Martinos, Haris. 1989: *Industrial and Business Space Development*. London: E. & F.N. Spon.

Morris, Charles R. 1980: *The Cost of Good Intentions*. New York: Norton.

Moss, Mitchell L. 1986: "Telecommunications and the future of cities." *Land Development Studies*, 3, 33–44.

Myers, Steven Lee. 1992: "The prime of 'Wall Street East.'" *New York Times*, May 15.

National Audit Office. 1988: *Department of the Environment: Urban Development Corporations*. Report by the Comptroller and Auditor General. London: HMSO.

Netzer, Dick. 1988: "Exactions in the public finance context," in Rachelle Alterman (ed.), *Private Supply of Public Services*. New York: New York University Press, pp. 35–50.

Neuwirth, Robert. 1990: "Amsterdam Theater falling down?" *The Voice*, October 2.

New York City, Department of Housing Preservation and Development (DHPD). 1989: *Ten Year Housing Plan, Fiscal Years 1989–1998*. New York: DHPD.

New York City Planning Commission (NYCPC). 1981: *Midtown Development*. New York: Department of City Planning.

New York City Public Development Corporation (PDC). N.d. [1984?] *Forty-second Street Development Project Fact Sheet*. New York: PDC.

New York State Office of the State Deputy Controller (OSDC) for the City of New York. 1991: *Review of the Financial Plan of the City of New York, Fiscal Years 1992 through 1995*. Report 4-92, June 17.

—— 1988: *New York City Planning Commission Granting Special Permits for Bonus Floor Area*. Report A-23-88, September 15.

Newfield, Jack, and Barrett, Wayne. 1988: *City for Sale*. New York: Harper & Row.

Newfield, Jack, and DuBrul, Paul. 1981: *The Permanent Government*. New York: Pilgrim Press.

Newman, Oscar. 1972: *Defensible Space*. New York: Macmillan.

Nissé, Jason. 1992: "Docklands tube link derailed." *Independent*, May 29.

O'Leary, Brendan. 1987: "Why was the GLC abolished?" *International Journal of Urban and Regional Research*, 11(2), 193–217.

O'Neill, Hugh, and Moss, Mitchell L. 1991: *Reinventing New York*. New York: Urban Research Center, Robert F. Wagner Graduate School of Public Service, New York University.

Oser, Alan S. 1992: "New York slashing an array of programs." *New York Times*, April 5.

—— 1988: "Lease gives impetus to Brooklyn project." *New York Times*, April 3.

—— 1987: "'Public housing' in abandoned buildings." *New York Times*, October 4.

Pahl, R.E. 1970: *Whose City?* London: Harlow, Longmans.

Parker-Jervis, George. 1992: "Olympia & York drop dead days." *Observer*, April 19.

Parkes, Michael, Mouawad, Daniel C., and Scott, Michael J. 1991: *King's Cross Railwaylands: Towards a People's Plan*. Draft. June 1991.

Parkinson, Michael (ed.). 1987: *Reshaping Local Government*. New Brunswick, NJ: Transaction.

—— and Evans, Richard. 1990: "Urban development corporations," in Michael Campbell (ed.), *Local Responses to Economic Development*. London: Cassell, pp. 65–84.

—— Foley, Bernard, and Judd, Dennis (eds). 1988: *Regenerating the Cities: The UK Crisis and the US Experience*. Manchester: Manchester University Press.

—— and Judd, Dennis. 1988: "Urban revitalisation in America and the UK – the politics of uneven development," in Michael Parkinson, Bernard Foley, and Dennis Judd (eds), *Regenerating the Cities: The UK Crisis and the US Experience*. Manchester: Manchester University Press, pp. 1–8.

Peston, Robert. 1992: "O & Y's Canary Wharf in administration." *Financial Times*, May 28.

Peston, Robert, and Simon, Bernard, 1992a: "Banks cautious on O & Y debt plan." *Financial Times*, April 14.

—— 1992b: "A victim of hubris falls at Canary Wharf." *Financial Times*, April 13.

Peterson, Iver. 1988: "Battery Park City: a new phase begins." *New York Times*, June 19.

Peterson, Paul. 1981: *City Limits*. Chicago: University of Chicago Press.

Pickvance, Chris. 1988. "The failure of control and the success of structural reform: an interpretation of recent attempts to restructure local government in Britain." Paper presented at the International Sociological Association RC 21 Conference on Trends and Challenges of Urban Restructuring. Rio de Janeiro, Brazil, September.

—— 1981: "Policies as chameleons: an interpretation of regional policy and office policy in Britain," in Michael Dear and Allen J. Scott (eds), *Urbanization and Urban Planning in Capitalist Society*. London: Methuen, pp. 231–66.

Polsby, Nelson. 1963: *Community Power and Political Theory*. New Haven: Yale University Press.

Ponte, Robert. 1982: "Building Battery Park City." *Urban Design International*, 3 (March/April), 10–15.

Port Authority of New York-New Jersey (PANYNJ). 1992: *Regional Economy: Review 1991, Outlook 1992 for the New York-New Jersey Metropolitan Region*. March.

—— 1991: *Regional Economy: Review 1990, Outlook 1991 for the New York-New Jersey Metropolitan Region*. March.

Potter, Stephen. 1988: "Inheritors of the new town legacy?" *Town and Country Planning*. November, 296–301.

Preteceille, Edmond. 1981: "Collective consumption, the state and the crisis of capitalist society," in Michael Harloe and Elizabeth Lebas (eds), *City, Class and Capital*. London: Edward Arnold, pp. 1–16.

Prokesch, Steven. 1992a: "New Jersey and New York collide in new competition to lure jobs." *New York Times*, December 1.

—— 1992b: "3 named to administer Olympia London Project." *New York Times*, May 29.

—— 1990: "London betting on itself and on Canary Wharf." *New York Times*, November 13.

Pryke, Michael. 1991: "An international city going 'global': spatial change in the City of London." *Environment and Planning D: Society and Space*, 9, 197–222.

Purdum, Todd S. 1992: "Olympia tax to be paid on property." *New York Times*, May 22.

Real Estate Board of New York (REBNY). 1990: *Real Estate Reporter*. Fall.

—— 1987: *Manhattan Market Profile*. New York: REBNY.

—— 1985: *Fact Book, 1985*. New York: REBNY.

Rees, Gareth, and Lambert, John. 1985: *Cities in Crisis*. London: Edward Arnold.

Retkwa, Rosalyn. 1992: "MetroTech a boon for Brooklyn environs." *Crain's New York Business*, April 20.

Richard Ellis. 1991: "The impact of the existing built form on the potential for change and growth in world cities," in LPAC, *London: A World City Moving into the 21st Century*, Annex N. 1991.

Robertson, David B., and Judd, Dennis R. 1989: *The Development of American Public Policy*. Glenview, IL: Scott, Foresman.

Robertson, Roland. 1990: "After nostalgia? Wilful nostalgia and the phases of globalization," in Bryan S. Turner (ed.), *Theories of Modernity and Postmodernity*. London: Sage, pp. 45–61.

Rodgers, Peter, and Nissé, Jason. 1992: "Canary Wharf may spurn tenants." *Independent*, May 29.

Rodriguez, Nestor P., and Feagin, Joe R. 1986: "Urban specialization in the world-system: an investigation of historical cases." *Urban Affairs Quarterly*, 22 (December), 187–220.

Rosenthal, Donald B. (ed.) 1980: *Urban Revitalization*. Beverley Hills, CA: Sage.

Rosslyn Research Limited. 1990: *Planning Gain*. Summary presentation for KPMG Peat Marwick Management Consultants. August.

Rudnitsky, Howard. 1992: "Survivor." *Forbes*, June 8, 48.

Rueschemeyer, Dietrich, and Evans, Peter B. 1985: "The state and economic transformation: toward an analysis of the conditions underlying effective intervention," in Peter B. Evans, Dietrich Rueschemeyer, and Theda Skocpol (eds), *Bringing the State Back In*. Cambridge: Cambridge University Press, pp. 44–77.

Rule, Sheila. 1988: "At new Docklands, a tale of 2 cities." *New York Times*, October 15.

Safdie, Moshe. 1987: "Collective significance," in Nathan Glazer and Mark Lilla (eds), *The Public Face of Architecture*. New York: Free Press, pp. 142–54.

Sanders, Heywood T., and Stone, Clarence N. 1987: "Developmental politics reconsidered." *Urban Affairs Quarterly*, 22 (June), 521–39.

Sassen, Saskia. 1991: *The Global City*. Princeton: Princeton University Press.

Saunders, Peter. 1986: *Social Theory and the Urban Question*. 2nd edn. New York: Holmes & Meier.

——. 1979: *Urban Politics*. Harmondsworth, Middlesex: Penguin.

Savitch, H.V. 1988: *Post-Industrial Cities*. Princeton, NJ: Princeton University Press.

Sbragia, Alberta. 1990: "Pittsburgh's 'third way': the nonprofit sector as a key to urban regeneration," in Dennis Judd and Michael Parkinson (eds), *Leadership and Urban Regeneration*. Newbury Park: Sage, pp. 51–68.

Schmalz, Jeffrey. 1987: "New York City reaches agreement on housing." *New York Times*, December 27.

Schwartz, Alex. 1992: "The geography of corporate services: a case study of the New York urban region." *Urban Geography*, 13(1), 1–24.

Sclar, Elliott, and Schuman, Tony. 1991: *The Impact of Ideology on American Town Planning: From the Garden City to Battery Park City*. Unpublished paper.

Sennett, Richard. 1990: *The Conscience of the Eye*. New York: Knopf.

SERPLAN. 1992. "The South East Region of England in Europe Post-1992." Draft policy statement from the Economic Strategy Group. November.

Shachtman, Tom. 1991: *Skyscraper Dreams*. Boston: Little, Brown.

Shefter, M. 1985: *Political Crisis, Fiscal Crisis*. New York: Basic Books.

Simmie, James M. 1981: *Power, Property and Corporatism*. London: Macmillan.

—— 1974: *Citizens in Conflict*. London: Hutchinson.

Simon, Bernard. 1992a: "Reprieve for Canary Wharf after Toronto court ruling." *Financial Times*, July 1.

—— 1992b: "Olympia & York ratings lowered." *Financial Times*, February 25.

Simon, Bernard, and Robert Peston. 1992: "O & Y tells Water Street investors they face big loss." *Financial Times*, May 20.

Sleeper, Jim. 1987: "Boom & bust with Ed Koch." *Dissent*, special issue: "In Search of New York." Fall, 413–19.

Smallwood, Frank. 1984: "The demise of metropolitan government? London and the metropolitan county councils." Paper presented at the annual meeting of the American Political Science Association, September.

Smith, Adrian. 1989: "Gentrification and the spatial constitution of the state: the restructuring of London's Docklands." *Antipode*, 21(3), 232–60.

Smith, Michael Peter. 1988: *City, State and Market*. Oxford: Blackwell.

Smith, Michael Peter, and Feagin, Joe R. (eds.) 1987: *The Capitalist City*. Oxford: Blackwell.

Smith, Neil. 1992: "Geography, difference and the politics of scale," in J. Doherty et al. (eds), *Postmodernism and the Social Sciences*. London: Macmillan, pp. 57–79.

—— 1987: "Dangers of the empirical turn: some comments on the CURS initiative." *Antipode*, 19, 59–68.

—— 1984: *Uneven Development*. Oxford: Blackwell.

—— 1979: "Toward a theory of gentrification: a back to the city movement by capital not people." *Journal of the American Planning Association*, 45 (October), 538–48.

Smyth, Hedley. 1985: *Property Companies and the Construction Industry in Britain*. Cambridge: Cambridge University Press.

Sobel, Robert. 1990: *Trammell Crow, Master Builder*. New York: John Wiley.

Soja, Edward W. 1989: *Postmodern Geographies*. London: Verso.

—— 1980: "The socio-spatial dialectic." *Annals of the Association of American Geographers*, 70, 207–25.

Sorkin, Michael. 1992a: "Introduction," in Michael Sorkin (ed.), *Variations on a Theme Park*. New York: Hill and Wang, pp. xi–xv.

—— (ed.). 1992b: *Variations on a Theme Park*. New York: Hill and Wang.

—— 1992c: "See you in Disneyland," in Michael Sorkin (ed.), *Variations on a Theme Park*. New York: Hill and Wang, pp. 205–32.

Squires, Gregory (ed.). 1989. *Unequal Partnerships*. New Brunswick, NJ: Rutgers University Press.

Squires, Gregory, Bennett, Larry, McCourt, Kathleen, and Nyden, Philip. 1987: *Chicago: Race, Class, and the Response to Urban Decline*. Philadelphia: Temple University Press.

Stasio, Marilyn. 1989: "Now playing on Broadway, the big squeeze." *New York Times*, July 9.

Stegman, Michael. 1988: *Housing and Vacancy Report, New York City, 1987*. New York: New York City Department of Housing Preservation and Development.

Sternlieb, George, and Hughes, James W. 1975: *Post-Industrial America: Metropolitan Decline & Inter-Regional Job Shifts*. New Brunswick, NJ: Rutgers University Center for Urban Policy Research.

Sternlieb, George, Roistacher, Elizabeth, and Hughes, James. 1976: *Tax Subsidies and Housing Investment*. New Brunswick, NJ: Center for Urban Policy Research, Rutgers University.

Stollman, Rita. 1989: "Borough's residences in revival." *Crain's New York Business*, July 10.

Stone, Clarence. 1993: "Urban regimes and the capacity to govern: a political-economy approach." *Journal of Urban Affairs*, 15(1), 1–28.

—— 1989: *Regime Politics*. Lawrence, KS: University Press of Kansas.

—— 1976: *Economic Growth and Neighbourhood Discontent*. Chapel Hill, NC: University of North Carolina Press.

Store, Clarence, and Sanders, Heywood, (eds). 1987. *The Politics of Urban Development*. Lawrence, KA: University Press of Kansas.

Stuckey, James P. 1988: "Letter to the editor." *New York Newsday*. December 7.

Sudjic, Deyan. 1992a: "Towering ambition." *Guardian*, April 17.

—— 1992b: *100 Mile City*. London: André Deutsch.

Sullivan, Lorana. 1992: "O & Y's learning tower of debt." *Observer*, May 17.

Sullivan, Lorana, Parker-Jervis, George, and Shamoon, Stella. 1992: "Nightmare in Docklands." *Observer*, May 31.

Swanstrom, Todd. 1988: "The effect of state and local taxes on investment: a bibliography." *Public Administration Series: Bibliography*. Monticello, IL: Vance Bibliographies.

—— 1987: "The Limits of Strategic Planning for Cities." *Journal of Urban Affairs*, 9(2): 139–57.

—— 1985: *The Crisis of Growth Politics*. Philadelphia: Temple University Press.

Sweeney, James L. 1977: "Economics of depletable resources: market forces and intertemporal bias." *The Review of Economic Studies*, 44 (February), 125–41.

Tabb, William K. 1982: *The Long Default*. New York: Monthly Review Press.

Taylor, Alex. 1986: "Smart moves for hard times." *Fortune*, December 8, 28–30.

Teitz, Michael B. 1989: "Neighborhood Economics: Local Communities and Regional Markets." *Economic Development Quarterly*, 3: 111–22.

Thornley, Andy. 1991: *Urban Planning under Thatcherism*. London: Routledge.

Thrift, Nigel, and Leyshon, Andrew, 1990: "In the wake of money: the City of London and the accumulation of value," in Leslie Budd and Sam Whimster (eds.), *Global Finance and Urban Living*. London: Routledge, pp. 282–311.

Thrift, Nigel, Leyshon, Andrew, and Daniels, Peter. 1987: "'Sexy greedy': the new international financial system, the City of London and the South East of England." University of Bristol and Service Industries Research Centre, Portsmouth Polytechnic. Working Papers on Producer Services no. 8. October.

Tierney, John. 1991: Era ends as Times Square drops slashers for Shakespeare. *The New York Times*, January 14.

Tobier, Emanuel. 1979: "Gentrification: the Manhattan story." *New York Affairs*, 5, 13–25.

Tocqueville, Alexis de. 1957 (orig. c. 1848): *Democracy in America*, trans. Henry Reeve and Phillips Bradley. New York: Vintage.

Townsend, Peter. 1987: *Poverty and Labour in London*. London: Low Pay Unit.

Travers, Tony. 1986: *The Politics of Local Government Finance*. London: Allen & Unwin.

Turok, I. 1992: "Property-led urban regeneration: panacea or placebo?" *Environment and Planning A*, 24, 361–79.

United Kingdom Department of the Environment (DoE). 1991: *Housing and Construction Statistics, 1980–1990: Great Britain*. London: HMSO.

—— 1989: "Strategic Planning Guidance for London." July.

United States Bureau of the Census. 1991: *Statistical Abstract of the United States*. Washington, DC: US Government Printing Office.

University College London (UCL), Bartlett School. 1990: *King's Cross Second Report*. London: UCL, Bartlett School.

Venturi, Robert, Scott Brown, Denise, and Izenour, Steven. 1977. *Learning from Las Vegas*. Rev. edn. Cambridge, MA: MIT Press.

Vizard, Mary McAleer. 1992: "Planning strategies for a new retail environment." *New York Times*, June 14.

Walls, Christopher. 1991: *The Central London Office Market, Interest Rates and Property Shares*. London: Salomon Brothers UK Equity Research – Property, April 22.

Warner, Sam Bass, Jr. 1968: *The Private City*. Philadelphia: University of Pennsylvania Press.

Weiss, Marc A. 1991: "The politics of real estate cycles." *Business and Economic History*, second series, 20, 127–35.

—— 1989: "Real estate history: an overview and research agenda." *Business History Review*, 63 (Summer), 241–82.

Westminster, City of. 1988: *District Plan*. London: City of Westminster.

Wheaton, William. 1987: "Cyclic behavior of the national office market." *Journal of the Real Estate and Urban Economics Association*, 14(4), 281–99.

Willensky, Elliot. 1986: *When Brooklyn Was the World*. New York: Harmony Books.

Wilson, James Q., ed. 1966: *Urban Renewal*. Cambridge, MA: MIT Press.

Wirth, Lewis. 1938: "Urbanism as a way of life." *American Journal of Sociology*, 44 (July), 1–24.

Wolfe, Alan. 1992: "Democracy versus sociology: boundaries and their political consequences," in Michele Lamont and Marcel Fournier (eds), *Cultivating Differences*. Chicago: University of Chicago Press, pp. 309–25.

Wolfe, Tom. 1987: *Bonfire of the Vanities*. New York: Farrar, Straus, Giroux.

Wolfinger, Raymond. 1974: *The Politics of Progress*. Englewood Cliffs, NJ: Prentice-Hall.

Yates, Douglas. 1977: *The Ungovernable City*. Cambridge, MA: MIT Press.

—— 1973: *Neighbourhood Democracy*. Lexington, MA: Lexington Books.

Young, Iris Marion. 1990: *Justice and the Politics of Difference*. Princeton: Princeton University Press.

Young, Michael Dunlop, and Willmott, Peter. 1957: *Family and Kinship in East London*. London: Routledge.

Zukin, Sharon. 1992: "The city as a landscape of power: London and New York as global financial capitals," in Leslie Budd and Sam Whimster (eds), *Global Finance & Urban Living*. London: Routledge, pp. 195–223.

—— 1991: *Landscapes of Power*. Berkeley: University of California Press.

—— 1982: *Loft Living*. Baltimore: Johns Hopkins University Press.

INDEX